T0305060

Corporate Technological Competence and the Evolution of Technological Diversification

For my mother and father

*'I still don't know if I am riding a cow or a horse,
but at least I have travelled a little further on my journey'*

Corporate Technological Competence and the Evolution of Technological Diversification

Felicia M. Fai

Lecturer, School of Management, University of Bath, UK

Edward Elgar

Cheltenham, UK • Northampton, MA, USA

Published by
Edward Elgar Publishing Limited
Glensanda House
Montpellier Parade
Cheltenham
Glos GL50 1UA
UK

Edward Elgar Publishing, Inc.
136 West Street
Suite 202
Northampton
Massachusetts 01060
USA

A catalogue record for this book
is available from the British Library

Library of Congress Cataloging in Publication Data
Fai, Felicia M., 1971–
    Corporate technological competence and the evolution of technological
    diversification / Felicia M. Fai.
        p. cm.
    Includes bibliographical references and index.
    1. Diversification in industry. 2. Technological innovations. 3. Technological
    innovations—Management. 4. Organizational change. I. Title.

    HD2756 .F35 2003
    658.5'14—dc21

2002035401

ISBN 1 84064 353 6
Printed and bound in Great Britain by MPG Books Ltd, Bodmin, Cornwall

Contents

Figures

Tables

Acknowledgements

This book is based on my PhD Thesis undertaken at the Department of Economics, University of Reading, UK and I am grateful for the financial scholarship they awarded me.

I would like to thank my supervisor, Professor John Cantwell for allowing me access to the database that this thesis relies upon and moreover for his support and guidance throughout what was a simultaneously frustrating, depressing, exhilarating and exciting few years. I learnt much from the academic process as well as much about my own strengths and potential.

I should like to thank Professor Nick von Tunzelmann for his kindly made criticisms, advice and continuous encouragement during my thesis and beyond, and for extending me the honour of his friendship and the opportunity to write with him on two papers that have contributed to chapters in this book.

Anyone who has undertaken a PhD or written a book will be aware of the enormous emotional roller coaster the process becomes and without the encouraging words of friends and family, this work might never have been completed. I should like to thank amongst others: Dr Birgitte Andersen, Dr Steve Brammer, Mrs Anne Cameron, Dr Helen Carrier, Professor Luigi Orsenigo, Mr Bob Pearce and Dr Tim Wakeley for their unflagging friendship during both the highs and particularly the lows. Also I am indebted to my parents and brother Kevin for their love and belief in me.

Finally I wish to thank Dymphna Evans and the staff at Edward Elgar for their infinite patience, help and good humour. All remaining errors are my own.

Felicia Fai

1. Introduction

This book examines technological diversification over the period 1930–90. By combining evolutionary economics and the resource-based perspective it considers the pervasiveness of technological diversification, its relationship to firm size and growing inter-relatedness between formerly distinct technologies. It also considers where relatedness between technologies lie – in their underlying scientific or engineering principles or in a firm-specific manner through their combination and use in production.

My interest in technological diversification arose from a curiosity about how large firms evolved over time; how they searched and selected from 'technological space'. Was technological diversity by firms deliberate or were they forced to diversify by changes in the prevailing technological paradigm? Did this have any implications for industrial boundaries as determined by technologies? Were constraints placed upon their choice of which trajectory to follow as determined by the possession of previous technological competencies in an earlier related paradigm or do firms have relative freedom to choose the technologies they combine? Essentially, these are questions that address the *nature* of corporate technological diversification. Whilst I go some way in answering them here, more questions have inevitably arisen in their place. These I have had to leave to another time, nevertheless, the significance of my findings lies beyond satisfying just my own curiosity.

For all the recognition that we exist in a rapidly changing technological environment there have been few economic studies that consider technological diversification explicitly, yet diversification at the industry, market and product levels has concerned economists for years. I suspect the inheritance of a predominantly neoclassical training where technology exists in that infamous 'black box' (Rosenberg, 1982) has led to the oversight of technological diversification in its own right. Nevertheless, studies in the evolutionary economic perspective have demonstrated that technology is important and must be considered as distinct from product and industrial diversification. This book at least attempts to address this general oversight.

For business policymakers the need to understand the nature of technological diversification arises because technology is not only changing rapidly, but is increasingly costly and complex too. Decisions about which technologies to move into may be partially determined by observing findings that emerge from the science base or trends being established by competitors. Nevertheless,

1

whether as trendsetters or follower-firms, management holds some discretionary power to determine whether to pursue these developments and should do so in the light of how they impact upon the overall corporate technological profile and its organizational coherence. In order to do this, they ought to understand the basis on which technologies are related. Such decisions cannot be taken lightly given that large amounts of resources must be committed to pursue these opportunities or defend against such threats. It is also important for strategic purposes given that, in the evolutionary perspective, technological innovation largely progresses in an incremental, cumulative and path-dependent manner. Not only are there implications for the immediate to long-term cost functions of the firm, but also there are potential opportunity cost considerations of moving into technologies today that are inappropriate for the firm's future development. The findings of this book relating to the nature of technological diversification and their implications for the firm should therefore be of some interest to other academics and business policymakers.

1.1 BACKGROUND

Neoclassicists traditionally study the behaviour of firms with respect to input factors of production; the quantity of goods produced and the price at which they should be sold in order to maximize profit. The consideration of these decisions is subject to any number of limiting assumptions, many of which are highly remote from reality. In this perspective, it is merely the combination and recombination of land, capital and labour ratios that determines what to produce, how to produce it, and in what quantities to maximize profits at the margin. There is no suggestion that how these factors relate to one another might be important in the production process or for the growth of the firm.

Nelson and Winter's 'An Evolutionary Theory of Economic Change' (1982) arose from their frustration with the limitations of the orthodox economic approach. They recognized that processes of economic change were much more subtle, involving the combination of firm-specific, endogenously generated factors with exogenous pressures for change generated by the environment within which firms are operating. Their work, combined with the perspectives on the theory of the firm put forward by resource-based theorists, provides a much richer view of the firm. The firm no longer remains simply a co-ordinating, profit-maximizing device. The firm has the ability to evolve and change by building on its prior competencies and resources; it is a repository of competence or productive expertise, and an institutional device for learning and accumulating such (Winter, 1991); it is the principal source of innovation and growth (Cantwell and Fai, 1999).

The technological environment is changing rapidly and becoming increasingly complex; different technological areas are fusing (Kodama, 1986, 1992) and others are becoming more inter-related (Patel and Pavitt, 1997). As a result, firms have found it necessary to increase the range of technologies with which they are familiar in order to sustain existing, or access new product markets; they have become 'multi-tech' (Granstrand et al., 1997). However, at the same time, the firm is constrained by the path-dependent, incremental and cumulative nature of technological change and the limits of the firm's ability to learn and manage its growth. These conflicting forces have implications for the phenomenon of technological diversification within firms and this, in turn, will impact upon the evolution of the firm's technological competencies.

Evolutionary economics helps us to understand the nature of technological change. When combined with resource-/competence-based perspectives (Foss, 1993, 1996; Eliasson, 1994; Montgomery, 1995; Pavitt, 1995) they both help to illuminate how firms might choose to engage in technological diversification and why they follow certain technological paths over others.

In the following sections I first briefly review three of the fundamental tenets of evolutionary economic theory developed by Nelson and Winter (1982) and some basic principles of resource-based theory (Penrose, 1959) before elaborating on how they help us understand the nature of technological diversification. I provide arguments as to why the firm is the appropriate level at which to examine technological innovation, then I review the literature that has enlightened our understanding of technological diversity and product diversity as separate, but interdependent phenomena before presenting my own thoughts on their potential relationships. In conclusion to this introductory chapter, I outline the contents of the rest of the book.

1.2 EVOLUTIONARY INFLUENCES

Nelson and Winter (1982) made the seminal theoretical contribution to evolutionary economic theory through their establishment of three basic concepts: routines, search and the selection environment. These fundamental concepts are particularly relevant to diversification in that they influence the generation of variety and hence diversity. I expand on each below.

1.2.1 Organizational Routines

At any time, organizations have built into them a set of ways of doing things and ways of determining what to do ... [this] is not to say it is unchanging or that it is ineffective ... it is to recognize that the flexibility of routinized behavior is of limited scope and that a changing environment can force firms to risk their very survival on attempts to modify their routines (op. cit., p. 400).

Firms have a set of rules/heuristics which are standardized within the organization and which enable the firm to go about its daily business. They are partially codified and partially tacit channels of communication within firms. Nelson and Winter's comment suggests that routines are at the very essence of the firm's strength, even its existence and that they tend to persist, although there is scope for incremental change. Because routines are developed from the firm's own experiences they will tend to be firm-specific and idiosyncratic in nature. With specific application to technology, the notion of routine may be applied at different conceptual levels.

It may suggest that firms embody technologies in processes and products in a routine manner, e.g. certain combinations of technologies will be used together, in the same way, time and time again to produce a product as they lie at the technological heart of the firm. Alternatively, routines may suggest that the firm uses the same technologies routinely to produce a range of products, but that the technologies are used in a different balance of combinations and in different ways. However, Nelson and Winter's definition also builds in scope for the existence of meta-routines that might bring about changes in subordinate routines. For example, firms may establish routines that require them to scan for new technologies that will enhance current technological combinations that then improve products and processes and so lead to incremental innovation where 'innovation' means a change in routine has taken place. The 'new' technologies need not be entirely 'new' in the conventional sense of the word to the firm or industry, just novel in their application to existing routines – as in the Schumpeterian concept of innovation involving the 'carrying out of new combinations' (Schumpeter, 1937, pp. 65–6).

1.2.2 Search

The example of the meta-routine described in the above example, in this instance, is synonymous with 'search' (Levinthal and March, 1981). Nelson and Winter (1982) describe search as:

> all those organizational activities which are associated with the evaluation of current routines and which may lead to their modification, to more drastic change or to their replacement (ibid., p. 400).

Thus, search itself may be routinized and predictable but may also stochastically generate mutations. Behaviour in all routines associated with success, including ones related to search, will tend to be repeated whilst behaviour which is associated with failure will either not become routinized, or if embedded in existing routines, these routines will be altered or ultimately dropped altogether and replaced by new ones. By keeping successful routines the firm builds persistence into its profile of competencies.

With respect to technological competencies and search, currently successful technologies and successful search routines for new ones will be maintained by the firm, possibly for long periods of time. On the one hand, currently successful routines might result in shortsighted firms who will, in time, suffer from organizational inertia. On the other hand, if the routinized search for new technologies is successful at identifying technologies of potential use to the firm and it is deemed that it is necessary for the firm to build up some level of competence in that area, or indeed own that technology, successful search routines may result in technological diversification.

However, diversified behaviour can also potentially arise because of failures; either the technology itself failed within the context of the firm sparking the need for renewed search, or the search and selection routines that led to this technology's adoption by the firm themselves failed in that these routines led them to choose an 'inappropriate' technology. Thus, routines tend to become modified through a process of incremental and cumulative learning (Stiglitz, 1987; Dodgson, 1991, 1993; Malerba, 1992; Marengo, 1992; Levinthal and March, 1993; Loasby, 1993; Cantwell, 1994).

Routinized search suggests that firms are continuously and actively looking for new solutions to threats and opportunities from both the technological environment and more conventionally, product markets. For the most part firms will engage in the same type of search – for example, looking for technological threats/opportunities within the realm of their competitors' and partners' activities in their own industry or sector, but perhaps occasionally, firms may find opportunities from areas where they would not have expected them, e.g. from neighbouring industrial sectors, from another distinct industry, perhaps a new country or particular scientific area within the science base. All these areas form part of the firm's 'selection environment'.

1.2.3 The Selection Environment

This is described as:

> the ensemble of considerations which affect its [the organization's] well-being and hence the extent to which it expands and contracts. The selection environment is determined partly by conditions outside the firms in the industry or sector being considered ... but also by the characteristics and behavior of the other firms in the sector (Nelson and Winter, 1982, p. 401).

This suggests that the firm has to look beyond its own sector for opportunities and solutions to current problems. The most suitable of these solutions are likely to lie 'close into' the firm's current competencies, activities and interests. In other words, they are likely to come with more frequency from the firm's own technological locality or industry. Patel and Pavitt (1994a) and Fai and von Tunzelmann (2001a) have demonstrated that profiles of industrial technological competencies are largely distinct and persistently so over time, with the exception of general-purpose technologies that pervade across industrial divides. However, the firm should still routinely search (and monitor) not only its immediate technological environment (upstream suppliers, downstream users and direct competitors) but also more broadly in other industrial areas and the science base. The extent to which effort is devoted in any of these areas may be industry-dependent, as suggested by Pavitt's taxonomy (1984).

Nelson and Winter's selection environment potentially has two meanings. First, it can be the environment from which the firms select potential opportunities to follow (Baum and Singh, 1994). Second, it can be the environment in which the firm itself is selected as a survivor or a victim because of its technological, or other, strengths or inadequacies. The two are linked in that consistent failure to do the first successfully ultimately means that the firm will become weaker and be selected out of the environment as in the second interpretation. My focus is on the first of these interpretations, although I am aware that the firm's environment is constantly changing and it is possible for successful routines developed from the firm's experiences in a particular environment to be misleading when the environment changes. Thus, here the selection environment represents the technological 'space' from which firms can select new technologies to use in the production process or embody in new/existing products and thereby diversify either or both their portfolios of technological competence and/or products.

1.3   RESOURCE-BASED THEORY AND COMPLEMENTARY ASPECTS

Resource-based theory has its foundation in the work of Edith Penrose (1959). Penrose perceived the firm as 'more than an administrative unit; it is also a collection of productive resources' (p. 24). Interest in this perception of the firm more or less lay dormant until the early 1980s (with the notable exception of George Richardson's contribution in 1972), but since then much interest in the approach has been stimulated by scholars such as Wernerfelt (1984), Dierickx and Cool (1989), Montgomery and Hariharan (1991) and Foss (1996, 1997). It considers a resource to be an asset of a given firm which at any given time, is tied semi-permanently to the firm (Wernerfelt, 1984). It addresses the assessment of firm resources, their accumulation (Dierickx and Cool, 1989) and how to focus these in such a way so as to convert distinctive competence into competitive advantages that match market opportunities. In particular, the approach concentrates on firm-specific resources that are long-lived and difficult to imitate, 'history matters, profits are persistent, and change most often occurs slowly and incrementally' (Peteraf, 1991, p. 14 from Foss et al., 1995, p. 8).

Because of the obvious attraction of the notions of firm-specific resources and the acknowledgement that historical events and past decisions are important, evolutionary theorists and business management scholars have become particularly interested in the view of competencies as resources and their implications for company performance and long-term economic growth (Prahalad and Hamel, 1990; Eliasson, 1994; Duysters and Hagedoorn, 1996). A competence-based theory of the firm has emerged from the more general resource-based approach (Richardson, 1972; Winter, 1987, 1991; Loasby, 1991; Nelson, 1992; Foss, 1993, 1997). However, within this body of literature, much of the discussion about competencies remains broad and addresses managerial, organizational and technological competencies together even though they have been recognized as being distinct from one another (Dosi and Teece, 1993). Technological competencies (Cantwell, 1991b) are a subset of the firm's entire profile of competencies and the competence-based theory is particularly appropriate for a study of technological change from an evolutionary perspective because in the former, 'the resources with which a particular firm is accustomed to working will shape the productive services its management is capable of rendering...' (Penrose, 1959, p. 5). Hence, past resources affect what managers can do today and current resources will affect what managers can do tomorrow. This accords with the evolutionary perspective in which technological change is perceived as an incremental, cumulative and path-dependent process in which history plays a key part (Nelson and Winter, 1982; Arthur et al., 1987; Arthur, 1989; Cantwell, 1991a; Kelm, 1995).

The evolutionary and resource-based approaches are also complementary in other ways such as their recognition of diversity among and within firms, etc., and in their mutual support lent to strengthen each other's weaker points. For example, the evolutionary approach essentially views firms from the industry level whilst the resource-based approach looks within firms themselves, although many of the fundamentals of evolutionary theory are as useful to the analysis of firm evolution as they are to the evolution of industries, or indeed nations (Nelson, 1988, 1992, 1993). Similarly, complementarity exists between the evolutionary approach's examination of the process of change whilst resource-based theory originally took a static equilibrium approach (Foss et al., 1995). Of particular interest are those works that have recognized the evolutionary characteristics of cumulative, incrementally changing but path-dependent knowledge embedded in organizational routines, and fused this with the idea that resources may also encompass accumulated knowledge bases. For example, Winter (1987) identified knowledge, competence, skills, know-how or capability as strategic assets, of which one specific form of particular interest here is technological competence (Cantwell, 1991b).

Competencies and technologies as resources have been recognized to be partially codified, partially tacit, but definitely context-specific, and tied to local skills and routines. As a result, a firm's portfolio of technological competencies is highly firm-specific. Each firm's history and, experiences differ and because there are initial differences between firms in terms of competencies and their context-specific development (in addition to their different input endowments in the more traditional economic sense), we would expect to observe highly idiosyncratic firm behaviour with respect to the direction and rates at which firms develop their technological skills.

One of the dangers of relying heavily on the resource-based perspective is the potential to ignore the external environment that will select among firms. In order not to be 'selected out' by the external environment firms need to have the competence to deal with change in both their own internal operations and the broader environment. Teece et al. (1990, 1997) and Teece and Pisano (1994) have identified such skills as 'dynamic capabilities'. Dynamic capability is the ability to 'demonstrate timely responsiveness and rapid and flexible product innovation, coupled with the management capability to effectively co-ordinate and redeploy internal and external competences' (Teece and Pisano, 1994, p. 1).

The possession of dynamic capability is a complement to the possession of a broad range of resources and competencies and might also be seen as a strategic asset (Markides and Williamson, 1994, 1996). It is insufficient for a firm's long-term survival to possess solely a broad range of complementary resources if it is unable to manage them in such a way that they afford the firm a source of competitive advantage in the longer term. Because the environment around them changes, firms must alter how they use internal prior accumulated competencies and in the process, create or acquire new ones (Nonaka et al., 2000). They must engage in the process of diversification.[1]

1.4   DIVERSIFICATION

What is diversification? The New Shorter Oxford Dictionary defines it as:

> the action of diversifying; the process of becoming diversified ... diversify ... a exhibit or produce diversity; vary, b of a company etc.; enlarge or vary its range of products, field of operations etc. to reduce its dependence on a particular market etc.

The idea of diversification in the traditional perspective was based very much on the need of firms to offset the economic risk and uncertainty of being dependent on a particular market. This diversification took place in two directions: vertical and horizontal. Diversifying vertically upstream would offset the risk of upstream factors of production coming to a sudden halt through problems in the contractual principal–agent relationship with suppliers of inputs. Similarly, diversifying downstream offsets risks associated with barriers to entry to markets by rival firms, e.g. the closure of distribution channels. Diversifying horizontally across markets offset the risk of profits being eliminated by the reliance on either a single product market or geographic region and, moreover, yield the benefits of economies of scope and/or scale in the use of factor inputs. Advocates of the transactions cost-based approach (Coase, 1937; Williamson, 1985) would require the internalization of many activities in order to reduce the costs and risks of non-ownership and control. As a result firms became larger, more bureaucratic and slower in their decision-making and reaction to changes in their environment. Only when the costs of internalization exceeded the costs of conducting the activity via the market did the boundaries of the firm end.

Interestingly, whilst the desire to offset risks and reach new markets for many firms remains, a number of authors (Gambardella and Torrisi, 1998; Andersen and Walsh, 2000; Piscitello, 2000) have empirically observed that, particularly in hi-tech industries, the product bases of firms have shrunk whilst their technological bases have broadened. This suggests the need to refine and define the levels at which we should be considering diversification.

Indeed, the recent past and current era sees diversification in a different light (Penrose, 1959; Montgomery and Hariharan, 1991; Granstrand and Oskarsson, 1994; Markides and Williamson, 1994; Markides, 1995; Argyres, 1996). Diversification is still a strategy for offsetting risk, however diversification has been recognized to exist not only at the levels of products and markets, but also at the level of technology itself. Diversity particularly across technologies is no longer a choice, but a necessity. The pace of development and change in many industries requires firms to be technologically agile. The sophistication of the production processes if not the products themselves involves high degrees of technological complexity. Firms need to develop competencies with a wide range of technologies, even if they do not directly engage in the design and production of the product or process that embodies that technology. They need to do this so that they can usefully engage in relationships with suppliers and partner firms who might be providing component inputs and services. In other words, firms must 'know more than they make' (Brusoni et al., 2001). Firms should no longer perceive diversification solely as a defensive strategy against risk and uncertainty, but a necessity for survival in a changing world. The possession of a wide range of technological competences and the combinative

ability to use them creatively is a way to offset the risks associated with the
current product market becoming unprofitable in the future. It forms a basis
which firms can leverage quickly to move into new areas in the future if they
need/want to without necessitating participation currently. Thus, efforts and
resources are able to fully focus on exploiting the currently profitable product
market without making the firm totally dependent upon it for its future.
Moreover, technological diversification might also be seen as an offensive
strategy because firms have been recognized as a principal source of innovation
and growth (Cantwell and Fai, 1999). Firms can shape the technological
trajectory of their own industries as well as be shaped by the technological
environment of the industry in which they operate. This technological creativity
within firms is a key ingredient of economic growth (Mokyr, 1990) and so the
perception of a firm as leading innovation-based economic growth is important.

1.5   THE FIRM AS A PRINCIPAL SOURCE OF INNOVATION AND GROWTH[2]

The essential idea is that technological innovation mainly takes the form of
firm-specific learning in production, through a process of cumulative and incremental problem-solving activity, as documented through extensive studies of
the history of technology by Rosenberg (1976, 1982, 1994). This technological learning is organized by, and occurs within firms but may also be facilitated
through inter-firm co-operation. Moreover, in developing their capability to
learn and in the problem-solving activities themselves, firms draw on their
interaction with other local institutions, with downstream markets, and with
the local science base (Nelson, 1996). Because each firm's technological
learning is to some extent particular to the problems encountered in its own
production facilities, each firm tends to follow a distinctive path or technological trajectory (Dosi, 1982, 1988).

   In this adaptation of the evolutionary perspective, the *firm* organizes and
initiates economic development in interaction with the growth of markets (a
view akin to that of Chandler – see Teece, 1993). It becomes a device for the
establishment of locally specific technological competence, and its continued
development over time, or in other words, a repository of competence or
productive expertise, and an institutional device for learning and accumulating such (Winter, 1991). As a result, the firm must be viewed as an institution
in its own right, irrespective of the inspiration for innovation sometimes
provided by markets, or the market's own success or failure as a general co-
ordinator of economic activity.

The evolutionary, competence-based view is concerned with how firms develop their own internal organizational routines, and inter-firm alliances for technological co-operation, so as to enhance the problem-solving efforts in production of each company. By comparison, in the transactions cost approach the central question is the extent to which alternative organizational forms increase the efficiency of the exchange process as such. The Coasian theory of the firm is founded upon market transactions arguments in which the (potential) existence of a market is presupposed, and the firm displaces the market only when it is capable of arranging transactions themselves more efficiently and therefore only partially breaks from the neoclassical approach.

During the nineteenth century and increasingly in the twentieth century, technological accumulation via the build up of tacit capability in collective learning processes has driven capital accumulation rather than the other way around. This reflects not just a greater capital stock, but a more complex and sophisticated type of social organization which is largely embodied within the routines and working practices of firms.

Continuous problem-solving or learning within production (documented by Rosenberg, 1982) gives rise to social or organizational capabilities, but also implies that production is technology-producing as well as technology-dependent (as noted by Richardson, 1972). Firms require specialized technological competence in order to produce attractive products by efficient methods in their respective industries, but it is by learning in production that they continue to develop their firm-specific capabilities. The evolutionary inheritance of firm-led economic development given to us by Marshall, Penrose and Richardson, as well as the more recent contribution of Nelson and Winter (Loasby, 1991) tells us that:

> The point is not that production is thus dependent on the state of the arts, but that it has to be undertaken (as Mrs Penrose has so very well explained) by human organisations embodying specifically appropriate experience and skill (Richardson, 1972, pp. 230–31).

In other words, technology is firm-specific and tied to the institutional structure of the countries in which it is developed due to its component of tacit capability. Technology is not merely a tradable factor of production, but is more in the nature of social organization or capability and is the outcome of an internal collective learning process within firms. This does not feature in conventional production functions, and is not reducible to individual 'human capital', but is embodied in the collective expertise and organizational routines of firms.

Marshall recognized that 'capital consists in great part of knowledge and organisation' (cited in Loasby, 1991, p. 39). Like in more recent evolutionary accounts, Marshall's firms used their knowledge of their trade to experiment with products and processes in the context of their own productive circumstances; and given the resulting variety between firms, inter-company networks were akin to each firm's 'external organization'. The firm's internal and external organization each defines a set of productive capabilities which are missed from the conventional production function – capabilities which are the outcome of active innovative learning on the part of the firms both in production within the firm, and production in interaction with upstream elements (the scientific base and corporate R&D), and downstream complementary or co-specialized assets and markets (Figure 1.1).

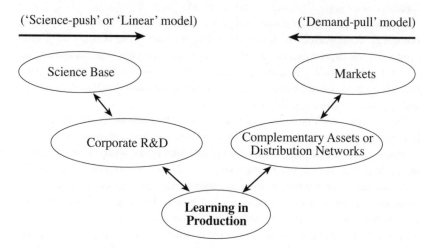

Figure 1.1   Learning as the principal source of innovation, in interaction with upstream and downstream assets

Corporate R&D and distribution networks may be vertically integrated within the firm (or involve inter-company networks), but the science base and product markets are external to it. The view that it is learning within production in the firm that should be seen as the centre of gravity of technological change might be contrasted with both the more traditional 'linear model' of causation of the early Schumpeter (from invention to commercialization), or the 'demand-pull' or market-led model of Schmookler (1966). These older theories based themselves on considerations largely external to individual firms – the push of new knowledge, or the pull of market growth. However, given that learning takes place within the production processes of firms and the purposeful organization of improved production is undertaken by firms, it is *the firm itself* which should be regarded as the principal source of innovation and growth.

1.5.1 The Role of Corporate R&D in Learning in Production within Firms

Specialized R&D laboratories devoted to the advancement of product and process technologies have become increasingly tied to particular firms since the end of the nineteenth century. Corporate R&D facilities have become the principle source of the design, problem-solving and development work leading to new products and processes across many industries, although their importance to firms differs from industry to industry (Nelson, 1992). Corporate R&D contributes to technological innovation by providing a supply of potentially public knowledge that is used in harness with the systematic development of tacit capability through the evolution of the collaborative skills and organizational routines of production teams. Therefore, it is misleading to think of R&D as in general driving innovation (even though it may play a leading role in the science-based sectors) since it also reflects what is achieved in the broader learning process, and thus what types of knowledge have become useful to the firm (perhaps resulting in diversification) or at least show enough potential to be worth exploring further. Industrial R&D laboratories both look inwards for guidance on priorities, but also outwards to monitor opportunities and challenges (Nelson, 1992).

Appreciating that innovation is a collective learning process organized by firms helps to resolve the old debate over whether the essential source of technological change is science or research-push (sometimes called technology-push by those using the old narrower 'engineering' or 'blueprint' definition of technology) or demand-pull (Mowery and Rosenberg, 1979). Innovative learning instead gathers a certain cumulative and incremental logic of its own, which interacts with but is not driven by the development of either science or market demand. Technology affects science and demand as much as the other way round. For example, the improvement of instrument technology has had a major impact on what is feasible in various branches of science (Rosenberg, 1994). Likewise, it is the steady progress of computer technology that has created the growth in demand for computerized equipment rather than some exogenous change in consumer tastes or preferences.

1.5.2 Learning in Production between Firms and Other Institutions

While the innovative learning activities of firms within production are not a simple response to market signals, they do interact with, and are facilitated by, market exchanges between firms themselves, and between firms and customers. These learning activities are also facilitated by the continuous gradual diffusion of new technological knowledge of a public kind, and by the non-market co-ordination of learning between firms, as well as interchanges between firms

and other institutions (such as universities). Each firm may follow a distinctive path of learning or technological trajectory, but certain aspects of its
learning activities may be commonly co-ordinated with other companies where
the activities are closely complementary to one another and can be arranged in
a mutually supportive fashion (Cantwell and Barrerra, 1999). Such close technological co-operation tends to arise more frequently over shorter geographical
distances, which at a country level may be associated with clustered combinations of firms and other local institutions constituting 'national systems of
innovation' (Nelson, 1993).

It is possible to distinguish between two types of technological co-operation
between firms. Co-operation may consist simply of an exchange of knowledge
which is akin to the transaction cost approach (each exchange being a discrete
act), or it may extend beyond this to co-operative learning, involving the co-
ordination of learning processes themselves (Cantwell and Barrerra, 1999).
While the market mechanism may be an adequate means of co-ordinating the
exchange of established items of knowledge or patents, etc., it is inadequate
for co-ordinating the learning process by which knowledge grows over time
(Loasby, 1991; Foss, 1993). Co-ordinating learning processes, as opposed to co-
ordinating a given set of goods or techniques, requires a mode of co-ordination
that has sufficient flexibility to allow for experimentation and the continuing
provision of variety. While co-operative learning encompasses contractual
exchanges such as cross-licensing agreements, these market exchanges tend to
become more a product of the common learning process rather than the other
way round.

The co-ordination of learning in production between firms becomes more
likely if the capabilities of firms are closely complementary to one another,
such that their learning activities are highly inter-related (Richardson, 1972).
The degree of complementarity between the technological traditions of firms
affects the costs of transferring knowledge between them, and the ease of imple-
menting knowledge generated out of one tradition in the context of another, as
well as the scale of potential benefits that may arise from co-operative learning.
For this reason, when the technological traditions of two companies are quite
different, the costs of imitation in a less amenable environment may exceed the
original costs of innovation (Mansfield et al., 1981; Klevorick et al., 1987).
Indeed, in such a situation imitation may not be attempted even if the potential
offered by the opportunity appears lucrative. Since it is in large part an outcome
of the firm's own problem-solving agenda, the new technological knowledge
generated by a firm tends to be more valuable in combination with the tacit
capability of the same firm, and firms whose capabilities are closely complementary to its own (Cantwell, 1995a).

Note that the usual dichotomy between the firm and the market may be
unhelpful in either of these contexts. Both a simple exchange of knowledge

and wider-ranging co-operative learning may occur within a firm (between business units) or between firms. It is only in the case of the exchange of discrete items of knowledge that a transaction cost analysis may play an important role in explaining whether the exchange occurs solely within the firm or through markets external to the firm. Even with a simple exchange of knowledge, there may be other inputs into the respective learning activities of partner companies, which are not exhausted or covered by market transactions (Richardson, 1972). With co-operative learning, market-like exchanges tend to become a by-product of the continuous learning process. Moreover, whether co-operation extends this far depends mainly on the conditions of learning in each firm (or in different parts of the same firm), rather than on the conditions of exchange arrangements (contracts) between firms (or between separate production facilities).

1.6 TECHNOLOGICAL DIVERSIFICATION

There is much work extolling the virtues of diversification across product markets, across strategic business units (SBUs), industries and geographically (Rumelt, 1974; Pearce, 1983; Porter, 1985; Chandler, 1990a; Markides and Williamson, 1994; Markides and Williamson, 1996) and across financial assets (as in portfolio theory). Even within the areas of resource-based and evolutionary approaches, diversification has largely focused upon the reasons for, and nature of product diversification (Rumelt, 1974; Teece, 1982; Pavitt et al., 1989). In the course of such studies the consideration of the notions of relatedness and coherence have arisen (Dosi et al., 1992; Teece et al., 1994; Foss et al., 1995; Langlois and Robertson, 1995). These concepts led to the perception that by diversifying into related product markets or other areas which lie 'close in' to the firm's existing profile of competencies and lines of business, firms could grow (Penrose, 1959) and also attain economies of scale and scope (Chandler, 1990a) in their (technological and other) competencies. In this way, with relatedness between products lying in the use of existing competencies in various complementary combinations, the firm is able to diversify and expand its product base whilst corporate coherence in resources is maintained.

More recently, within the strategic management literature, Markides and Williamson (1994, 1996) expanded upon these rather simple concepts of relatedness to identify three types of 'dynamic relatedness'. Essentially, the competencies used to develop strategic assets in one strategic business unit may be applied in any of the following manners:

- from an existing SBU to improve another existing SBU;
- from an existing SBU to aid a new SBU;
- from a new SBU to improve an existing SBU.

The dynamism here exists in the spread of the asset from one SBU to another and the learning generated in each instance, whilst the sharing of this asset creates relatedness between the SBUs and in the outputs they each produce. Markides and Williamson, however, still consider diversification through the application of a rather non-specific notion of competencies across business units rather than diversification of technologies per se. The specific subject of corporate technological diversification itself is less mature, even in the evolutionary perspective.

Granstrand (1999) has identified that technological diversification can simultaneously lead to growth in the firm's R&D expenditures and growth in the technology-based firm in the form of increased sales in five different and partly complementary ways (p. 126):

i.   static economies of scale (using same technology in several products);
ii.   dynamic economies of scale (multiple uses of a technology lead to learning and consequently should lead to improvements in the technology);
iii. economies of scope (cross-fertilization of technologies can yield new innovations and improve performance of existing ones);
iv.   economies of speed (intra-firm technological transfer is faster and more effective than inter-firm transfer); and
v.   economies of space (a technologically diversified company can benefit from operating in multiple locations which have a high concentration and diversity of technologies that yield spillovers).

Furthermore, academic interest in technological diversification has been stimulated by (i) the observation that artefacts and processes are becoming more technologically complex over time (Pavitt et al., 1989; Granstrand and Sjölander, 1990, 1992; Cantwell, 1993) but that (ii) amongst the largest firms, diversity in technological competencies has become broader than across product ranges with some firms even deliberately refocusing and narrowing their product ranges in the late 1980s and early 1990s (Markides, 1995; Granstrand et al., 1997; Pavitt, 1998) and (iii) technologies that were once quite distinct are being combined together in new ways, and 'fusing' to form new technological areas of their own (Kodama, 1986, 1992).

Indeed, few products are made with simple processes these days and recent studies suggest that technological complexity (and hence by implication, diversity) is essential to produce even once simple products (Rycroft and Kash, 1999). Firms are becoming more 'multi-tech' (Granstrand and Sjölander, 1990; Oskarsson, 1993; Granstrand et al., 1997). Moreover, the technological complexity involved in producing even some simple, let alone complex, products is more than one firm alone can handle (Patel and Pavitt, 1997; Rycroft and Kash, 1999). Thus, whilst managerial capability remains a constraint to the growth rate of the firm, just as Penrose pointed out, it is not the only constraint. Sometimes firms require a highly specialized depth of technological knowledge; sometimes they merely require access to a breadth of technological knowledge. However, few firms can adequately address both needs simultaneously (von Tunzelmann, 1995a; Wang and von Tunzelmann, 2000) due both to a lack of resources to do so and the inability to manage such complexity in a single organization. Over-diversification, or diversification into inappropriate technological directions may cause the firm to lose control over their competence leveraging and combinative capabilities, in other words, their organizational coherence (Dosi et al., 1992; Teece et al., 1994; Langlois, 1995; Pavitt, 1998). Pavitt (2001) has highlighted that entrepreneurship in practice is inseparable from the knowledge on which it is based and in the face of the high levels of complexity today, new knowledge requires the assimilation of specialized professionals. Moreover, major technological breakthroughs are increasingly based on publicly funded research in universities and so corporate entrepreneurship will depend increasingly on academic entrepreneurship. Firms, in other words, will have to rely more on their external network organization (Loasby, 1991).

One of the ways in which firms might simplify the complexity of issues they are facing is to consider whether technological diversification also requires them to engage in further product diversification. It certainly might enable them to do so, but is there the desire to do so when the issues at the technological level are so complicated? The necessity to cope with technological diversity has meant, particularly in some technologically dependent industries such as electronics and chemicals, increased technological diversity within firms, accompanied by a reduction in the diversity of product types produced by these firms (Gambardella and Torrisi, 1998; Andersen and Walsh, 2000; Piscitello, 2000). This makes some sense when the products in these markets appear to be exposed to radical market change more often than technological competencies are subject to radical technological change. Whilst distinctive products are competitive assets they may be short-lived. Technologies on the other hand may be regarded as strategic assets in that they are firm-specific resources in which, through learning processes, capabilities and competencies can be developed (Wernerfelt, 1984; Peteraf, 1993; Montgomery, 1995; Markides and Williamson, 1996; Foss, 1997). Hence, investment in the largely cumulative, incremental and path-dependent nature of technology provides a better strategy for long-term survival and competitive advantage than investment in a particular product market. The shifts in this type of thinking have meant that technology has risen to the top of the strategic agenda instead of being confined to the research and development departments of firms.

1.7   TECHNOLOGICAL DIVERSIFICATION –
IMPLICATIONS FOR THE FIRM

The issue of technological diversification is not addressed by traditional neo-classical economic approaches. By treating technology as a 'black box' (Rosenberg, 1982, 1994) – an exogenous factor that can be drawn upon at any time from a population of technologies – technological diversification becomes an ad hoc and random activity. When the firm realizes that market forces are telling it that demand is falling for its current products, the firm merely selects a different combination of factor inputs to produce a new product that suits the market's demands. Similarly, when the price mechanism tells it that its goods are priced uncompetitively the firm is assumed to be able to adjust the mix of its capital–labour ratio, thus employ a new technology and produce the same goods more efficiently and at lower cost than before. The causality in both cases runs from changes in relative prices in either factor or product markets towards technological change as a mere response to such market processes. This is a major fundamental weakness of traditional economic approaches as it allows the oft-cited scenario of a manufacturer of high fashion shoes becoming a producer of personal computers to become a possibility (Patel and Pavitt, 1994a). The firm is assumed to be able to just 'pluck' these electronic technologies from the exogenous technological space and apply them with relative ease, which is clearly not the case.

Business strategists (Markides and Williamson, 1994; Markides, 1995; Argyres, 1996), as mentioned earlier, have more directly addressed the subject of diversification at the firm level. However, here technological diversification has been subject to a high degree of managerial discretion. Managers (as opposed to the dictates of the markets) decide which technologies they need to use and in which combinations. Here again, there is little, if any, consideration of the endogeneity of technological change and its path-dependent, incremental and cumulative nature. Hence, there is no consideration of how the processes of search and selection are affected by these characteristics. Nor has technology in this arena been regarded much as a firm-specific resource, despite the competence that is generated from its use within production. Yet this build up of competence through routines and learning will both enable and limit managers in their choices with respect to the selection environment they are able to search within for new technologies, and this is where the strength of a technological trajectory-based argument holds promise.

The fact that firms are at least partially responsible for generating innovation and enhancing technological progress means that technologies cannot be 'plucked' from a general technological space under the pressures of market forces. Both the evolutionary and resource-based perspectives propose that by developing technologies and innovation themselves, firms accumulate large amounts of tacit knowledge that is complementary to the more codified aspects which might be more generally available. The accumulation of tacit knowledge both enables firms to generate new innovations and absorb technologies that are related to their prior capabilities and to draw upon those technological areas that are close to these capabilities. In this way firms will incrementally and cumulatively progress down particular technological trajectories whilst at the same time, their lack of tacit knowledge and underlying competence in other technological areas will prevent them from being able to follow other pathways. In this way, firms are limited to an extent in the directions in which they move and managers do not have sole discretion over the technological orientation of the firm, but may in fact be quite heavily constrained (Tidd et al., 1997).

Whilst there is constraint over the direction of a firm's technological pathway, there is considerable room for managerial discretion over the timing and rate at which firms diversify (Patel and Pavitt, 1997). Ultimately though, it is the limits of managerial competence (Penrose, 1959) and organizational constructs that will constrain the growth of the firm. Contemporary firms face what von Tunzelmann calls 'the entrepreneurial problem of scale and scope in the late 20th century' (von Tunzelmann, 1995a, p. 279) whereby increasingly, many (complementary and related) technologies can, or even must, be used to make one product yet a single technology may also be applied in many ways to produce a range of different products. The manager needs to exercise discretion over how many of these technologies he wants to embody, in how many products, in what combinations and balances at any particular time. This separation of discretion over the extent of product diversity from discretion regarding technological diversity represents a significant development over Penrose's concept of diversification. Similarly, the manager needs to decide which technologies need to be maintained in-house and which can be sourced from market or quasi-market relationships.

Brusoni et al. (2001) have argued that the definition of the firm's boundaries in terms of the activities performed in-house fails to distinguish between the decision to outsource production from decisions to outsource technological knowledge. Firms 'know more than they do' and this enables them to engage in a number of organizational constructs dependent upon the state of product interdependencies (predictable/unpredictable) and their relationship with the rate of change of component technologies (even/uneven). Essentially, if product interdependencies are predictable and the rate of change of component tech-nologies is even, the firm can use decoupled organizational structures, i.e. use arm's length relationships with other firms. If product interdependencies are unpredictable and technological change uneven, the firm should engage in tight organizational coupling, i.e. internalize the production and other activities. In the other two circumstances, either unpredictable product interdependencies with even rates of change in component technologies, or predictable product interdependencies with uneven technological rates of change among components, the firm should engage in loose organizational coupling. In other words, outsource production and detailed engineering, use contracts and in-house R&D and co-ordinate the two with systems integration. Moreover, firms will move between these types of coupling over time. In what follows I present my own thoughts on the relationship between technological diversification and product diversification alone.

1.8 RELATIONSHIPS BETWEEN PRODUCT DIVERSIFICATION AND TECHNOLOGICAL DIVERSIFICATION

Neoclassical economics sees diversification as just a change or an increase in variety of products to offset the risk of dependency on a single market. There is no consideration of how products are related to one another, no concept of firm-specific technological competencies and hence no regard for the relationship between products and resources. However, we now recognize that a firm is composed of a set of businesses and a set of resources forming two separate but inter-related bases. As such, the firm can enter into business/product diversification and/or resource diversification. It can focus on one or the other. However, the important source of dynamics in the evolution of the firm is formed by their interaction. Diversification in businesses and resources can occur in a sequential manner or concurrently. Since each business has a resource base which may, in turn, be exploited in different businesses, over time both the firm's resource and business base may shift with some resources, businesses or resource–business couplings being scrapped, some being kept and others added. Typically, there is more addition than scrapping, so this net addition results in diversification (Granstrand, 1999, pp. 123–4). Using this resource–product base framework, I look at technological diversification and its relationship to product diversification, both in a horizontal and vertical manner, and trace how our understanding of the relationship has evolved over time.

In the neoclassical economic perspective, firms that possessed the technology (call it '1') to produce product A and wanted to horizontally diversify their product range just selected a new combination of inputs, which effectively determined the use of technology 2 to make product B. The relationship between products is nil, the relationship between technologies is nil and the relationship between products and technologies is simple and direct (Figures 1.2a and b).

Similarly, if the firm decided that it needed to diversify vertically (e.g. downstream) from component A into component B, then there need not be any

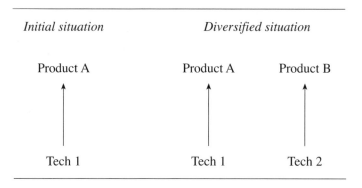

Figure 1.2a   Relationship Type I – neoclassical (horizontal diversification)

technological relationship between the two, see Figure 1.2b. The incentive to own both technologies and products was cost-efficiency driven. There is no scope for the concepts of routine, search and selection, as explained earlier.

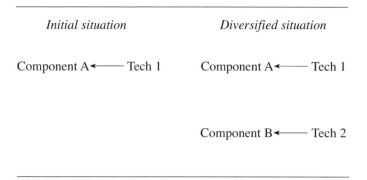

Figure 1.2b   Relationship Type I – neoclassical (vertical downstream diversification)

Penrose's (1959) concept of diversification recognizes that entry into new product markets may be related through common resources, but does not really encompass the issue of technological diversification. Within her view, firms should exploit their excess capacity in resources, including technological competencies. This would imply that diversification of Type II occurs as illustrated in Figures 1.3a and b. Although simplistic, this was a considerable improvement upon the type of diversification neoclassical doctrine would suggest. A limited role for Nelson and Winter's three major contributions starts to emerge. By learning through the repeated use of routines, firms generate economic 'slack', which can be used for product diversification. Search and selection take place at the level of the product base, and moreover these are limited to areas in which the firm already possesses technological competency.

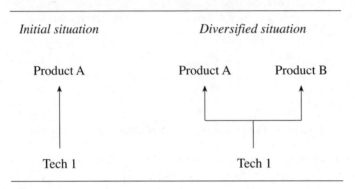

Figure 1.3a   Relationship Type II – Penrosian mark I (horizontal diversification)

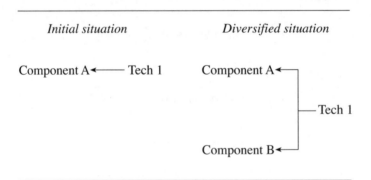

Figure 1.3b   Relationship Type II – Penrosian mark I (vertical downstream diversification)

Type II is pure product diversification with no technological diversification involved. Technology 1 is used efficiently for the production of product/component A. Excess capacity in technology 1 exists because of the effectiveness of specialization and learning processes so this becomes a source of innovation and facilitates the innovation and production of product/component B. In Granstrand's (1999) terms, we have static economies of scale arising in the use of technology 1. In extending the application of technology 1 to a second product/component B, it is likely that the firm engages in an incremental learning process so dynamic economies of scale arise in its efficient use to produce both A and B, or in Markides and Williamson's (1994) terms 'amortization advantages' arise through related (product) diversification. A relationship is formed between A and B via their mutual dependence on technology 1. However, Penrose herself noted that:

> Where diversification involves not only entry into new markets but also the establishment of a new production base, the competitive advantage in the new field can often be traced to the fact that the firm has developed productive services in its existing productive activities which are especially valuable in the new activity. These services may arise from the high development of a particular type of engineering skill, or a particular kind of chemical process, or from an extensive knowledge of some material or waste product that the firm has discovered can be profitably used. Of hundreds of examples of diversification examined in the course of this study only a handful could be found where there appeared to be no technological link whatsoever between the new production base and the old, and this held true even though a large proportion of diversification was effected through the acquisition of other firms (1959, p. 130).

This implies that there is scope within Penrose's theory to consider diversification Type III (Figures 1.4a and b).

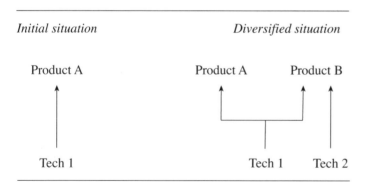

Initial situation   *Diversified situation*

Product A   Product A   Product B

Tech 1   Tech 1   Tech 2

Figure 1.4a   Relationship Type III – Penrosian mark II (horizontal diversification)

Here the starting point is the firm's diversification from product A into product B (or component A into component B in the vertical case) using excess capacity in technology 1 just as in Penrose mark I. However, in the process of innovating B, the firm finds that it needs to develop competence in technology 2. The firm engages in economies of scope and cross-fertilization (Granstrand,

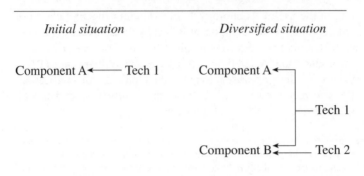

Figure 1.4b   Relationship Type III – Penrosian mark II (vertical downstream diversification)

1999). By diversifying into further products or downstream components, the firm has also become technologically diversified. Relationships have been created between the two products/components via their common dependency on technology 1, but a relationship arises between the two technologies through their complementary contributions in use, to product/component B – their relatedness arises through their use.

This fits with Chandler's discussions of diversification of firms in the early twentieth century and their pursuit of new markets and in the process diversifying their technological bases (Chandler, 1990a; Cantwell and Fai, 1999; Fai and Cantwell, 1999; Fai and von Tunzelmann, 2001b). Furthermore, it demonstrates that routines facilitate learning in technology 1, which enables the firm to spot the opportunity for horizontal or vertical product diversification. However, the search and selection processes are no longer limited to the product base, but also required at the technological level. Here, search and selection of new technologies (tech 2) is constrained by their need to be appropriate to the new product/component. The relationship between technologies 1 and 2 exists entirely through their complementary use in production, rather than any direct relation to existing technological competencies.

The contributions of research into technological trajectories in the evolutionary perspective, however, have led to the recognition that technological diversification can occur independently of product diversification – a notion that is not picked up by Penrose. So, we now have a fourth type of relationship between product and technological diversification (Figures 1.5a and b).

Here technological relatedness is the driving force of diversification in that the two technological areas are related by some underlying scientific/engineering principle, skill or knowledge (Breschi et al., 1998). At least two

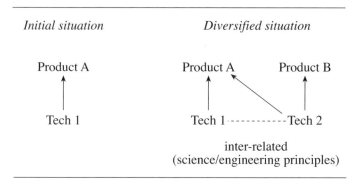

Figure 1.5a   Relationship Type IV – 'Pure' technological diversification (horizontal)

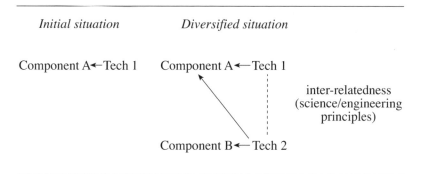

Figure 1.5b   Relationship Type IV – 'Pure' technological diversification (vertical downstream)

scenarios are possible. Firstly, through an extension of its understanding of and experiences with technology 1, the firm is able to build up competencies in a related technology, 2. Technology 2 may initially be required to improve product A. Here we have the case of technological diversification in the absence of product diversification. Over time, experience with technology 2 may enable the firm to pursue horizontal product diversification into product B (or vertical diversification downstream into component B), which it would not have been able to do without the prior underlying expertise it had accumulated with technology 1. A sequential, stepwise process of technological diversification followed by product diversification has taken place. In a second scenario, technological diversification into technology 2 may have been deliberately undertaken for the express purpose of enabling the firm to produce B, in which case the diversification of the technological and product base is concurrent. This exposition that technological diversification can occur in the absence of product diversification, or that it may indeed spur product diversification, is a further and important development in our understanding about the relationship between product and technological diversification.

Application of the concepts of routine, search and selection suggests that experience in routines associated with technology 1 enables the firm to develop their expertise and knowledge in the underlying scientific or engineering principles behind technology 1. It is this underlying knowledge which enables the firm to search and select for further technological opportunities. These new technologies may allow the firm to produce A more efficiently, to improve the technical aspects embodied within A or facilitate searches at the product level so that diversification into product B may occur either as a deliberate strategy, or as a positive spillover effect.

Thus, the above serves to illustrate that at least three types of diversification can occur. First, the resource-based approach challenges the neoclassical approach to diversification by introducing relatedness between the products based upon the utilization of excess capacity in existing resources. Second, there can be product diversification that leads to technological diversification where relatedness between products relies on a degree of overlap in their use of technological inputs and relatedness between technologies lies in their innovative combination within a single product. Third, the evolutionary perspective allows for technological diversification that subsequently enables product diversification. The products are again related in their overlapping use of technologies, but here, the relatedness between technologies is based on their similar underlying scientific principles and engineering concepts. As a result of these developments, the emergence of the multi-technology firm (Granstrand and Sjölander, 1990) has been recognized as a distinct entity to the better-recognized multi-product firm, although most large firms today are likely to be a combination of both. This is a significant distinction given that the importance of product diversification (Penrose, 1959; Rumelt, 1974) relative to technological diversification appears to have diminished in recent times. In fact, Piscitello (2000) has observed that whilst coherence in product diversification concerned firms in the late 1970s and mid-1980s, coherence in technological diversification has become a stronger feature among firms from the mid-1980s onwards. Given this background, I believe that the lack of research specifically on technological diversification in its own right is a point of weakness in our understanding of technological change and its implications for firm competitiveness and development, and this is what I attempt to start tackling in this book.

1.9 STRUCTURE OF THE BOOK

Chapter 2 examines the data used for the empirical basis for this research. Patents are the proxy measure used to measure innovation here. These reflect the codified knowledge firms have accumulated about certain technologies, but as codified and tacit knowledge are complements in the process of accumulating technological competence, patents not only reflect codified knowledge but are also a proxy for the underlying know-how. There are many well-documented arguments regarding the strengths and limitations of patent data as a proxy for technology, and these are recapped briefly. I then describe the specific structure of the database and the selection criteria applied to derive the dataset used in this particular research. Chapter 3 looks at industry-specific profiles of technological competence and the degree to which there is convergence. Technological profiles of large firms are recognized to be industry-specific and long-lived (Patel and Pavitt, 1997) but at the edges, there may be some convergence in their broad areas of technological activity as implicitly suggested by the pervasiveness of meta-paradigms and general-purpose technologies. Chapter 4 moves down from the industry level to look at the profiles of technological competence at the level of the firms. Given the cumulative and path-dependent nature of technological change adopted in the evolutionary approach, this chapter examines just how strong these characteristics are in their combined impact and looks at the endurance of firm-specific technological profiles over the period 1930–90. In essence, it considers the role of the firm as a repository of technological competence. However, in this chapter I also recognize the presence of incremental change and seek to examine how strongly this is reflected in corporate bases of technological competence and whether this causes firms to become more concentrated or diversified.

Building upon the findings of Chapter 4, technological diversification and its nature become the main focus of Chapters 5 to 7. Chapter 5 seeks to introduce the notion of technological diversification more strongly; the extent to which it is reflected in firms' competence portfolios and the strength with which it has been engaged in over time. Chapter 6 examines the influence of scale on technological scope and suggests whilst scale and scope are still strongly positively associated in general terms, in more recent years the influence of scale has diminished relative to other pressures associated with technological complexity and relatedness. This in turn has affected motives for engaging with technological diversification. Following this, Chapter 7 examines the implications of technological complexity upon the type of technological diversification engaged in by large firms. It explores whether there has been a trade-off of technological breadth against technological depth as these two facets together serve to increase the rising complexity of relationships between technologies, as embodied in products and processes that we observe today. The latter part of Chapter 7 attempts to bring in the notions of size or relatedness motivated technological diversification from Chapter 6 to establish the relation between technological depth and breadth on the one hand, and size or relatedness on the other, and the temporal dimension to the associations that arise. Finally, Chapter 8 presents a summary of the findings, implications these may have for academics and policymakers and some points for future consideration.

NOTES

1. I am assuming that firms discard some technologies, retain some and acquire others over time but the net result will be diversification given the rise of the multi-technology firm.
2. This section is taken from Cantwell and Fai (1999), with permission from Springer-Verlag.

2.   The data

2.1   INTRODUCTION

This research utilizes an accumulated patent stock database drawn from patents registered at the US Patent and Trademark Office. Professor John Cantwell compiled the database at the University of Reading, with the assistance of the US Patent and Trademark Office. In this chapter I shall explain the construction of the database and the selection criteria used to select data for this particular research. First though, it is necessary to explain why patent data provide a suitable empirical basis for the arguments put forward in this research.

The notion of 'core' competencies (Prahalad and Hamel, 1990) is broad as well as vague. It may include managerial and organizational competencies as well as technological ones and although the three are inevitably inter-linked, I am specifically interested in the latter. At the firm level, Granstrand et al. (1997) have demonstrated how the term 'core' is misleading because a firm's profile of technological competence tends to be 'distributed' across a wide range of technologies, rather than focused upon a few that might be considered 'core'. In order to trace the evolution of this profile of distributed technological competencies within firms, an indicator that allows the assessment of technological competence over many years must be used. A number of indicators are available, but all are indirect measures with the ability to enlighten us only about certain aspects of the process of technological change. Thus any indicator used will only be a proxy indicative of trends (Basberg, 1987).

2.2   THE INDICATORS OF TECHNOLOGICAL INNOVATION AND THE VALIDITY OF PATENTS

The first of these proxy indicators could be the use of scientific papers, enhanced in their individual significance by the use of bibliometric citation data. However, such measures more accurately capture scientific, as opposed to technological, output. Discoveries made in the science base are far removed from the arena of commercial viability and counts of scientific papers listing scientific discoveries may be criticized for being uncertain and uneven with respect to their individual commercial viability and impact. Scientific papers are also more likely to be written and used by those in scientific and educational institutions rather than firms (Archibugi, 1992). Scientific papers and bibliometric measures are therefore unsuitable as a measure of the technological competencies of firms.

The main indicators of technological, as opposed to scientific, activity are research and development (R&D) expenditure and patents. Here the arguments for and against each measure are well documented (Pavitt, 1988; Griliches, 1990; Cantwell, 1991a; Patel, and Pavitt, 1991; Archibugi and Pianta, 1992). Both measures are imperfect with arguments against the use of R&D data being that much expenditure goes towards research down avenues that end up being 'dead-ends' and R&D expenditures were not captured in any systematic manner prior to the 1950s. Arguments against the use of patents place the focus on the (in)ability of patents to capture innovation as opposed to invention and the variance in the propensity to patent amongst firms and across industries. Given their imperfections, the remaining arguments centre on the equivalency of R&D and patent data and the findings here are inconclusive (Scherer, 1983) and the arguments for and against each measure seem to be equally compelling.

Pakes and Griliches (1984) found that the relationship between patents and R&D was strong in cross-sectional analysis both across firms and industries, and a significant but weaker relationship existed between the two indicators within firms over time. Pavitt (1988), on the other hand, found that national rankings for OECD countries in the rates of increase in industrial R&D in firms were virtually the same as the rates of increase of foreign patenting activity in the US. Thus, there is some evidence supporting the equivalency of R&D and patents.

Conversely, there is evidence to show that R&D and patents are not closely correlated. Criticism of the use of patents versus R&D generally targets arguments towards the diminishing returns to R&D, i.e. as R&D expenditures increase, the output measure of invention and innovations in the form of patents declines. It does seem that there is a lower concentration of technological activities among large firms when considered by US patenting than R&D expenditures (Patel and Pavitt, 1991, p. 10). However, this may be because well-established major firms are less dependent upon current patenting for their market positions (Griliches, 1990, p. 1677). Alternatively, smaller firms appear to patent more on smaller R&D expenditures. This is due to the greater proportion of informal development work that is not accounted for in the formal R&D expenditure figures in firms of this size (Pavitt, 1988; Archibugi and Pianta, 1992).

There are also inter-industry differences in the balance of the firm's propensity to patent against its R&D expenditure. Pavitt (1988) found that R&D and patenting were both high in chemicals, electrical and electronic firms, that R&D exceeded patents in motor vehicles and aerospace, but that shares of patents in mechanical engineering, instrumentation and fabricated metal products were much greater than shares of R&D.

As mentioned above, patents are often criticized as being a measure of invention rather than innovation and so uncertain and uneven with respect to their individual commercial viability and impact. However, whilst it is also acknowledged that not all inventions are patentable, Mansfield (1986) found that firms apply for patents for 66 to 87 per cent of their patentable inventions and similarly, Archibugi (1992) showed that of those inventions that are patented, 40 to 60 per cent become innovations. Criticism has also been levied at the motives lying behind patent applications; they may be taken out to form strategic barriers to entry or be used as bargaining chips in cross-licensing agreements as well as to prevent and defend infringement lawsuits in the protection of intellectual property rights (Jaffe, 2000). Rossman and Sanders (1957, from Griliches, 1990, p. 1679) found that a surprisingly large fraction of all sampled patents were reportedly 'used' commercially, either currently or in the past. Consequently, it is untrue that most patents are not associated with a significant economic event.

2.2.1 Improving Patent Count Data

Despite patent statistics presenting a potentially very rich source of empirical evidence on questions related to technology (see Scherer et al., 1959; Schmookler, 1966; Pavitt, 1988; Griliches, 1990) the weaknesses of patent data have been well recognized. Considerable effort has been invested in improving patent data proxies of technological change. A major contribution to this field has been the application of bibliometric techniques to patent citations (Narin et al., 1984; Harhoff et al., 1997; Hall et al., 2001). The use of patent citations improves data on patent numbers in that the frequency with which a patent is cited in new patent applications/grants is indicative of the earlier patent's significance and quality. Patent citation-related indices have been suggested as alternative proxies to patent number counts, although there are a number of problems associated with this approach. These include the fact that innovative bottlenecks exist; patents may be granted but their significance may only be realized after a considerable time lag. Citations are frequently made more than 10 years after the original patent was issued (Hall et al., 2001). As frequency involves a time dimension, it is necessary to determine an interval over which the patent's appearance will be counted, e.g. how are we to determine whether the significance of a patent cited 10 times over 5 years is greater than that cited 10 times over 10 years? The first might be counted as significant to that particular 5-year time frame through the frequency of its observation, but the latter might be counted as significant through its durability. The second problem is that existing patents cited in new patents are not always cited because the inventor actually utilized these earlier patents, but because either the patent attorney wants to avoid possible lawsuits, or patent examiners believe the earlier patent to have some relevance or relation even though the inventor may not have been aware of the cited patent (Hall et al., 2001). Nevertheless, measures based upon patent citations are particularly useful for strategic purposes because network linkages may be traced (Narin et al., 1984, 1992) and potential strategic alliances may be spotted (Harhoff et al., 1997; Hall et al., 2001) as well as being indicative of the general existence, nature and direction of knowledge spillovers.

A second contribution to the improvement of the measurement of techno-logical change through patent data has been the use of indicators of employees' educational levels and backgrounds as pioneered in studies of Swedish companies by Jacobsson and Oskarsson (1995) and Jacobsson et al. (1996). They define technology as knowledge about the application of natural science and mathematical principles, rather than that embodied in artefacts like machines. Thus, the firm's technological base is the set of competencies it has and this is embodied in individuals who possess technological knowledge. In this sense, the measurement of technology is quite distinct to that measured by patents. Still, Jacobsson et al. (1996) found that educational indicators of engineering backgrounds and patents were more closely related to each other in what they said about technological concentration than they were to R&D, at least in the Swedish case. There was, however, discrepancy over the technological competence of firms with educational data better mirroring the multi-disciplinary character of the process of technological change, whilst patents were better at capturing the specific focus of a firm's technological endeavours and what the firms themselves saw as their prime source of competitive strength.

There are nonetheless a number of problems with educational data. For example, such statistics are not collected as efficiently, or in as great detail, in all countries as they are in Sweden, so accessibility for international compar-isons will be difficult. Relatedly, the intrinsic value of degrees from different countries would make direct comparisons problematic, e.g. German first degrees are considered to be significantly different from British first degrees. Studies might also be limited to more scientific or engineering functions because graduates often do not work in an area directly related to their degree, e.g. engineers and scientists may enter the financial services sector as city analysts and stockbrokers.

Both patent citations and educational statistics[1] can enhance patent numbers-based measures of technological change. Their use as complementary indicators to improve the variable quality of patents should be encouraged whenever suitable. However, it remains that few indicators can match patents in their ease of accessibility, availability over long time periods, and level of detail.

2.2.2 Measuring Invention versus Innovation

Often inventions are regarded as distinct from innovations, and patents tend to be criticized for capturing a measure of the former only. The distinction follows from Schumpeter's view that invention is the idea or the knowledge that precedes development, commercial exploitation and diffusion of the new and better products and processes that are innovations (Pavitt, 1988). However, a patent is granted to the inventor (of a device, apparatus, or process) on the basis of novelty and *potential utility* (Griliches, 1990, p. 1662); the invention must be non-trivial (i.e. not obvious to the skilled practitioner of the relevant technology) and useful (i.e. have potential commercial value, Hall et al., 2001). Therefore, patents not only provide a measure of inventions themselves, but are also a vehicle to facilitate the invention's commercial exploitation and the diffusion of knowledge. Furthermore, the learning process that facilitates the accumulation of capability that in turn enables new innovations to be made relies on inputs of new knowledge and inventions. As long as the pattern of knowledge requirements thus reflects the underlying distribution of techno-logical competence across firms, corporate patents may be used as a proxy for the underlying pattern of technological change, and not merely as a direct measure of inventions (Cantwell and Fai, 1999). Therefore, here, patents will be taken as a proxy for both inventions and innovations as in Pavitt (1988).

2.2.3 Capturing Codified versus Tacit Knowledge

In addition to the invention–innovation issue, there is the argument that patents merely capture codified knowledge whereas technological change is a process that is propagated by the incremental and cumulative generation of knowledge in both its codified and tacit form. However, codified and tacit knowledge are complements and both are important for technology transfer (Taylor and Silberston, 1973). Arora (1995, 1997) has shown that as long as patent protection is strong enough, simple contracts can transfer know-how as well as codified knowledge. Andersen (2001) argues that innovative new technology is mainly the outcome of the interaction process between scientists, inventors, engineers, innovators and entrepreneurs, learning and market diffusion. So, by using accumulated patent stocks, an appropriately broad view of technology can be seen to include the interaction between codified knowledge, tacit knowledge and the market diffusion of knowledge.

In general, patents are an appropriate indicator of technological innovation in that they measure technological (as opposed to scientific) contributions, compare well to alternative measures of technical change, are easily available, provide highly detailed information, may be used as a proxy for both innovation as well as invention and also indirectly account for both elements of codified and tacit knowledge. Having argued that patents are a useful measure of innovative activity, the following section considers why they are a suitable measure for use in the evolutionary economic approach.

2.3   THE VALIDITY OF PATENTS TO THE EVOLUTIONARY APPROACH AND THE RESOURCE-BASED/ COMPETENCE-BASED THEORY OF THE FIRM

Nelson and Winter (1982) pioneered the evolutionary approach to economic change. Within this they characterize technological change as an incremental, cumulative, path-dependent process. This approach lends itself to longitudinal analysis, as the impact of these incremental changes and their cumulative significance will only be recognized after a considerable length of time. Few innovations lead to radical technological changes. As such, patents are valid as an indicator for a number of reasons. The first being that patents are available over very long time frames.[2] It is true that the quantity of patents may have increased over time bringing issues about small number problems to the fore, particularly in any analysis of earlier periods. However, there are no records of R&D data of any generality before the late 1950s (Griliches, 1990) and data on the employment of scientists or distribution of the technically trained labour force is sketchy (Mowery, 1983). The mere fact that patent data exist for very significant periods favours them for use in a long-term approach, albeit with care.

The second reason why patents are suited to long-run analysis is related to the argument put forward by Griliches (1990) that:

> The relatively low correlations in the time dimension (between R&D expenditures and patent numbers) ... imply that patent numbers are a much poorer indicator of short-term changes in the output of inventive activity or the 'fecundity' of R&D (op. cit., p. 1674).

In an inverse manner, this suggests that patents are more suitable for long-run analysis and so supports their use in this particular research.

Patents, as mentioned earlier, are frequently criticized for their variance in economic impact, most being of only small significance. Whilst patents are required to possess the characteristics of novelty and potential use, these demands are in reality not very high (ibid., p. 1663). However, this might work in the favour of patents as a suitable indicator in the evolutionary perspective because in this approach, technological change is an incremental process, so patents seem to be a suitable proxy for its measurement. The cumulative nature of technological change is also to some extent overcome in this research by the use of accumulated patent stocks rather than flows. The choice to use stocks as opposed to flows in this research is given in greater detail in a later section in this chapter. Suffice it to say for now that using accumulated patent stocks has two benefits: it accounts for the cumulative nature of technological progress and additionally, the impact of a radical innovation and its diffusion is substantially ameliorated by the use of large numbers of patents (Cantwell and Barrerra, 1999).

This book is concerned primarily with the evolution of corporate patterns of diversification so it is necessary to utilize data that allow us to investigate patterns at the firm level. Moreover, because it is concerned particularly with technological diversification, any such data must be able to identify a technology with both a firm and a specific technological area. Whilst R&D data will indicate the research interests of the firm, it is not generally provided at the level of detail necessary to identify which technological competencies, areas and fields the firm utilizes in the R&D programme/project. Patents are more useful for representing the specific technological focus of firms and thus the extent of their competence in various technological areas.

The use of patents to trace the technological evolution of firms is a fairly recent innovation in itself (Patel and Pavitt, 1997; Cantwell and Fai, 1999). Previous work concentrated on using patents to consider macro-level characteristics at the level of the country, regional or industrial sector (Schmookler, 1966; Soete and Wyatt, 1983; Archibugi and Pianta, 1992; Cantwell, 1993; Patel and Pavitt, 1995; Zander, 1997; Cantwell and Janne, 1999, 2000; Cantwell and Santangelo, 2000). However, research into technological trajectories was recognized to have implications for firm-level competencies (Pakes and Griliches, 1984) As technologies follow certain paradigms and trajectories, it followed that the technological development of firms was also subject to such limiting factors and hence firms themselves would progress technologically in an incremental, path-dependent manner and the acquisition of new technologies would be cumulative. The level of detail afforded by patents at the very micro level (to specific technological areas within firms, not just the firms themselves) means that they probably provide the best means of measuring the concepts of accumulated technological capabilities and competencies as shown by the use of patent proxies at the firm level in recent work (Cantwell, 1993; Patel and Pavitt, 1994a, 1995, 1997; Breschi et al., 1998; Cantwell and Fai, 1999).

2.4   US PATENT DATA

It has been argued that US patent data provide the most useful basis for international comparisons of technological change (Soete, 1987; Pavitt, 1988). There are several reasons for this. Firstly, the US has been the world's largest single market and a country that welcomed and encouraged new ideas and innovation. It is likely that firms (especially large ones) will register for a patent there after patenting in their home countries. The US Patent and Trademark Office imposes common screening procedures on all patent applications. This implies that firms originating from different countries must also meet the requirements of the official US patent assessment criteria and so there is a common standard of comparison and to this extent, some of the variability in the quality of the patents is reduced.

The data available in the US also cover a very long period of time.[3] The US enacted their first patent law in 1790 and patents from this date onwards are available from the US Patent and Trademark Office. However, there is a cautionary note to consider when looking at the patenting of non-US firms in the US because the use of foreign patenting activity in the US before 1914 is likely to be much less reliable than it is when working only with recent data (Cantwell, 1991a, p. 43). Nevertheless, when a foreign patent is registered in the US, it is likely to be of higher quality and significance (on average) than domestic patents (Basberg, 1987) whilst domestic US patents will still satisfy some common basic level of novelty.

2.5   THE READING UNIVERSITY DATABASE

This database is composed of both individual and corporate patents granted in the US between 1890 and 1995. Each patent allows the identification of the year it was granted, to which firm it was assigned, the firm's nationality and the type of technological activity it is associated with at various levels of aggregation.

For the period 1890–1969, information was collected manually from the *US Index of Patents* and the *US Patent Office Gazette* on all patents that were assigned to a selection of large US-owned and European-owned firms. From 1969 onwards, equivalent information has been computerized by the US Patent Office and incorporated into the database, and the Patent Office also provided a technological classification of all patents granted from 1890 onwards at a detailed level of disaggregation using the US patent class system.

Technological activity is measured here using a count of patents granted in the period 1901–90, which is accumulated into 30-year stocks over the period 1930–90 using the perpetual inventory method, as in vintage capital models. Straight-line depreciation for the separate contribution of each new item of technological knowledge is allowed for over this period, 30 years being the normal expected lifetime of the capital in which the knowledge is partially embodied.[4] It also represents a proxy measure of the life of the underlying technological knowledge and tangible devices with which it is associated, rather than the lifetime of a US patent which is generally recognized to last only 17 years (Griliches, 1990, p. 1662). Hence, the stock of patents in 1930 represents a weighted accumulation of patenting between 1901 and 1930 with weights rising on a linear scale from 1/30 in 1901 to 30/30 in 1930.

It has been recognized that since the nineteenth century patents have taken on tremendous economic significance (Liebenau, 1988, p. 135), but there are two major problems in using patents for economic analysis: classification and variability (Griliches, 1990). The variability issue has been dealt with above to a considerable extent in the discussion of both using citations and educational data to support patent count analysis where appropriate. Also, the use of cumulative patent stocks over sufficiently large numbers ameliorates the impact any single patent of particular significance has.

In order to aid the classification procedure, the database is organized in a manner that recognizes that whilst firms may be separated into broadly defined and distinct industrial areas, the range of technologies these firms are active in may be far more diverse, reflecting distributed competencies. Hence, I emphasize that firms for, and from, the database have been selected in a manner distinct from the way in which the patents received by these firms have been allocated to various technological areas. I deal with each separately below.

2.5.1 Allocation of Firms to Industrial Sectors in the Database

The firms selected for the patent database were identified in three ways. The first group consisted of those firms which have accounted for the highest levels of US patenting after 1969; the second group comprised other US, German or British firms which were historically among the largest 200 industrial corporations in each of these countries (derived from lists in Chandler, 1990a); and the third group was made up of other companies which featured prominently in the US patent records of earlier years. In each case, patents were counted as belonging to a common corporate group, or firm where they were assigned to affiliates of a parent company. In total, the US patenting of 867 companies or affiliates was traced historically and together they comprise 284 corporate groups or firms. Births, deaths, mergers and acquisitions as well as the occasional movement of firms between industries (sometimes associated with historical changes in ownership) have been taken into account.

Instead of facing the ambiguity of classifying patents according to the industry that is most likely to produce the invention (industry of origin), or to the industry that is most likely to use it (industry of destination) (Griliches, 1990), the Reading database utilizes an approach similar to that pursued by Scherer (1965a, b). Each *corporate group* (as opposed to patent) is allocated to an industry on the basis of its primary field of *production*. These industries have then been combined into four major industrial groups on the basis of the types of technology that have been most characteristically developed by the firms in question:

1. Chemicals [chemicals, pharmaceuticals, textiles and clothing, coal and petroleum products (oil)];
2. Electrical [electrical equipment, office equipment (computing)];
3. Mechanical [food, drinks, metals, mechanical engineering, paper and paper products, printing and publishing, non-metallic mineral products, profes- sional and scientific instruments, other manufacturing]; and
4. Transport [motor vehicles, aircraft (aerospace), other transport equipment, rubber and plastic products (tyres)].

Collectively these will be referred to as the CEMT industrial groups. Of the 284 corporate groups in total, 82 are in Chemicals, 45 in Electrical, 107 in Mechanical and 50 are allocated to Transport (Figure 2.1).

**Four Broad Industrial Groupings
(CEMTIND)**

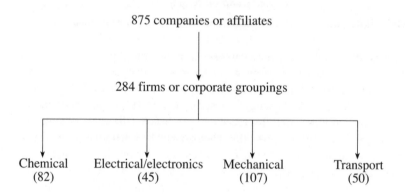

Figure 2.1   Classification of firms and affiliates to industrial groupings in Reading University Patent Database

2.5.2   Allocation of Patents to Technological Fields in the Database

The US Patent Office classifies patents into many classes (300+ in mid-1950s and 400+ in 2000) and even many more subclasses (over 50 000), but as the system of patent classes used by the US Patent Office changes, the Patent Office reclassifies all earlier patents accordingly, so fortunately the classification is historically consistent. Furthermore, where patents were assigned to several fields, the primary classification was used in all cases. Allocating classes or subclasses can derive various broad categories of technological activity to common groups of activity. For this purpose patents registered in subclasses have been allocated to one of 399 technological classes within the Reading database, which in turn have been subsumed into one of 56 technological fields. To illustrate, patents belonging to some of the subclasses that fall within US patent class 62, 'refrigeration', comprise a group that has been assigned to the technological field 'chemical processes', while the remaining patents that fall under other subclasses within refrigeration constitute a different field which has been allocated to 'general electrical equipment'. These 56 technological fields can in turn be allocated to one of five broad technological groups – Chemical, Electrical and Electronic, Mechanical, Transport and 'Other' non-industrial fields – CEMTO collectively (Figure 2.2). A full list of the five technological groups, 56 fields and 399 classes is given in the Appendix.

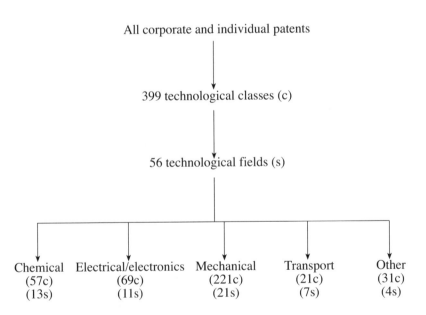

Five Broad Technological Groups
(CEMTO)

All corporate and individual patents

399 technological classes (c)

56 technological fields (s)

Chemical	Electrical/electronics	Mechanical	Transport	Other
(57c)	(69c)	(221c)	(21c)	(31c)
(13s)	(11s)	(21s)	(7s)	(4s)

Figure 2.2   Classification of patent subclasses to technological fields in Reading database

Once again I assert that the classification of patents into five broad techno-logical groups, in terms of the types of technological activity with which each patent is associated, must be distinguished from the main industrial output of the companies which form the four broad industry groups. However, most large companies have engaged in at least some development in most of the general spheres of technological activity, irrespective of the industry in which they operate. This is the case both for the relatively mature industries – like petro-chemicals in which the obvious need to draw upon organic chemistry is combined with the need to be skilled in electronic technology – and in more modern industries such as the rigid disk drive industry where electronic, mechanical and materials-based technologies are all required (Christensen, 1993).

2.6　THE RESEARCH-SPECIFIC DATASET

2.6.1　Selection of Firms

For this particular research only firms that were active throughout the relevant historical period were included – that is, those that have been patenting throughout the period 1930–90 either as firms in their own right or as part of a larger corporate grouping. As corporate patenting took off in the inter-war period, a cut-off point earlier than 1930 would significantly reduce the number of firms considered in this research. Also, in an effort to reduce the small number problems that may arise, especially in relation to the earlier part of our period of analysis, selected firms were required to possess an accumulated stock of at least 225 patents by 1930.[5] The trade-off is that we may be left with some 'industrial dinosaurs' however, 17 of the 32 firms were in the Fortune 500 companies in 2000, and a further seven could be traced as major business units or subsidiary divisions of such companies. Only three have broken up more or less beyond recognition in recent times. For the purposes of analytical continuity, the following firms are referred to under the heading of their earliest and historically most important company name within the period under study, e.g. Allied Chemical, Standard Oil (New Jersey), United Aircraft and West-inghouse Air Brake, or have either been consolidated into the relevant historical corporate groups despite subsequent de-mergers or separations: IG Farben/Bayer/BASF/Hoechst, Swiss IG/Ciba/Geigy/Sandoz. Similarly, they are referred to as individual companies when appropriate. Hence, although Ciba-Geigy and Sandoz subsequently merged in 1997 to form Novartis, this lies outside my time frame of 1930–90 in this research. This gave 32 firms and corporate groups in total, for the year 1930 (six chemical, nine electrical, 11 mechanical, and six transport firms) although the changing composition of the corporate groups alters the number of firms over time (Table 2.1).

As can be seen from Table 2.1 there is a large American bias in the firms selected. This is due to the problem of comparing foreign patenting in the US by non-US firms, with the domestic patenting of the American firms. While

Table 2.1   List of firms and corporate groups as at 1930

Industry Group	Name (1930)	HQ Country	Now
Chemical (6)	Allied Chemical	USA	part of Honeywell International
	Du Pont	USA	Du Pont
	Standard Oil (NJ)	USA	Exxon Mobil
	Union Carbide	USA	Union Carbide
	IG Farben[†]	Germany	Bayer, BASF, Hoechst (Aventis)
	Swiss IG[††]	Switzerland	Novartis
Electrical/ electronic (9)	AT&T	USA	AT&T
	Burroughs[‡]	USA	part of Unisys
	General Electric	USA	General Electric
	RCA	USA	part of Thomson Multimedia
	Singer	USA	broken up late 1980s
	Sperry[‡]	USA	Unisys
	Westinghouse Electric	USA	part of BNFL
	AEG-Telefunken	Germany	part of Siemens
	Siemens	Germany	Siemens
Mechanical (11)	Allis Chalmers	USA	broken up late 1980s
	American Can	USA	broken up late 1980s
	Bethlehem Steel	USA	Bethlehem Steel
	Deere	USA	Deere
	Eastman Kodak	USA	Eastman Kodak, Eastman Chemicals
	Emhart	USA	Emhart Fastening Teknologies
	International Harvester	USA	Navistar International
	US Steel	USA	part of USX Corporation
	Westinghouse Air Brake	USA	WABTEC
	Vickers	UK	part of Rolls-Royce
	Krupp	Germany	part of Thyssen- Krupp
Transport (6)	Bendix	USA	part of Honeywell International
	Firestone Tire & Rubber	USA	part of Bridgestone Corporation
	General Motors	USA	General Motors
	BF Goodrich	USA	BF Goodrich
	Goodyear Tire & Rubber	USA	Goodyear Tire & Rubber
	United Aircraft	USA	United Technologies

Notes:
[†]   952 split into Bayer, BASF and Hoechst.
[†]   1952 split into Ciba, Geigy, Sandoz; 1960 merger of Ciba, Geigy.
[‡]   1986 merger of Burroughs and Sperry into Unisys.

this is problematic in some senses, it is also reflective of the technological leadership and economic dominance of American business for much of the twentieth century, although this is more true historically than in contemporary times. However, it does seem that a number of European firms (German, Swiss and British), particularly in the chemical industry, have patented strongly in the US historically. This accurately reflects the patenting patterns of such firms in the late nineteenth and early twentieth centuries (Liebenau, 1988, pp. 139–44) and their national patterns of technological specialization.

2.6.2   Selection of Technological Fields for this Research

As mentioned earlier, although US patents are available over long periods, their quantity has changed over time and there is a potential for small number problems to arise in any analysis of the pre-1960s period. In order to reduce problems associated with small numbers, the analysis of the technological activity of the firms of each industrial group from 1930 to 1990 was conducted in two alternative ways. In the first case, a restriction on the minimum size of corporate patenting for a technological field to be included was imposed on the volume of activity in 1930, to facilitate a consistent comparison between the 1930–60 and 1960–90 periods; while in the second case, the restriction applied to the year 1960, to enable a comparison in the light of any changes in the composition of corporate technological activity in the period 1960–90 in its own right.

The first criterion required fields to possess an accumulated patent stock of 100 patents or more in 1930 (pat30>100), and this restriction gave the following number of relevant fields for each industrial group: 11 out of a possible 56 for chemical firms, 24 for electrical, 22 for mechanical, 15 for transport firms. This was the basis of analysis for both subperiods, 1930–60 and 1960–90, and the entire 1930–90 period. The second criterion for selection was that fields had to have 500 patents or more by 1960 (pat60>500). This gave 22 relevant fields in chemicals, 21 in electrical, 16 in mechanical and 14 in transport. Obviously in a number of cases, the relevant fields on this second criterion did not have sufficient numbers of patents in the earlier subperiod (1930–60) to be analysed without encountering small number problems, consequently, the analysis has been confined to the 1960–90 subperiod. The full list of the relevant fields under both criteria is given in Table 2.2.

2.7   SUMMARY

This chapter has outlined why the use of patent statistics is suited to the analysis of corporate technological change. Despite a number of weaknesses, patents represent a very rich, detailed and relatively easily available source of infor-

Table 2.2 Technological areas and fields and industrial sector competencies

Tech. Area	Tech. Field	Inds. (pat30>100)				Inds. (pat60>500)			
		C	E	M	T	C	E	M	T
Chemical	chemical processes	X	X	X	X	X	X	X	X
	distillation processes					X			
	inorganic chemicals	X				X			
	agricultural chemicals								
	explosives								
	photographic chemistry					X		X	
	cleaning agents, etc.	X		X		X			
	disinfecting + preserving								
	synthetic resins + fibres	X		X		X		X	X
	bleaching + dyeing	X				X			
	other organic compounds	X				X		X	
	pharmaceutical + biotech.	X				X			
	coal + petroleum prods.	X				X			
Electrical/ electronic	telecommunications		X				X		
	other elect, communic.		X				X		
	special radio systems		X				X		
	image + sound equip.		X				X		
	semiconductors						X		
	office equipment + DP		X				X		
	calculators + typewriters		X				X		
	photographic equipment			X					
	illumination devices		X				X		
	elect. devices + systems		X	X			X	X	X
	other general elect. equip.	X	X	X	X	X	X	X	X
Mechanical	metallurgical processes		X	X	X	X	X		X
	misc. metal products		X	X	X	X	X	X	X
	metalworking equip.		X	X	X		X	X	X
	chemical + allied equip.	X	X	X	X	X	X	X	X
	building material equip.		X						
	material handling equip.		X	X		X	X	X	
	construction equip.								
	mining equip.					X			
	agricultural equip.		X				X		
	food + tobacco equip.								

Table 2.2   continued

		Inds. (pat30>100)				Inds. (pat60>500)			
	textile machinery		X	X		X	X	X	
	papermaking equip.								
	printing equip.			X					
	woodworking machinery								
	other special machinery		X	X	X	X	X	X	X
	other general ind. equip.	X	X	X	X	X	X	X	X
	elect. lamp manufact.								
	power plants		X						X
	other instruments		X	X	X	X	X	X	X
Transport	internal combustion			X	X				X
	motor vehicles				X				
	aircraft				X				X
	ships + marine								
	railway equip.		X	X					
	other transport equip.		X	X	X				
	rubber + plastic prods.				X	X			
Other	nuclear reactors								
	textiles + leather			X					
	wood products								
	building materials		X	X		X	X	X	
	food + tobacco products								
	other + non-industrial		X	X			X		
		11	**24**	**22**	**15**	**22**	**21**	**16**	**14**

mation. According to Griliches (1990) nothing else even comes close in the quantity of available data, accessibility, and the potential industrial, organizational and technological detail. Its quality can be improved by a number of means, but even without this, patents can serve to enlighten us further about the process (and directions) of technological change at a level of detail that R&D cannot.

Further to this, rather than play negatively upon the observation that many patents are not radical in their impact upon technological change, here the fact that a patent requires a small degree of novelty and commercial potential is seen to enhance it positively as an indicator of the incremental, cumulative nature of technological progress from an evolutionary approach. It has also been noted here that the level of detail afforded by patents allows us to trace not only the firms that are engaging in particular innovative activities, but also the areas of technological competence they will use or develop in doing so, hence it is an appropriate measure for the competence, or resource-based approach, to the theory of the firm.

To some extent the problems associated with the use of patents as a proxy for technical change have been eased with the use of accumulated patents stocks and the particular configuration of the database at Reading University. There are other issues calling for caution in the use of patents regarding inter-industry, inter-firm and inter-sectoral differences in the propensity to patent. I am aware of these but will deal with the issues appropriately in the proceeding chapters as and when they arise. For this research and at this time however, patents provide the most appropriate, detailed and comprehensive data source on technology despite their weaknesses and problems, so they are utilized here with caution to learn from them what we can.

NOTES

1. There are other ways of clarifying the relative significance of individual patents such as the use of patent renewal fees. For an overview see Griliches (1990, pp. 1679–82).
2. The US patent system is one of the oldest in the world and became a distinct bureau under the US government in 1802.
3. Although most European countries set up their own national patent systems between 1800 and 1882 and those of the UK and France can be traced to well before this time, the European Patent Office was only established in 1977. The first of the EPO applications arrived in 1978, the first being granted in 1980. The growth rate in European patents granted, however, has been strong with the 300 000th being granted in 1995 (http://www.european-patent-office.org/).
4. It is stressed that 30 years is the average expected lifetime given the huge variance of capital life expectancy between different items.
5. This criterion was selected pragmatically after experimenting with a number of possible cut-off points.

3 Industry-specific competencies and industrial convergence[1]

3.1 INTRODUCTION

This chapter is the backdrop to the focal interest of this book, the issue of firm-level technological diversification. It considers technological competencies and the extent to which they remain industry-specific over time. Technological competency is defined here as the ability to create and use a particular field of technology effectively, which is gained through extensive experimentation and learning in its research, development and employment in production. This is distinct from capabilities, which I use to define activities the firm engages in with less intensity and at which the firm may potentially become competent with experience. Firms exist within industries and are subject to industrial pressures. These may manifest themselves at both the technological level and the product level.

We generally define industries by the products (goods and services) they produce even though industries, and the large firms included within them, have typically produced multiple products over the past century or more (Chandler, 1990a). The production of each of these products however, typically requires multiple technologies, as explained further below. The relationship between technologies, as 'inputs', and products, as outputs, in large firms – and *a fortiori* in industries – is hence normally not one-to-one or even one-to-many, but many-to-many (Rycroft and Kash, 1999; Piscitello, 2000). As a result, the products firms produce can be identified strongly with a particular industry whilst the range of technologies the firm uses to produce this output is probably less industry-specific. With this in mind, I examine here whether there has been a process of 'convergence' in technological competencies between large firms in different industries.

A review of the existing literature might leave the reader feeling ambivalent as to whether technological competencies are industry-specific or whether there should be any convergence in technological competencies across industries. On the one hand, it has been suggested that technological activity is highly industry-specific (Patel and Pavitt, 1994a, 1997). That is, industries are characterized by a certain set of technologies that are common to, and dominant for, those firms operating within that industry. These technologies may be labelled as 'core' technological areas for that industry. For example, it would be expected that most chemical firms, even when broadly defined, would have some skill in technologies such as 'distillation processes' and that electrical firms would have skill in the technologies associated with 'electricity, conductors and insulators'. However, we probably would not expect an electrical firm to possess great competencies in distillation processes, nor the reverse. As these differences between firms and industries are expected to persevere over time, I label this the 'path-dependency' view. In this view, most spillovers of technology between firms would arise within specific industries.

On the other hand, literature at the firm level has recognised that firms operate in a broader range of technological areas now than historically – the notion of core competencies is replaced by distributed distinctive competencies (Granstrand et al., 1997) – and that there has been corporate technological diversification (Fai and Cantwell, 1999). This view has most commonly been allied with the notion of 'long waves' in cross-industry technological 'paradigms' (e.g. Freeman et al., 1982; Dosi, 1988; Freeman and Louca, 2001). For example, whilst Henry Ford's Model T relied primarily on mechanical technologies (relating to engines, gearing, etc.) and chemical technologies (relating to fuel consumption, metallurgy, etc.), present-day Ford models combine these with digital and electronic systems for the more sophisticated control of temperatures, fuel regulation, braking systems, etc. In addition, the adoption of programmable computers on the vehicle assembly line, in order to make rapid changes in the models produced and their components, alters the structure of process technologies involved. Thus in both product and process technologies, the new digital–electronic 'paradigm' surfaces as an important technological input in the vehicle industry as well as in its original home in the electrical–electronic industry. The 'long wave' view supposes that all industries will come to be influenced sooner or later by these new technological paradigms, and I will refer to this as a process of technological convergence between industries.

These two interpretations are, however, rather crude, and when read in a more considered and subtle light the two literatures are not really at odds. For example, the 'path-dependency' view does not deny the importance of new fast-growing technologies, but the way it encompasses the idea is through assuming the continuation of a division of labour between firms and industries producing those technologies, and firms and industries using them. Conversely, the 'long wave' view does not reject substantial path-dependency in the medium term, as its protagonists explore the conditions for conflict between old and new paradigms (Freeman and Perez, 1988). The 'technological convergence' view also has the capacity to accept that there may be a continual division of labour in the face of new technologies and that much of the actual manufacturing of such component parts might be outsourced or developed via strategic alliances. However, the proviso could be made that these represent only the formal organizational modes that carry out such activities. Firms participating in such partnerships still need to be able to integrate the underlying technologies into a compatible whole. Thus, at the very least, the car manufacturer (in this example) will need a level of 'absorptive capacity' (Cohen and Levinthal, 1989) to combine the subtechnologies embodied in constituent parts into a marketable vehicle. Hence, during this process the firm is likely to diversify in technological terms. Furthermore, the strongest trends in this increasing technological diversity at the firm level, when aggregated, ought to be reflected in part at the industry level. In other words, increasing technological diversity within and across firms should be reflected in a changing technological structure at the industry level, with spillovers occurring across industry boundaries. It seems that the ambivalence that might arise is due to a perceived gap between these two literatures, rather than these literatures falling into divided camps. The gap however already has a number of tentative bridges built across it from both a theoretical and a historical perspective.

Within theory, Schumpeter's work brought the notions of path-dependency and diversification together as it progressed and developed over time. The 'early-Schumpeter' view (e.g. Schumpeter, 1911/1934) is highly path-dependent and supposes that the advent of new products and technologies leads to the 'creative destruction' of older products and hence of the firms which produce them. Any firms that survive become 'industrial dinosaurs', though they may endure an undistinguished old age before they eventually collapse. The 'late-Schumpeter' view (e.g. Schumpeter, 1943) instead suggests the adaptability of large older enterprises, and their ability to initiate as well as passively absorb new advances. In this case the notion of path-dependence remains, but it is a less rigid concept and allows for technological diversification to occur within the same enterprise. These have their counterpart in the management literature in the coexistence of, yet contrast between, 'competence-destroying' and 'competence-enhancing' technologies (e.g. Tushmann and Anderson, 1986).

The historically based literature also gives support to these views. There has been a strong focus on the persistent specificity of competencies at the firm level (e.g. Patel and Pavitt, 1997; Cantwell and Fai, 1999), which is widely regarded as symptomatic of path-dependency in firms' technological structures. The notions of 'core competencies' and of 'sticking to the knitting', which dominated management thinking in the area in the 1980s and early 1990s (Peters and Waterman, 1982; Prahalad and Hamel, 1990), attest to the practical as well as theoretical significance of such ideas.

However, in the course of the twentieth century, new scientific areas such as electronics and genetics have emerged, firms have been developed and driven new technological fields forward (Cantwell and Fai, 1999), and consumers have demanded new products like increasingly sophisticated software. According to this view, the world has become more technologically complex – opportunities are dispersed across a broad range of technological areas, technologies are increasingly used as complements, new technologies are used to extend the life of older ones, and firms that seek to exploit these opportunities have become more multi-technological (Granstrand and Sjölander, 1990; Oskarsson, 1993). As a result, many once relatively simple artefacts or processes no longer draw upon just a few technologies, but upon a widened range of technologies (Feldman and Audretsch, 1995).

As well as firms developing technological competencies in new areas, their existing technological capabilities may, over time, come to have multiple uses both within and outside their primary industrial sector of activity (Langlois and Robertson, 1995). This represents an enlarged range of applications or uses of the firm's outputs. Again, the result might be that the technology profiles of firms from various industries become more similar over time, blurring the industry-specificity of technologies. Because of lack of data, the breakdown between the widening range of technologies required for an existing range of products and the widening adoption of existing technologies in products new to the firm is inferred (cf. von Tunzelmann, 1995a, ch. 8).

The notion of general-purpose technologies (GPTs), recently popularized (e.g. Bresnahan and Trajtenberg, 1995; Helpman, 1998), draws on this latter view of inter-industry spillovers. The GPT notion tends to stress technologies as key artefacts, such as the steam engine or the laser, which in the fullness of time come to be adopted in several 'application sectors'. The long wave view accepts that these GPTs may well be strongly represented among the spillover technologies, but raises the wider issue of new knowledge about how and where to advance technologies and how to solve the problems raised by existing technologies. For example, the production of microprocessors remains concentrated in specialist producers using expensive dedicated equipment, but simpler or application-specific (ASIC) chips may be embedded in advances made by users and reflected in patenting by user industries. The latter are led more generally to solving technological problems through miniaturization and information technology as encouraged by advances in semiconductors, i.e. the new paradigm spills over to them as well. Hence the GPT view stresses the demand side for new applications of potentially generic technologies, whereas the long wave view adds this to a greater emphasis on the supply or input side, of major breakthroughs in scientific or technological thinking.

The progression of a technological paradigm as described above would suggest that paradigms are characterized by a period of rapid technological growth through innovation in a particular industry, followed by a period of somewhat slower growth, forming an 'S-curve' of technological development (Andersen, 2001, ch. 4) (Figure 3.1). However, when the industry in which the technology was most immediately relevant is positioned in the section of its pathway where there are decreasing returns, there may come a greater diffusion of the technology to other industries. This has implications for our expectations about patterns of technological convergence over time at the industry level, where technological convergence is regarded as the process by which different industries come to share similar technological bases.

When the rate of innovation in a new technological area is highest, technological innovation will occur predominantly in the industry that can most easily and readily exploit the opportunities that arise, which is the industry that has this area as its 'core competence'. This will coincide with increased technological divergence between industries (or at least a slowing in the degree of convergence), and over this period, industry-specific path-dependency dominates. However, at some point there will come a point of inflexion and the growth rate of the technology will slow in the initial industry, but in some cases its pervasiveness across industries may rise as the diffusion process occurs (Figure 3.2). As the technology diffuses, we would expect increased technological convergence between industries (or at the minimum, a decrease in the degree of divergence between industries).

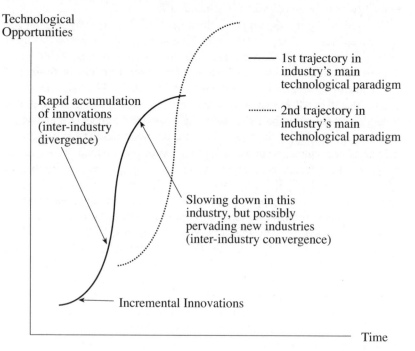

Figure 3.1   S-shaped path of technological trajectories within an industry-specific paradigm

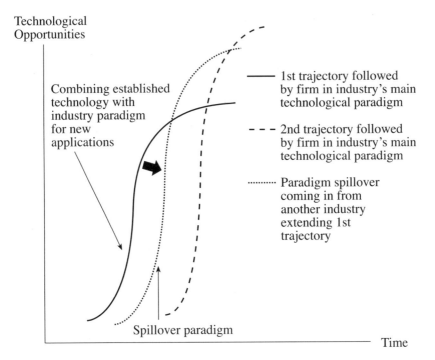

Figure 3.2 S-shaped paths for firms in particular industries, adopting industry-specific and spillover technologies

Many sources of literature hint that technological diversification within firms, path-dependency and technological convergence between industries are not necessarily opposing or conflicting forces but that they can in fact work together in the same direction, perhaps in a sequential manner. However this has not been formally demonstrated in any general way. Here I attempt to make their linkages explicit through the use of empirical data.

This chapter will show that the 'profiles' of technological competencies are quite distinct between broad industrial sectors and these endure, in the sense that firms and industries continue to be recognizable from their technological profiles, even though these change over time. However, empirical evidence of technological convergence between industries is also presented, because on average these changes have been in similar directions though at different points of time. Following this, I focus on the technologies themselves and discuss which technologies have been the causes of the greatest degrees of convergence or divergence between industrial sectors over different historical time intervals before concluding.

3.2 METHODOLOGY

Despite their shortcomings, patents reveal ownership and so the patents a corporation holds highlight the range of technological interests the firm has. This,
in turn, enables us to trace how the technological areas of interest to firms in
different industries change over time. With increasing technological complexity
in products and production processes (von Tunzelmann, 1995a) and the presence
of widely dispersed technological opportunities (Andersen, 2001), we might
expect growing inter-firm and inter-industry division of labour in patenting, if
the strict 'path-dependency' view is valid, or alternatively growing intra-firm
and intra-industry diversity in patenting, if the 'technological convergence'
hypothesis holds. The 'S-curve' argument would predict a sequence in which
the former was followed by the latter.

This chapter works primarily at the level of 56 technological fields (see
Chapter 2). In the preparation for this chapter, different levels of patent aggregation were compared, but the general results were fairly insensitive to
reasonable variations in the level of disaggregation.[2] One of the criticisms levied
at patents is the existence of variable propensities to patent both at the firm and
industry levels. Inter-firm differences are not a major issue here as the analysis
is conducted at the level of the industrial sectors, whilst the effects of inter-
industry differences in the propensity to patent are reduced as far as possible
through the use of the revealed technological advantage (RTA).

The RTA index has been used to measure the relative specialization of
corporate and national technological competencies (Cantwell, 1991a, 1993;
Patel and Pavitt, 1995; Zander, 1997). In the case of industries, it alleviates a
degree of the inter-industry difference to patent in different fields by weighting
an industrial sector's patenting in a particular field by the overall propensity of
that industrial sector to patent in general. Each industrial sector's RTA (IRTA)
in any technological field is given by the following formula:

$$\text{IRTA}_{ik} = (P_{ik}/\Sigma_k P_{ik})/(\Sigma_i P_{ik}/\Sigma_{ik} P_{ik}) \tag{3.1}$$

where P_{ik} is the number of patents held in technological field i by broad
industrial sector k.

The value of the index centres around unity, such that a value greater than
one in a particular technological field indicates that the industrial sector
possesses a relative technological advantage in that field, i.e. it is technologically competent in that technological field relative to other industrial sectors.
A value of less than one indicates relative disadvantage.

3.3   INDUSTRY-SPECIFIC COMPETENCIES AND PATH-DEPENDENCY

A casual perusal of Table 2.2 in the previous chapter will reveal the simple correlation between industries and the technologies in which they conduct the significant part of their patenting. Both the pat30>100 and pat60>500 criteria show indications of a 'diagonal' relationship between the industry and the technological fields in which it does the majority of its patenting. The chemical industry patents primarily in chemical technologies, similarly the electrical/electronic industry is important in developing most of the electrical/electronic fields, mechanical in most mechanical fields and the transport industry in transport technological fields. However, at the same time, we can see that the chemical industry is also technologically strong in the mechanical and transport fields pertaining to equipment, the electrical/electronic industry is strong in many mechanical technologies, as is the transport industry (which is not surprising). We also see that the mechanical industry is active in several of the fields in all four of the other technological areas (CETO). This begins to suggest that technologies are less industry-specific than might be expected from the industry-specificity argument. In this case, the pervasiveness of mechanical technologies to all industrial sectors is clear (albeit to different degrees).[3] This is reflected in the presence of mechanical technologies in the profiles of all four industries and, on the other side of the same coin, by the more limited diversification of the mechanical industry into non-mechanical technological fields.

While some changes are evident between the 1930 criterion and that for 1960, Table 2.2 nevertheless gives some support to the path-dependency view that the overall technological profiles of different industries are rather distinct and persist over time. Such path-dependency in the evolution of industrial technological competencies is further demonstrated by the strength of the correlation in the RTA distribution (in the technological fields selected on the pat30>100 criterion) between the years 1930–60, 1960–90 and 1930–90 (Table 3.1).

From Table 3.1 it is clear that industry-specific competencies for each industrial sector endure even over time horizons of 60 years, although this is less so for the transport sector in 1930–60, and for both the mechanical and transport sectors in 1930–90. However, over this time frame, industry-specific competencies in historically significant technological fields do erode.

The erosion in the persistence of industry-specific competencies may work in two possible directions. One would be that the industry is becoming more technologically focused over time. The chemical industry would become increasingly strong in chemical technologies, and weaker in, say, the mechanical technologies which it had earlier developed. This would mean that the industries would appear to become more technologically divergent. The alternative is that industries are becoming more technologically diversified. In this view, the chemical industry still patents predominantly in chemicals, but increasingly patents in mechanical technologies, suggesting that the industries are becoming technologically convergent. The correlations are therefore equally compatible with the alternative long wave view. Moreover, the findings in this section hinge upon the adequacy of the rather arbitrarily chosen criteria for cutting off small numbers of patents in order to avoid major biases in the RTA calculations. The proportion of technological fields common to more than one industry can turn out to be small if these criteria are too stringent. Further study is thus required.

Table 3.1   The persistence of industry-specific competencies (value of $\hat{\rho}$)

Broad Industrial Sector	$IRTA_{1960}$ on $IRTA_{1930}$	$IKTA_{1990}$ on $IRTA_{1960}$	$IKTA_{1990}$ on $IRTA_{1960}$	$IRTA_{1990}$ on $IRTA_{1930}$
	(pat30>100)	(pat30>100)	(pat60>500)	(pat30>100)
Chemical	0.914	0.977	0.972	0.902
Electrical/electronic	0.923	0.987	0.986	0.913
Mechanical	0.861	0.817	0.894	0.695
Transport	0.688	0.977	0.984	0.689

Note: All correlations are significant at the 1% level.

3.4   INTER-INDUSTRY TECHNOLOGICAL CONVERGENCE

According to the technological convergence view, as time progresses industries move out of technological fields which were of importance in a past period, into other areas which are of importance in a later period. Using patent stocks in all of the 56 fields allows us to capture the essence of this type of technological shift. For these reasons, the analysis in this section considers all 56 technological fields, rather than a subsample chosen on historically based criteria.

Table 3.2 shows the estimated inter-industry correlation ($\hat{\rho}$) matrices that have been compiled using patent stock counts across *all* 56 technological fields. It also provides more detail with respect to the timing of any convergence between industrial sectors by considering them across 15-year rather than 30-year intervals. As the RTA is not being considered here but rather the correlation of patent stocks, the problem of the distorted emphasis of the importance of certain fields through small number problems is not an issue. A positive coefficient reflects that a pair of industries place the 56 fields in more or less the same order of technological importance; a negative value indicates that they rank the technological fields in the opposite order. The greater the actual value of the coefficient, the greater the degree to which the relationship holds.

Table 3.2   Inter-industry correlation coefficient matrices and technological convergence between industries

Year		C	E	M
1930	E	–0.039	—	—
	M	–0.010	0.205	—
	T	0.033	0.213	**0.539**
1945	E	0.081	—	—
	M	0.141	0.143	—
	T	0.032	**0.330**	**0.646**
1960	E	–0.059	—	—
	M	**0.373**	0.239	—
	T	0.087	**0.414**	**0.656**
1975	E	–0.025	—	—
	M	**0.399**	**0.305**	—
	T	0.133	**0.471**	**0.693**
1990	E	0.007	—	—
	M	**0.353**	**0.367**	—
	T	0.131	**0.498**	**0.717**

Note: Figures in bold are statistically significant from zero at the 5% level.

In 1930, only the mechanical and transport industries were significantly correlated (figures in bold type). Given their common bases in mechanical engineering, this result might have been expected. By 1945 a significant but low correlation arises between the electrical and the transport industrial sectors. This might be indicative of the advances being made in the military transport industries at that time, with respect to the improvement of instrumentation and transmission systems, etc. In 1960 some convergence occurs between the technologies that the chemical and mechanical industrial sectors are developing. This corresponds well with Landau and Rosenberg (ch. 10 in Rosenberg, 1994), who comment that, although chemical engineering as a discipline emerged in the early twentieth century, specialized engineering firms (SEFs) played a critical role after World War Two. As these firms learned more about the field through working for various chemical firm clients, they are likely to have become more innovative at this time.[4] By 1975 the electrical and mechanical industries also became similar to the point of statistical significance, probably through the application of electrical and electronic processes to formerly mechanized equipment, so that either industry might plausibly be producing it.

No further new significant correlation between pairs of industries occurred by 1990. However, over the whole 60 years, each time a pair of industries became statistically significant, this coefficient grew stronger in each subsequent period; the only (and minor) exception being the correlation between the chemical and mechanical industrial sectors between 1975 and 1990, which weakened marginally.

Table 3.2 therefore supports the proposition that technological convergence has emerged between broadly defined industries over the period 1930–90. The illustrations provided are based on what is described in the literature on the history of technology and industrial histories. However, in order to provide some details on the sources of any such convergence we need to examine what the pervasive paradigms in each industry were over the period. Furthermore, we need to examine whether any of these have spread from their industry of origin into wider usage elsewhere, as a complementary or enabling technology which provided new opportunities for innovation in the second industry.

3.5   IDENTIFYING EMERGING TECHNOLOGICAL PARADIGMS AND FIELDS OF CONVERGENCE

3.5.1   Emerging Paradigms

Indications of the changing paradigms considered in the literature referred to in the Introduction are reflected in the patent data given in Table 3.3. This table ranks technological fields according to their proportionate increases in patent stocks over the specific 15-year intervals (1930 to 1945, etc.). Emerging technological paradigms are assumed to show up in fast growing patenting, and therefore be visible by obtaining high rankings. The level of the patent stock in the initial year, of course, influences the rankings so a high rate of growth from a tiny initial base may not mean very much. Thus 'semiconductors' get top ranking in 1930/45, i.e. in the years *before* the invention of the transistor, and again in 1945/60; but by 1975/90 when the microprocessor revolution was in full sway, they are almost halfway down the table, because the base (1975) is so much higher than in 1930 or 1945 (as indicated in the first two data columns of this table).

Allowing for this, we can see the relatively rapid growth of many chemicals fields in 1930/45 and 1945/60, though some, such as 'distillation processes', then drop away. The rise of 'pharmaceuticals and biotechnology' (which has subsequently transformed the chemical industry) gets top ranking in 1975/90. In the electrical/electronics area, the case of 'semiconductors' has just been

Table 3.3   Ranking of the 56 technological fields (based on relative percentage increase in patent stocks over 15-year intervals)

Tech. Area	Tech. Field	Share of Total Patent Stock, %		Ranking in Proportionate Increase			
		1930	1990	1930/45	1945/60	1960/75	1975/90
Chemical	chemical processes	1.72	4.35	19	13	16	11
	distillation processes	0.07	0.20	3	11	54	47
	inorganic chemicals	1.19	1.21	32	35	23	24
	agricultural chemicals	0.05	0.85	8	3	12	2
	explosives	0.24	0.11	42	49	10	56
	photographic chemistry	0.33	1.82	6	20	9	16
	cleaning agents, etc.	1.21	2.68	7	22	42	20
	disinfecting + preserving	0.02	0.05	22	17	15	6
	synthetic resins + fibres	0.73	7.53	4	7	18	14
	bleaching + dyeing	0.64	0.60	12	53	40	17
	other organic compounds	5.21	9.31	13	16	29	41
	pharmaceutical + biotech.	0.30	4.65	11	8	7	1
	coal + petroleum prods.	0.99	1.97	5	24	49	37
Electrical/	telecommunications	7.94	2.19	47	52	50	15
electronic	other elect, communic.	0.64	1.28	27	15	14	18
	special radio systems	0.38	0.60	9	12	52	38
	image + sound equipment	1.42	1.50	29	42	41	5
	semiconductors	0.02	1.55	1	1	3	25
	office equipment + DP	0.51	4.03	15	5	4	7
	calculators + typewriters	1.03	0.31	48	50	48	13
	photographic equipment	0.65	0.95	25	48	6	9
	illumination devices	2.81	1.52	18	29	55	50
	elect, devices + systems	1.73	5.65	37	41	45	39
	other general elect, equip.	8.14	4.27	45	33	38	31
Mechanical	metallurgical processes	1.95	2.20	26	36	19	22
	misc. metal products	3.37	2.44	33	34	31	36
	metalworking equip.	4.01	1.81	46	45	28	34
	chemical + allied equip.	2.90	3.49	21	26	34	21
	building material equip.	0.86	0.19	44	55	43	51
	material handling equip.	2.10	1.76	28	27	27	45
	construction equip.	0.03	0.08	24	9	5	44
	mining equip.	0.07	1.00	2	6	8	28
	agricultural equip.	1.22	0.44	38	38	46	52
	food + tobacco equip.	0.11	0.08	23	31	33	55
	textile machinery	6.16	0.83	50	54	53	53
	papermaking equip.	0.51	0.69	20	18	22	46
	printing equip.	1.30	0.32	53	46	37	32
	woodworking machinery	0.12	0.02	55	47	32	40
	other special machinery	2.65	1.67	39	32	25	48
	other general ind. equip.	8.07	5.11	34	39	36	33
	elect, lamp manufact.	0.20	0.11	41	28	39	43
	power plants	0.41	0.99	17	4	35	35
	other instruments	6.26	7.68	30	23	30	10

Table 3.3   continued

Tech. Area	Tech. Field	Share of Total Patent Stock, %		Ranking in Proportionate Increase			
		1930	1990	1930/45	1945/60	1960/75	1975/90
Transport	internal combustion	1.05	1.12	35	30	44	4
	motor vehicles	0.45	0.51	31	25	20	30
	aircraft	0.57	0.39	36	10	51	42
	ships + marine	0.17	0.14	49	51	2	29
	railway equip.	1.15	0.19	54	43	47	54
	other transport equip.	1.17	0.51	51	44	24	26
	rubber + plastic prods.	0.67	1.39	14	19	21	19
Other	nuclear reactors	0.00	0.43	—	2	1	3
	textiles + leather	0.50	0.06	43	56	56	49
	wood products	0.10	0.13	40	21	13	27
	building materials	1.57	3.21	16	40	17	8
	food + tobacco products	0.18	0.79	10	14	11	23
	other + non-industrial	2.09	1.04	52	37	26	12
TOTAL		100.00	100.00				

mentioned, but office equipment (including those patent classes pertaining to information storage and retrieval, computers and data processing systems) predictably grows rapidly after 1945. After 1960 there is some switch of emphasis to electronic products including consumer electronics, with 'telecommunications' also picking up after 1975. The mechanical technologies tend to have a middling performance with the weaker ones, like 'textile machinery', reflecting the slow growth of user sectors. Much the same is true in the transport area, but there is a resurgence of growth in the 'internal combustion engine' after 1975 mainly reflecting fuel crises (the impact of fuel efficiency in patents data from the 1970s is confirmed by Meliciani, 1998). 'Nuclear reactors' are another odd case, because of having no patents at the outset.

Overall, and allowing for the exceptions mentioned, the rankings, together with the changes in overall shares (the difference between the first two data columns), do appear to reflect prevailing views about the most striking technological and industrial changes.[5] But do technological paradigms originating in one industry eventually pervade into other industries and so lead to the convergence of technological systems?

3.5.2   Identifying Areas of Industrial Technological Convergence

To identify areas of industrial technological convergence, we need to relate the areas and fields of convergence to the paradigm shifts previously adumbrated.

Table 3.4 provides an assessment of the spread of technological paradigms across industries by restricting the attention to the 12 fastest-growing fields over the whole period 1930–90 (subject to the restriction that the share in the total patent stock in 1990 was greater than 0.5 per cent, cf. Table 3.3). Certainly a number of these (at least) are closely identified with the usual notions of what constituted paradigmatic change over this interval – 'pharmaceuticals and biotechnology', 'semiconductors', 'data processing equipment', 'rubber and plastic products', etc.

The figures in Table 3.4 represent rankings of percentage-point increases, relative to all technological fields (there were altogether 55 of these fields in 1930/45 and 56 thereafter with the addition of 'nuclear reactors'). Initially the impact of these fast-growing fields is predominantly in the chemical industry, and as the majority of them (seven out of 12) are classified as chemicals technologies, this reflects a concentration in the associated industry. Over time, the median rankings for the fast-growing fields rise in both electrical/electronics industries and in the transport industries (see bottom row).

The rankings for electronic technologies are not surprisingly the highest in the electrical sector, but there is also some increased impact on other sectors of fast-growing fields, especially in regard to 'data processing equipment'. The mechanical sector overall shows less indication of convergence, although there is some indication of it for the most obvious new technologies.

The table on the whole thus supports Andersen's notion of an S-shaped pattern of initial divergence and then subsequent convergence, at least so far as the fastest-growing technologies are concerned. Nevertheless, the pattern in Table 3.4 is far from being as smooth as might have been expected. Table 3.5 looks at the full range of technological fields, not just the fastest growing. In this table the median scores of the percentage-point increases of each technological area in each industrial sector, at 15-year intervals, have been computed. The medians are derived from the equivalent scores for the 56 technological fields. The fastest patenting increase of a broad technological area for the chemical industry in 1930/45 would score 1, and so on. As a group, the median of 'other' technologies increased fastest in this industry in 1930/45 while the median of 'chemicals' technologies increased slowest (top-left data panel). I have also computed the quartile deviation (QD) around these rankings to reveal the amount of dispersion. In the example given, though the 'other' technologies increased fastest on average in the chemical industry in 1930/45, there was some spread around the median, as shown by a 2= ranking of the QD; conversely, though the 'chemicals' technologies increased slowest on average, there was a very high dispersion around this median, so *some* chemicals technologies would have risen quite rapidly.

The rows for the chemical industrial sector in Table 3.5 show that chemical technologies were not growing very rapidly on average in the first subperiod

Table 3.4 Top 12 fastest growing fields (as identified from across all industries over the interval 1930/90) and their specific ranking in each industrial sector (at 15-year intervals)

Industry	12 fastest growing fields 1930/90	Chemical				Electrical/electronic				Mechanical			Transport			
		30/45	45/60	60/75	75/90	30/45	45/60	60/75	75/90	45/60	60/75	75/90	30/45	45/60	60/75	75/90
1. Chemical proc.	38	3	8	6	14	6	3	5	7	6	2	5	55	53	1	17
2. Agric. chems.	19	7	15	3	32	32	25	30	27	25	21	25	33	13	27	33
3. Photog. chems.	8	46	5	8	20	12	4	8	3	7	11	53	29	22	23	24
4. Cleaning agents	3	52	55	11	22	13	14	44	11	44	14	35	14	30	17	10
5. Synthetics	2	1	1	5	7	17	11	4	10	2	3	43	4	15	41	5
6. Pharm. + bio.	39	4	2	1	25	24	16	27	18	11	38	3	15	16	26	15
7. Coal + petroleum	1	55	56	55	30	42	36	22	20	24	33	40	47	40	16	25
8. Semiconductors	28	26	22	32	12	2	2	21	35	21	19	36	31	12	4	41
9. Data proc.	15	13	14	12	4	1	1	2	24	27	17	4	28	9	2	2
10. Plastics	7	41	16	43	45	19	18	10	13	19	26	17	51	47	38	7
11. Building mats.	5	49	3	4	17	28	15	7	4	49	1	1	12	49	22	3
12. Food prods.	13	17	19	33	29	30	27	33	8	10	6	13	25	19	29	36
Median	**10.5**	**21.5**	**12.5**	**9.5**	**21**	**18**	**14.5**	**15.5**	**12**	**20**	**15.5**	**21**	**28.5**	**20.5**	**22.5**	**16**

(1930/45), as just stated. By this time, what might be termed the 'second generation' of chemical technologies was maturing and the 'third generation' (pharmaceuticals, etc.) still relatively small. The median score was thus low, but as just pointed out, some chemical technologies being developed by the chemicals firms were growing quite rapidly. The high median score recorded by 'other' technologies mainly represents users of chemicals (food products, etc.). So by this stage, one is seeing the diffusion of chemical technologies to user industries being incorporated within the technological ambit of the supplier companies. Electrical technologies also score quite highly in the chemical industry, indicating the fusion between electrical and chemical technologies previously mentioned. This pattern generally intensifies over the next two subperiods, down to 1975. The median score for the chemical technologies themselves even declines, and the dispersion remains very high, as fast-growing and slow-growing fields coexist. In the final subperiod, the 'third generation' of chemicals really comes through, and pulls chemical technologies up to first place in terms of the median, though with a continuing high dispersion.

In the electrical/electronics industrial sector, electrical technologies appear to have been less mature in the first subperiod than were the chemicals technologies, as reflected in the high median score for electrical technologies in their own industry at that time (median = 11, ranking = 1). Examination of the individual technological fields suggests that some electrical technologies had indeed matured, e.g. electric lamps, but new branches were still emerging. Thus the dispersion was high (QD = 29, rank = 5). The pattern of maturation and dispersion, as found for the chemical industries, becomes more evident in the following periods, especially 1960/75. As with chemicals, the rise of new-generation electrical technologies (especially information technology and semiconductors) leads to a high median and high dispersion in the years after 1975. The effect of users for the electrical industries is less clearly apparent than for chemicals, except in some branches of mechanical engineering. The high ranking for chemicals technologies in later subperiods does, however, probably reflect the orientation of use of electrical technologies to chemical purposes rather than the reverse, if we take into account the individual technological fields involved (not shown in the table).

Mechanical technology inputs continue to be important throughout this period into many user fields, as Patel and Pavitt (1994b) have shown. The relative importance of the technological areas in the mechanical industry thus mostly reflects the 'demand-pull' of growth of user activities (I noted earlier the decline of branches of mechanical engineering in branches like textile machinery where demand was comparatively stagnating). The 'third generation' of chemicals however had less impact on mechanical firms than other radical technological departures, as one might predict from the nature of pharmaceutical production

Table 3.5   Median changes in rankings of relative patent stocks by broad technological area within each industrial sector, 15-year intervals

Industrial Sector	Tech. Areas	1930/45 Median/QD	Rank	1945/60 Median/QD	Rank	1960/75 Median/QD	Rank	1975/90 Median/QD	Rank
Chemical	C	36	5	46	5	38	4	13	1
		(40)	(5)	(46)	(5)	(45)	(5)	(39)	(5)
	E	25	2	19	1	22	2	26	2
		(22)	(2=)	(10.5)	(2)	(16.5)	(3)	(17)	(3)
	M	31	4	29	2	39	5	40	5
		(26)	(4)	(25.5)	(4)	(24.5)	(4)	(29)	(4)
	T	27	3	35	3	31	3	27	3
		(12)	(1)	(7)	(1)	(8)	(1)	(8.5)	(1)
	O	17.5	1	37	4	19	1	28.5	4
		(22)	(2=)	(15.5)	(3)	(15)	(2)	(13.5)	(2)
Electrical/ electronic	C	28	3	24	2	17	1	22	2
		(12)	(3)	(21)	(2)	(18)	(2=)	(11)	(1)
	E	11	1	22	1	51	5	14	1
		(29)	(5)	(49)	(5)	(47.5)	(5)	(41)	(5)
	M	35	4	26	3	29	3	41	5
		(23)	(4)	(26)	(4)	(28)	(4)	(19.5)	(3)
	T	45	5	43	5	38	4	36	4
		(8.5)	(1)	(22.5)	(3)	(18)	(2=)	(16)	(2)
	O	27.5	2	33	4	28.5	2	26	3
		(11.3)	(2)	(8.25)	(1)	(10.5)	(1)	(21)	(4)
Mechanical	C	18	1	24	2	25	2	33	4
		(13)	(1)	(27)	(4)	(22)	(2)	(15)	(1)
	E	30	2	27	3	23	1	20	1
		(15)	(2)	(11.5)	(1)	(18.5)	(1)	(19)	(3)
	M	32	3	38	4	34	5	41	5
		(31)	(5)	(34.5)	(5)	(34.5)	(5)	(34)	(5)
	T	42	5	23	1	27	3	22	3
		(21)	(3)	(21)	(3)	(26.5)	(3)	(15.5)	(2)
	O	35.5	4	41	5	32.5	4	21.5	2
		(25.5)	(4)	(15)	(2)	(32)	(4)	(22.3)	(4)
Transport	C	27	3	25	2	21	2	23	1
		(19)	(3)	(17)	(3)	(10)	(1)	(16)	(2)
	E	24	2	11	1	15	1	30	3
		(21)	(4)	(12.5)	(2)	(33)	(4)	(27.5)	(3)
	M	32	4	34	4	37	4	35	5
		(29.5)	(5)	(25.5)	(5)	(21)	(3)	(29)	(4)
	T	49	5	41	5	38	5	34	4
		(8)	(1)	(10.5)	(1)	(36.5)	(5)	(29.5)	(5)
	O	22	1	31.5	3	30	3	27.5	2
		(18)	(2)	(21.3)	(4)	(16.3)	(2)	(15.3)	(1)

Notes:
Figures are medians of the 56 technological fields for each sector, or their intra-sector ranks.
Quartile deviations (Q3–Q1) or their ranks are in parentheses.

processes. The rise of knowledge-based industries seems bound to amplify this effect in the recent past and future. The high level of electrical technologies in this sector, especially in later years, appears to be brought about by the adoption of the electromechanical paradigm in the mechanical engineering industries, rather than by supplying machinery to electrical activities; so representing the extension of the 'S-curve' as in Figure 3.2.

Finally, the transport sector is inherently more 'downstream' than the others considered, so that the impact of paradigm changes 'upstream' is quite strongly in evidence here, e.g. the importance of electrical technologies. The low growth of transport technologies themselves, together with low dispersion, suggests that the sector was technologically quite mature from the beginning of our time span. However, as there is no aircraft or similar company among the included companies, our results may be somewhat biased as a reflection of the sector as a whole.

To summarize Table 3.5, the 'S-shape' pattern appears to be confirmed by these data for the companies of this dataset. Maturing technologies showed low median scores with low dispersion. At this stage, the main fields of growth tend to be in user activities, as applications of the upstream technologies progress steadily. As new generations of technologies appear, they show up mainly as high dispersion in the associated sectors (chemical technologies in the chemical industry, etc.). It can take 30–60 years for the new generations to dominate the growth of technologies in the associated industry. Meanwhile, the impact begins to spill over into other user activities, so bringing eventual convergence in those respects.

3.6   SUMMARY AND CONCLUSIONS

This chapter sought to discover whether there has been a growing overlap of the technological areas in which different industrial sectors are operating, or whether technological profiles at the industry level remain specific and distinct. The recognized trends of increasing technological complexity and the increasing emergence of 'multi-technology' firms would suggest that the technological profiles of firms have become more diversified, but whether these phenomena have been pervasive enough to blur industry boundaries was uncertain. Moreover, the erosion of an existing profile of technological competencies does not by itself indicate whether firms and industries retreated into their heartland 'core competencies', or instead diversified into areas of overlap through the rise of new technological paradigms with generic implications.

First it was found that the overall technological profiles of the four broadly defined industrial sectors indeed remained highly distinct and somewhat persistent over the period 1930–90, and that, by and large, the industrial sectors tended to patent most in their corresponding technological fields, as judged by RTAs (Tables 2.2 and 3.1). Such a measure confirms the 'path-dependency' view related to enduring industry specificity.

However, when explored more generally, across all the technological fields, much stronger support emerged for the alternative view of an increased convergence between the industrial sectors (Tables 3.2 to 3.5). Both views set out in the Introduction can therefore be supported from the historical evidence. If we envisage a matrix with 'industrial sectors' forming columns and 'technological fields' forming rows (as in Table 2.2), path-dependency is evident when looking at the levels of patenting across the technological fields within each industrial sector (i.e. within columns) whilst technological convergence over time is more apparent when looking at changes in patenting within the technological fields across all industrial sectors (i.e. within rows). In terms of firm behaviour, as the technologies fundamental to the industry matured within firms, firms would mainly look downstream to user applications as a first way of diversifying. However the advent of new technological paradigms, initially in their own industry and later elsewhere, would eventually redirect their efforts. This confirms the existence of 'S-shape' behaviour here at the level of large firms, which Andersen (2001) previously found at the technological level. The situation emerging from the results here for firms is as set out in Figure 3.2, with the flatter sections corresponding to periods mainly devoted to developing applications, and the steeper finer dashed section to absorbing inter-industry spillovers. The latter follow as a counterpart to the former; for example, firms in the transport industry may first buy in data-processing hardware from the electronic industry, but subsequently develop their software in-house, the linking arrow in Figure 3.2 suggests the relationship. Firms which fail to absorb the inter-industry spillovers (new paradigms) become consigned to 'dinosaur' status even though they may continue to develop downstream applications; a pattern that was beginning to emerge at the very end of our observation period.

The chapter therefore extends the work recently undertaken on GPTs, which emphasizes new applications of generic technologies, to the 'long wave' context of incorporating new technological paradigms into the ways in which firms develop new processes and products. The spillover effects of innovations that are made in one industrial sector may be positive, and contrary to some views, eventually become large when applied (with some adaptation) to other industrial areas.[6] However the time intervals involved may be very long, as firms balance path-dependency on the one side against increasing technological complexity from the absorption of new technological areas on the other.

NOTES

1. This chapter is based on Fai and von Tunzelmann (2001a), with permission from Elsevier Science.
2. The 50 000 or so subclasses of the 399 USPTO classes are not examined here, but the great majority of these disaggregations have little or no economic meaning.
3. Patel and Pavitt (1994b) demonstrated the pervasiveness of older mechanical technologies.
4. Freeman found that by the 1960s nearly three-quarters of all major new chemical plants were engineered, procured and constructed by specialized plant contractors (Rosenberg, 1994, p. 200).
5. For further analysis of similar data, the reader is referred to Andersen (2001).
6. It might be that inter-industrial spillovers are largely of principles contained within innovations, rather than the actual innovations themselves. The paper by Feldman and Audretsch (1995) is a good review of the issues involved, as noted in the Introduction.

4. Technological persistence in the evolution of corporate technological competence[1]

4.1 INTRODUCTION

The previous chapter demonstrated that technological competencies are highly industry-specific. Yet, at the same time, they have experienced technological convergence as the technologies typically associated with the industry of origin pervade further afield into applications in other industries, with the result that these application industries increase the technological breadth of their patenting. For the remainder of this book, I attempt to identify this broader trend with behaviour at the firm level. Firms and industries are, to some degree, inevitably, although not directly, inter-linked in their behaviour (Langlois and Robertson, 1995). So whilst there is some evidence of an increase in technological breadth within each of the industrial groups, and hence convergence between them, does this affect and/or reflect behaviour at the level of the corporate groups and firms within them?

4.2 THE PERSISTENT CHARACTERISTICS OF INNOVATION WITHIN FIRMS, BUT VARIETY BETWEEN FIRMS

Within the literature, it is known that national technological specialization is persistent (Cantwell, 1991a; Archibugi and Pianta, 1992), furthermore, this persistence is strong over time and often the current technological strengths of countries can be traced back historically to the beginning of the twentieth century (Cantwell, 1991a). It has also been found that technological competence persists for about 25–30 years at the level of the firm within a specific industry (Cantwell, 1993; Patel and Pavitt, 1997). These firm-level studies, however, are limited in that they only study persistence in the post-1960 period. This chapter builds on this work by looking more historically at the issue of persistence in firms and seeks to examine whether persistence has broken down over time within them.

When the *firm* is considered to be the principal source of innovation and growth, as it is here, the essential idea is that technological innovation mainly takes the form of firm-specific learning in production and that learning for firms is a cumulative process and an incremental problem-solving activity (Rosenberg, 1976, 1982, 1994). To this extent, a firm's current profile of competencies is, at least in part, a reflection of the firm's own particular past problems and current interests. As problems are particular to each firm, learning experiences are distinctive and cumulative, hence unique path-dependency will tend to be a feature of the development of each firm's technological trajectory (Dosi, 1982, 1988).

A number of insights emerge from focusing upon the path-dependent nature of the evolution of profiles of corporate technological competence, as the outcome of internal learning processes in the production of firms. One that will be emphasized below concerns the elements of stability that may characterize economic growth, despite the unpredictable and open-ended nature of technological change. Firms evolve typically along paths in which their own past history plays a critical role, rather than through a series of discrete and unrelated steps. At the level of industries, technological competence is sustained over long periods. This is because there are a variety of technological paths or lines of experimentation across firms, and so stability is increased at times when the principal fields of technological opportunities change, since the new growth areas will be in the portfolios of at least some existing companies (Nelson and Winter, 1982; Eliasson, 1991). This need not imply dramatic substitution effects between firms. Firms interact with each other and it is this interaction in their learning activities which means that although corporate paths are distinct they are not entirely independent of one another; it also means that the industry-level pattern appears relatively more stable.

Allied to this are insights with respect to the nature of technological co-operation between firms, which from the competence-based perspective of the firm (Teece et al., 1994) is not reducible to market-like exchanges of technological knowledge. Firms may co-operate directly with each other in their learning activities, within which context exchanges of technological knowledge (sometimes embodied in patents or machinery) are just part of a broader story. Corporate problem-solving in production, however, is also facilitated by a wider public diffusion of certain types of generic knowledge, and by co-operation with other institutions such as universities. As argued by Loasby (1991), the well-developed principles of the co-ordination of a given set of activities through the exchange of some given set of items (normally through the market mechanism) are unlikely to be applicable to the analysis of the co-ordination of evolutionary learning and novelty-generating processes, the latter being an open-ended and continuous process.

The implication of this interpretation of the firm is that as a result of the cumulative nature of learning, the underlying fields of technological competence (or social capability) tend to change only very slowly. Competence or capability evolves gradually within the production processes of established firms, even though markets and products themselves may change quite dramatically over longer historical periods and will influence the direction taken by firms. Thus, the firm provides elements of institutional continuity over time in its function as a repository of specific fields of competence.

Arising out of this is the hypothesis that competence within firms will tend to persist over quite long periods of time having evolved gradually in a path-

(a) technological persistence, technological diversification, no change in product diversity

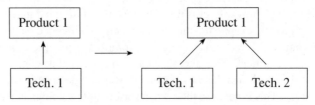

(b) technological persistence, technological diversification, switch to new product

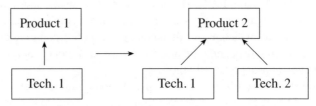

(c) technological persistence, technological diversification, product diversification

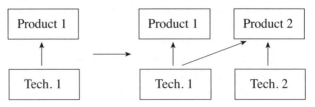

Figure 4.1   Examples demonstrating the persistence of technology 1 despite technological diversification and irrespective of activity at the product level

dependent manner, providing there is institutional continuity. Within the same firm, competence may evolve into related areas or may become relatedly diversified from an established base, but the firm's technological origins will remain identifiable in its subsequent trajectories irrespective of the presence or absence of product diversification. For example, Figures 4.1a–c relate to the possible relationships between product and technological diversification outlined in Chapter 1. Figure 4.1a reproduces the Type III relationship discussed in Chapter 1 and shows how technological diversification can occur independently of product diversification – a notion not regarded by Penrose (1959). The remaining illustrations in Figure 4.1 show a number of other ways in which technological diversification and product diversification may evolve together; each demonstrates how technological competencies will tend to persist despite what happens at the product level.

The comment above regarding institutional continuity is significant because, where the institution itself changes more dramatically, technological persistence may be severely disrupted, e.g. where there are major mergers or acquisitions, or as in Germany, post-war reconstruction. I examine the strength of technological persistence below.

4.3 METHODOLOGY

4.3.1 The Selection of Firms and Technological Sectors

In this chapter I continue using 32 consolidated firms or corporate groups and technological fields selected on the basis of two criteria: pat30>100 and pat60>500. With reference to potential problems associated with patent data, the chapter deals with intra-industry comparisons only so inter-industry differences in patenting propensity are eliminated, although admittedly the industrial groups are defined very broadly, especially the 'mechanical' group. The remaining inter-sectoral or inter-firm differences in the propensity to patent that may arise are controlled for here, by the use of the *intra*-industry RTA and applied to the level of *the firm* (as opposed to the industrial sector's RTA used in Chapter 3).

The intra-industry RTA relates a firm's technological advantage in a spectrum of technological activity to that of other firms in the same industry. It shows the firm's (*j*) share of US patents granted to all companies in the same industrial group, in a technological field (*i*), relative to the firm's overall share of all US patents assigned to all firms in the industry in question. If P_{ij} denotes the number of US patents granted in activity *i* to firm *j* in a particular industry, the RTA index is defined as:

$$RTA_{ij} = (P_{ij}/\Sigma_j P_{ij})/(\Sigma_i P_{ij}/\Sigma_{ij} P_{ij}) \qquad (4.1)$$

Again, the index varies around unity. In this manner inter-sectoral differences in the propensity to patent are normalized in the numerator of the RTA index, and inter-firm differences are normalized in the denominator. There still remains the possibility of intra-firm and intra-sectoral differences in the propensity to patent, but it is likely that the respective variances of these two factors are systematically lower than the inter-firm and inter-sectoral differences.

The intra-industry RTA distribution for each firm is calculated for 1930, 1960 and 1990 and the correlation between the sectoral distribution of the RTA index at time t and an earlier time period $t-1$ (or $t-2$) is estimated through a simple linear cross-sector regression of the following kind:

$$RTA_{it} = \alpha + \beta RTA_{it-1} + \varepsilon_{it} \qquad (4.2)$$

where i refers to the sector of technological activity at time t, and the residual ε_{it} is independent of RTA_{it-1}. Three regressions are considered: RTA_{1960} on RTA_{1930}, RTA_{1990} on RTA_{1960} (this one is run twice, for each of the technological field selection criteria), and RTA_{1990} on RTA_{1930}.

4.4   MEASUREMENT INDICATORS

4.4.1   The Measurement of Persistence

Persistence is taken here to mean that the cross-sectoral profile of a company's pattern of technological specialization is stable and not subject to much inter-sectoral mobility in the RTA distribution over time. The extent of mobility can be measured by Pearson's correlation coefficient ρ (Hart, 1983). If the estimate of ρ is given by $\hat{\rho}$ then $(1-\hat{\rho})$ measures the size of the 'mobility effect', while the magnitude of $\hat{\rho}$ gives a positive indicator of the degree of persistence. In an equation with a single independent variable the t-test of whether $\hat{\beta}$ is significantly different from zero is equivalent to the F-test of the significance of $\hat{\rho}$ (persistence) and hence constitutes an inverse test of the extent of mobility:

- If $\hat{\beta}$ is significantly greater than zero, then $\hat{\rho}$ is significant and there is persistence in the firm's profile of technological specialization.
- If $\hat{\beta}$ is significantly less than zero, the t-test implies that $\hat{\rho}$ is significantly less than one and the mobility effect $(1-\hat{\rho})$ is thus significantly greater than zero. In fact, the ranking of the sectors becomes reversed; that is, previously disadvantaged sectors tend to become areas of technological advantage and vice versa. However, this goes totally against the expec-

tation that patterns of technological specialization tend to persist over time, which implies that $\hat{\beta} > 0$.

- When $\hat{\beta}$ is not significantly different from zero in either direction, neither persistence nor a reversal of sector rankings can be said to exist in the profile of technological specialization of the firm.

4.4.2 The Measurement of Diversifying Incremental Change

In the case of countries, it has been observed that technological profiles tend to persist for approximately 20 years (Pavitt, 1987; Cantwell, 1991b), but to diversify incrementally and hence to shift more significantly over longer periods (of say 50 years, or more). Here I explore whether the same tendency towards diversification is also true at the firm level.

The process by which this tendency is expected to occur is that of *diversifying incremental change*. By diversifying incremental change, I am referring specifically to the tendency for a firm to gradually move into new areas in which it has made comparatively little effort in the past, and hence to become more evenly balanced in terms of its relative advantage among the sectors of technological activity over time. Another kind of 'incremental change' would be small changes in a firm's technological profile that lead it to become even more specialized and advantaged in its existing areas of strength, which would constitute a 'reinforcement' of the firm's existing pattern of technological specialization. Thus diversifying incremental change is to be distinguished from reinforcing incremental change. The extent of incremental change may be measured by $(1-\hat{\beta})$ – the 'regression effect'. This can operate in two directions and its significance is measured by the *t*-test of whether $\hat{\beta}$ is significantly different from *one:*

- If the *t*-test of $\hat{\beta}$ is significantly greater than one, this implies that there has been regression *away* from the mean RTA; thus *reinforcing* incremental change has taken place in the firm's profile of technological competencies.
- If the *t*-test of $\hat{\beta}$ is significantly less than one, there has been a regression effect *towards* the mean and *diversifying* incremental change has occurred. That is, the firm has dispersed its technological advantage more evenly across sectors than in a previous period.
- If the *t*-test of $\hat{\beta}$ is not significantly different from one in either direction, the firm cannot be said to have really experienced any incremental change in its profile of competencies.
- If, however, a weak positive regression effect $(1-\hat{\beta})$ still outweighs a weak mobility effect $(1-\hat{\rho})$ diversifying incremental change may still occur.

In what follows, I shall focus on the evidence for the notion of persistence in the profiles of technological specialization as depicted in Tables 4.1 to 4.5. For those firms that display non-persistence, the issue of diversifying incremental change is less relevant in this context.

4.5   RESULTS OF TESTS FOR PERSISTENCE IN PROFILES OF CORPORATE TECHNOLOGICAL SPECIALIZATION

4.5.1   Industrial Group-level Observations

Table 4.1 highlights two main features. First, it clearly shows that persistence was a dominant feature of the technological profiles of the selected very large firms of the CEMT groups in all three time periods. In accordance with theoretical expectations, persistence eroded somewhat over the period 1930 to 1990. However, this was not as great as one might have anticipated since the number of firms displaying significant persistence only fell from 28 and 26 (in the two subperiods respectively, pat30>100 criterion) to 22 in the overall period. Persistence was both widely spread across all selected firms and persisted over long periods of time – at least 60 years in many cases. The second major feature illustrated by Table 4.1 is the presence of diversifying incremental change over time. Taking incidences of both diversifying incremental change given by a $\hat{\beta}$ significantly less than one, and the weaker change given by a positive, but statistically insignificant regression effect outweighing a smaller mobility effect, then from the totals of these two rows, diversifying incremental change is also widespread across the selected firms (22, 18, 20 and 21 firms) over each interval and basis respectively. A substantial number of the firms even displayed persistence in the face of diversifying incremental change together.

Looking more closely at temporal effects, diversifying incremental change within a persistent technological profile was at least as, if not more, strong in the earlier subperiod 1930–60 than in the later subperiod, 1960–90. This calls into question whether diversification in modem times is truly occurring with increasing frequency within firms, due to formerly distinct branches of technology becoming more inter-related (Granstrand and Sjölander, 1990).

Instances of persistence in the absence of incremental change, in either direction, were relatively few although incidences were slightly more frequent in the subperiod 1960–90. If anything, the combined outcome supports extremely strong persistence within these firms; not only were competencies in technologies held for a long time, they were held with the same relative levels of emphasis over the periods as well. Firms narrowing and hence specializing their techno-

Table 4.1   Persistence and incremental change – all industrial groupings

(i) RTA_{60} on RTA_{30} (pat30 > 100)

	Persistence			
Incremental Change	$\hat{\beta} > 0$ Persistent rankings	$\hat{\beta} < 0$ Reversed rankings	$\hat{\beta}$ not significantly different from zero	**Row Total**
$\hat{\beta} > 1$ Reinforcing incremental change	1E 2M (3)	—	—	**3**
$\hat{\beta} < 1$ Diversifying incremental change	1C 6E 8M 2T (17)	—	1C IT (2)	**19**
$\hat{\beta}$ not significantly different from one	2C 2E 1M (5)	—	1C IT (2)	**7**
$(1 - \hat{\beta}) > (1 - \hat{\rho})$ Diversifying incremental change	1C 2T (3)	—	—	**3**
Column Total	**28**	**—**	**4**	**32**

(iia) RTA_{90} on RTA_{60}(pat30 > 100)

	Persistence			
Incremental Change	$\hat{\beta} > 0$ Persistent rankings	$\hat{\beta} < 0$ Reversed rankings	$\hat{\beta}$ not significantly different from zero	**Row Total**
$\hat{\beta} > 1$ Reinforcing incremental change	2M 2T (4)	—	—	**4**
$\hat{\beta} < 1$ Diversifying incremental change	3C 2E 7M IT (13)	—	1C 1E 1M IT (4)	**17**
$\hat{\beta}$ not significantly different from one	2C 3E 1M 2T (8)	—	—	**8**
$(1 - \hat{\beta}) > (1 - \hat{\rho})$ Diversifying incremental change	1E (1)	—	—	**1**
Column Total	**26**	**—**	**4**	**30**

(iib) RTA_{90} on RTA_{60} (pat60 > 500)

	Persistence			
Incremental Change	$\hat{\beta} > 0$ Persistent rankings	$\hat{\beta} < 0$ Reversed rankings	$\hat{\beta}$ not significantly different from zero	**Row Total**
$\hat{\beta} > 1$ Reinforcing incremental change	2M 2T (4)	—	—	**4**
$\hat{\beta} < 1$ Diversifying incremental change	3C 3E 5M (11)	—	1C 1M IT (3)	**14**
$\hat{\beta}$ not significantly different from one	2C 2E 1M IT (6)	—		**6**
$(1 - \hat{\beta}) > (1 - \hat{\rho})$ Diversifying incremental change	2E 2M 2T (6)	—	—	**6**
Column Total	**27**	**—**	**3**	**30**

(iii) RTA_{90} on RTA_{30} (pat30 > 100)

	Persistence			
Incremental Change	$\hat{\beta} > 0$ Persistent rankings	$\hat{\beta} < 0$ Reversed rankings	$\hat{\beta}$ not significantly different from zero	**Row Total**
$\hat{\beta} > 1$ Reinforcing incremental change	IE 1M (2)	—	—	**2**
$\hat{\beta} < 1$ Diversifying incremental change	2C IE 6M 2T (11)	—	1C 3E 1M IT (6)	**17**
$\hat{\beta}$ not significantly different from one	1C 2E 2T (5)	—	1C IT (2)	**7**
$(1 - \hat{\beta}) > (1 - \hat{\rho})$ Diversifying incremental change	1C 3M (4)	—	—	**4**
Column Total	**22**	**—**	**8**	**30**

Note: 32 firms reduce to 30 over time due to the merger of Sperry and Burroughs into Unisys, which, through data issues, was omitted for the 1960–90 and 1930–90 intervals.

logical competencies (persistence with reinforcing incremental change) were rare, as were firms seemingly engaging in more radical changes in their profiles by engaging in diversifying incremental change in the absence of persistence.

Comparing across industry groups in Table 4.1, persistence was strongly displayed within all CEMT groups in every period. However, in the electrical group there was a tendency for persistence to be eroded over very long periods and for the selected transport firms persistence strengthens very slightly in the later subperiod. The number of historically large chemical and mechanical firms displaying persistence over time was more or less stable in each period, but it is necessary to convey a caveat regarding the highly heterogeneous mechanical industrial group.

As the mechanical group is more broadly defined and heterogeneous than any other, as a by-product of aggregation across a wider range of companies, each firm would be measured as having a historically narrower, more concentrated focus of technological specialization. For example, the photographic companies were strongly focused in photographic instruments relative to, for example, textile and other firms. Because the firms of each separate industry exhibit a distinct profile of technological specialization (Patel and Pavitt, 1997) firms in the more heterogeneous mechanical group will tend to show particularly persistent technological profiles.

4.5.2 Firm-level Observations

4.5.2.1 Chemical
Table 4.2 highlights that among large chemical firms, persistence was a strong feature, particularly during 1960–90.[2] The exception was Allied Chemical (and to a lesser extent Du Pont). Allied Chemical maintained a non-persistent profile in each period. This is not surprising as Allied Chemical underwent major changes in its structure during this time. During the early subperiod, Allied Chemical found itself without strong guidance from a competent chairman but nevertheless pursued its earlier profitable activities in basic chemical production, however, it neglected to invest in R&D leaving its activities to become obsolete. Coinciding with diversifying incremental change in the later subperiod, two sequential chairmen (Connor in 1969 and Henessey in 1979) embarked Allied Chemical upon forays into oil, gas and high value-added products based on advanced technology. As a consequence, the company's interests are now highly diversified, lying in aerospace, electronic materials, polymers, speciality chemicals, automotive products, etc. (*International Directory of Company Histories, 1988–1992*). In fact, Allied Chemical is no longer strictly classifiable as a chemical company based on its products (which was the basis for industry classification of firms as they were in 1930 in this dataset – see Chapter 2), so we must regard its results with due caution.

Table 4.2   Chemical group

(i) RTA_{60} on RTA_{30}(pat30 > 100)

Incremental Change	Persistence		
	$\hat{\beta} > 0$ Persistent rankings	$\hat{\beta} < 0$ Reversed rankings	$\hat{\beta}$ not significantly different from zero
$\hat{\beta} > 1$ Reinforcing incremental change			
$\hat{\beta} < 1$ Diversifying incremental change	Standard Oil (NJ)		Du Pont
$\hat{\beta}$ not significantly different from one	IG Farben (Bayer/BASF/Hoechst) Union Carbide		Allied Chemical
$(1 - \hat{\beta}) > (1 - \hat{\rho})$ Diversifying incremental change	Swiss IG (Ciba/Geigy/Sandoz)		

(iia) RTA_{90} on RTA_{60}(pat30 > 100)

Incremental Change	Persistence		
	$\hat{\beta} > 0$ Persistent rankings	$\hat{\beta} < 0$ Reversed rankings	$\hat{\beta}$ not significantly different from zero
$\hat{\beta} > 1$ Reinforcing incremental change			
$\hat{\beta} < 1$ Diversifying incremental change	Bayer/BASF/Hoechst (IG Farben) Du Pont Union Carbide		Allied Chemical
$\hat{\beta}$ not significantly different from one	Ciba/Geigy/Sandoz (Swiss IG) Standard Oil (NJ)		
$(1 - \hat{\beta}) > (1 - \hat{\rho})$ Diversifying incremental change			

(iib) RTA$_{90}$ on RTA$_{60}$(pat60 > 500)

Incremental Change	Persistence		
	$\hat{\beta} > 0$ Persistent rankings	$\hat{\beta} < 0$ Reversed rankings	$\hat{\beta}$ not significantly different from zero
$\hat{\beta} > 1$ Reinforcing incremental change			
$\hat{\beta} < 1$ Diversifying incremental change	Bayer/BASF/Hoechst (IG Farben) Du Pont Union Carbide		Allied Chemical
$\hat{\beta}$ not significantly different from one	Ciba/Geigy/Sandoz (Swiss IG) Standard Oil (NJ)		
$(1 - \hat{\beta}) > (1 - \hat{\rho})$ Diversifying incremental change			

(iii) RTA$_{90}$ on RTA$_{30}$(pat30 > 100)

Incremental Change	Persistence		
	$\hat{\beta} > 0$ Persistent rankings	$\hat{\beta} < 0$ Reversed rankings	$\hat{\beta}$ not significantly different from zero
$\hat{\beta} > 1$ Reinforcing incremental change			
$\hat{\beta} < 1$ Diversifying incremental change	Standard Oil (NJ) Union Carbide		Du Pont
$\hat{\beta}$ not significantly different from one	Ciba/Geigy/Sandoz (Swiss IG)		Allied Chemical
$(1 - \hat{\beta}) > (1 - \hat{\rho})$ Diversifying incremental change	Bayer/BASF/Hoechst (IG Farben)		

Diversifying incremental change was less prevalent than persistence, although half to more than half of the selected firms experienced it during the intervals considered. Unsurprisingly, Du Pont is the one firm to display constant significant diversifying incremental change. This has been documented by more qualitative investigations into the company's history and development (Hounshell and Smith, 1988; Hounshell, 1992; Loasby, 1996). Also of note is the entire lack of reinforcing incremental change in this group of firms.

4.5.2.2 Electrical/electronic
Among electrical/electronic firms (Table 4.3) persistence was an overwhelming trend in both subperiods but this trend was somewhat weaker when viewed over the longer period – Siemens, RCA and AEG all displayed non-persistent technological profiles. This suggests that the technological evolution of these firms was more akin to the observed behaviour of countries, in which technological profiles tended to persist for approximately 20 or 30 years, but to break down over longer periods of 60 years (Pavitt et al., 1987; Cantwell, 1991a).

For Siemens the result reflects more qualitative accounts. Their continued prominent role in the production of military goods and equipment during both world wars probably dominates their earlier subperiod profile, despite having moved towards more commercial areas such as consumer radio receivers in the inter-war period. Post World War Two, the company moved more into railroad, medical, telephone and power-generating equipment and consumer-electronics products, becoming a dominant global player in many product areas by the late 1970s. Further ambitious programmes of acquisitions and R&D took place in the 1980s (*International Directory of Company Histories*, Vol. 2, pp. 97–100; Feldenkirchen, 1998).

Closer analysis of the regression results (not reported here) showed that RCA and AEG both had significant but weaker persistence in 1930–60 than in 1960–90, when it was very strong. However, persistence in 1930–90 overall was very weak.

Diversifying incremental change was less prevalent across the selected firms, although it affects more firms in the late subperiod on the pat60>500 basis, suggesting that where diversification strategies have gained importance among electrical/electronic firms in recent decades, it is in technological sectors of more recent patenting activity than the historically important ones (patenting in power and transport technologies has been squeezed out by that in semiconductors by this industry – see Table 2.2). AT&T stands out for its constant persistence and diversifying incremental change in each period, even though it was dogged by the US Department of Justice in the 1950s, anti-trust lawsuits in the 1970s and an eventual break up of its businesses in the 1980s (*International Directory of Company Histories*, Vol. 5, pp. 239–64). The other electrical/electronic firms largely exhibit persistence but are also much more variable in the incremental change behaviour they exhibit.

Table 4.3   Electrical/electronic group

(i) RTA_{60} on RTA_{30}(pat30 > 100)

Incremental Change	Persistence		
	$\hat{\beta} > 0$ Persistent rankings	$\hat{\beta} < 0$ Reversed rankings	$\hat{\beta}$ not significantly different from zero
$\hat{\beta} > 1$ Reinforcing incremental change	Singer		
$\hat{\beta} < 1$ Diversifying incremental change	Siemens AT&T RCA AEG-Telefunken Sperry Burroughs		
$\hat{\beta}$ not significantly different from one $(1 - \hat{\beta}) > (1 - \hat{\rho})$ Diversifying incremental change	General Electric Westinghouse Electric		

(iia) RTA_{90} on RTA_{60} (pat30 > 100)

Incremental Change	Persistence		
	$\hat{\beta} > 0$ Persistent rankings	$\hat{\beta} < 0$ Reversed rankings	$\hat{\beta}$ not significantly different from zero
$\hat{\beta} > 1$ Reinforcing incremental change			
$\hat{\beta} < 1$ Diversifying incremental change	AT&T Westinghouse Electric		Siemens
$\hat{\beta}$ not significantly different from one	General Electric RCA AEG-Telefunken		
$(1 - \hat{\beta}) > (1 - \hat{\rho})$ Diversifying incremental change	Singer		

(iib) RTA_{90} on RTA_{60}(pat60 > 500)

Incremental Change	Persistence		
	$\hat{\beta} > 0$ Persistent rankings	$\hat{\beta} < 0$ Reversed rankings	$\hat{\beta}$ not significantly different from zero
$\hat{\beta} > 1$ Reinforcing incremental change			
$\hat{\beta} < 1$ Diversifying incremental change	Siemens AT&T Singer		
$\hat{\beta}$ not significantly different from one	Westinghouse Electric RCA		
$(1 - \hat{\beta}) > (1 - \hat{\rho})$ Diversifying incremental change	General Electric AEG-Telefunken		

(iii) RTA_{90} on RTA_{30}(pat30 > 100)

Incremental Change	Persistence		
	$\hat{\beta} > 0$ Persistent rankings	$\hat{\beta} < 0$ Reversed rankings	$\hat{\beta}$ not significantly different from zero
$\hat{\beta} > 1$ Reinforcing incremental change	Singer		
$\hat{\beta} < 1$ Diversifying incremental change		AT&T	Siemens RCA AEG-Telefunken
$\hat{\beta}$ not significantly different from one	General Electric Westinghouse Electric		
$(1 - \hat{\beta}) > (1 - \hat{\rho})$ Diversifying incremental change			

Note: Sperry and Burroughs cannot be calculated for the regressions of 1990 on an earlier period, because by 1984 the two had merged to form Unisys.

4.5.2.3 Mechanical

Persistence in the mechanical firms' technological profiles was again dominant as Table 4.4 shows, although the earlier caveat on heterogeneity applies. Krupp is the exception but its lack of persistence in the later subperiod can be explained by the fact that post-World War Two, the allied forces ordered the divestiture of Krupp's coal and steel assets. This may have forced/enabled Krupp to rebuild and consolidate its interests in fabrication, trading and engineering and may have initiated the move in its interests into the technological fields which were of importance in 1960–90 on the pat60>500 basis. These areas subsequently became the focus of Krupp's production in the late 1970s and 1980s and such behaviour might account for why in 1960–90 on the pat30>100 basis, Krupp possesses a diversifying but non-persistent technological profile.

Diversifying incremental change, although again slightly less pronounced than persistence, does appear to get more widespread across the firms over the longer time frame. With the exception of Westinghouse Air Brake, all firms show an element of diversifying incremental change in the longer period.

4.5.2.4 Transport

In the transport industrial grouping (Table 4.5), persistence and diversifying incremental change were equally prevalent in 1930–60. However, in 1960–90, persistence was the much stronger trait. The exceptions to persistence were Firestone and United Aircraft.

However, like Allied Chemical above, this outcome for United Aircraft is not entirely unexpected, as it is well known that the firm is a substantially different entity now (as United Technologies) to that which it was in 1930. At that time, United Aircraft was a monopoly in the US aeronautics industry and it continued to grow through a process of acquisition and merger. This policy appears to have led to diversifying incremental change, but a lack of techno-logical persistence in the early subperiod. United Aircraft continued to diversify in the 1960s and 70s to the extent that by 1975, its original company name no longer reflected the diversity of its interests and so they renamed themselves United Technologies. Growth through acquisitions continued until the mid-1980s after which a programme of business rationalization and organizational restructuring was implemented. It also appears that automotive firms experi-enced diversifying incremental change in the presence or absence of persistence, whereas the tyre companies have had an apparent tendency to concentrate over time. This would fit intuitively given that automotives are systems-based products, whilst tyres are much more focused, perhaps therefore requiring less breadth of technological knowledge by comparison.

Table 4.4   Mechanical group

(i) RTA_{60} on RTA_{30} (pat30 > 100)

Incremental Change	Persistence		
	$\hat{\beta} > 0$ Persistent rankings	$\hat{\beta} < 0$ Reversed rankings	$\hat{\beta}$ not significantly different from zero
$\hat{\beta} > 1$ Reinforcing incremental change	Emhart Westinghouse Air Brake		
$\hat{\beta} < 1$ Diversifying incremental change	Eastman Kodak Deere US Steel Allis Chalmers International Harvester American Can Bethlehem Steel Vickers		
$\hat{\beta}$ not significantly different from one	Krupp		
$(1 - \hat{\beta}) > (1 - \hat{\rho})$ Diversifying incremental change			

(iia) RTA_{90} on RTA_{60} (pat30 > 100)

Incremental Change	Persistence		
	$\hat{\beta} > 0$ Persistent rankings	$\hat{\beta} < 0$ Reversed rankings	$\hat{\beta}$ not significantly different from zero
$\hat{\beta} > 1$ Reinforcing incremental change	Deere International Harvester		
$\hat{\beta} < 1$ Diversifying incremental change	Emhart US Steel Allis Chalmers American Can Bethlehem Steel Vickers Westinghouse Air Brake		Krupp
$\hat{\beta}$ not significantly different from one	Eastman Kodak		
$(1 - \hat{\beta}) > (1 - \hat{\rho})$ Diversifying incremental change			

(iib) RTA_{90} on RTA_{60} (pat60 > 500)

Incremental Change	Persistence		
	$\hat{\beta} > 0$ Persistent rankings	$\hat{\beta} < 0$ Reversed rankings	$\hat{\beta}$ not significantly different from zero
$\hat{\beta} > 1$ Reinforcing incremental change	Deere International Harvester		
$\hat{\beta} < 1$ Diversifying incremental change	US Steel Allis Chalmers Krupp American Can Bethlehem Steel		Vickers
$\hat{\beta}$ not significantly different from one	Eastman Kodak		
$(1 - \hat{\beta}) > (1 - \hat{\rho})$ Diversifying incremental change	Emhart Westinghouse Air Brake		

(iii) RTA_{90} on RTA_{30}(pat30 > 100)

Incremental Change	Persistence		
	$\hat{\beta} > 0$ Persistent rankings	$\hat{\beta} < 0$ Reversed rankings	$\hat{\beta}$ not significantly different from zero
$\hat{\beta} > 1$ Reinforcing incremental change	Westinghouse Air Brake		
$\hat{\beta} < 1$ Diversifying incremental change	Eastman Kodak US Steel Allis Chalmers American Can Bethlehem Steel Vickers		Krupp
$\hat{\beta}$ not significantly different from one			
$(1 - \hat{\beta}) > (1 - \hat{\rho})$ Diversifying incremental change	Emhart Deere International Harvester		

Table 4.5 Transport group

(i) RTA_{60} on RTA_{30}(pat30 > 100)

Incremental Change	Persistence		
	$\hat{\beta} > 0$ Persistent rankings	$\hat{\beta} < 0$ Reversed rankings	$\hat{\beta}$ not significantly different from zero
$\hat{\beta} > 1$ Reinforcing incremental change			
$\hat{\beta} < 1$ Diversifying incremental change	General Motors Bendix		United Aircraft
$\hat{\beta}$ not significantly different from one			Firestone Tyre & Rubber
$(1 - \hat{\beta}) > (1 - \hat{\rho})$ Diversifying incremental change	Goodyear Tyre & Rubber BF Goodrich		

(iia) RTA_{90} on RTA_{60}(pat30 > 100)

Incremental Change	Persistence		
	$\hat{\beta} > 0$ Persistent rankings	$\hat{\beta} < 0$ Reversed rankings	$\hat{\beta}$ not significantly different from zero
$\hat{\beta} > 1$ Reinforcing incremental change	Goodyear Tyre & Rubber BF Goodrich		
$\hat{\beta} < 1$ Diversifying incremental change	Bendix		United Aircraft
$\hat{\beta}$ not significantly different from one	General Motors Firestone Tyre & Rubber		
$(1 - \hat{\beta}) > (1 - \hat{\rho})$ Diversifying incrementalchange			

(iib) RTA$_{90}$ on RTA$_{60}$(pat60 > 500)

Incremental Change	Persistence		
	$\hat{\beta} > 0$ Persistent rankings	$\hat{\beta} < 0$ Reversed rankings	$\hat{\beta}$ not significantly different from zero
$\hat{\beta} > 1$ Reinforcing incremental change	BF Goodrich Firestone Tyre & Rubber		
$\hat{\beta} < 1$ Diversifying incremental change			United Aircraft
$\hat{\beta}$ not significantly different from one	Goodyear Tyre & Rubber		
$(1 - \hat{\beta}) > (1 - \hat{\rho})$ Diversifying incremental change	General Motors Bendix		

(iii) RTA$_{90}$ on RTA$_{30}$(pat30 > 100)

Incremental Change	Persistence		
	$\hat{\beta} > 0$ Persistent rankings	$\hat{\beta} < 0$ Reversed rankings	$\hat{\beta}$ not significantly different from zero
$\hat{\beta} > 1$ Reinforcing incremental change			
$\hat{\beta} < 1$ Diversifying incremental change	General Motors Bendix		United Aircraft
$\hat{\beta}$ not significantly different from one	Goodyear Tyre & Rubber BF Goodrich		Firestone Tyre & Rubber
$(1 - \hat{\beta}) > (1 - \hat{\rho})$ Diversifying incremental change			

4.6   SUMMARY AND CONCLUSIONS

In accordance with theoretical expectations, this chapter found that persistence was a strong characteristic of historically large firms lending support to the existence of path-dependency in the technological development of firms. The strength of persistence appears to be tied with the degree of institutional continuity among large firms because a lack of persistence has tended to occur largely in those firms which have experienced post-war restructuring or those which experienced a disruption in corporate organizational activity (i.e. Allied Chemical, United Aircraft). In the case of the latter, the behaviour of the firm is much more akin to that of a country (see Cantwell, 1991a). However, the degree to which persistence was widespread amongst firms did fall a little over much longer periods of time. This suggests that persistence did erode gradually, at least in some firms. However, the length of time over which persistence remained was found to be at least 60 years in the majority of cases – much longer than has been tested for before. This confirms the hypothesis that very large firms provide considerably more stability over time than has been found for the case of countries, despite possibly profound changes in the composition of the science base and of market demands.

Diversifying incremental change is a fairly widespread phenomenon among very large companies, with about two-thirds of the selected companies exhibiting such traits in their profiles of competencies over time. Moreover, it appears to have been just as widespread (if not marginally more so) historically as in recent decades. However, given that in recent times the motivation for technological diversification has been perceived to be growing inter-relatedness between formerly distinct technologies, the motivation for the historical tendency needs to be examined to see if this motivation also holds true in the earlier part of the period.

It seems that strong persistence in the technological profile of a firm's competencies does not preclude the occurrence of incremental change that leads firms to become more diversified. The two are not mutually exclusive. Although the tendency towards technological diversification has been a prevalent feature among very large firms it has been incremental in nature, and is unlikely to undermine the persistence of the principal technological activities of large companies, even over very long timescales of 60 years or so. Despite persistence, the firm's profile of specialization does tend to broaden through a process of incremental diversification in the majority of the largest US and European firms. There are incidences of persistence and either a lack of diversifying incremental change or even reinforcing incremental change, but for the most part, these are rare. However, what is notable is that diversifying incremental change is not a process of continuous drift as sometimes implicitly supposed, but tends to occur in phases in the face of occasional shifts across various firms, driven perhaps by either technological and/or organizational issues. This is a matter that I shall explore further in Chapter 6.

Many writers on technological change have emphasized its tendency to transform and disrupt economies from time to time and over longer periods, not least Schumpeter in his notion of 'creative destruction'. This chapter offers a rather different perspective. Other authors have focused on spheres of activity that are largely exogenous to individual firms: the science and the knowledge base, and the composition of products and markets. These spheres of activity do indeed change quite dramatically over time, and especially over longer periods, but many large firms survive despite these changes. This is because whilst the products may change, 'the firm develops a basic strength above or below the end product level as it were – in technology of specialized kinds and in market positions' (Penrose, 1959, p. 150); the firm is in effect a 'pool of resources' and its products at any one time merely reflect the way the firm chooses to combine those resources at that moment. In this way, the firm potentially provides a vehicle for institutional continuity, a means by which tacit capability or competence can be transformed (through learning and experimentation) to relate to and encompass a new body of knowledge; knowledge required in order to produce different products, to serve and help to create new markets. Such a transformation may imply that the survival of the firm depends in the longer term upon the management of divisional and other organizational restructuring, but the firm's productive and technological system itself is potentially more stable. Thus, the firm provides a means for preserving a greater social continuity, and a device for managing technological transitions within the economic system. Just as an inter-firm variety of technological paths may serve as an aid to stability in a changing environment (Eliasson, 1991), so too will the path-dependency itself of technological learning within each firm.

NOTES

1. This chapter is based on Cantwell and Fai (1999), with permission from Springer-Verlag.
2. I acknowledge that it is somewhat misleading to continue to treat the consolidated corporate groups of IG Farben and Swiss IG as single entities in their own right in the post-war period. This formulation was necessary to have a consistent basis for comparison between 1930 and 1990. The persistence in these firms after the war is therefore merely hypothetical. However, analysis of the individual firms that made up these consolidated corporate groups (not provided here) suggested that within the individual firms themselves, persistence in their individual technological profiles continued to be a strong feature in the post-war period to 1990.

5. Technological diversification

5.1 INTRODUCTION

By looking at the balance of the regression and mobility effects, the previous chapter found that large firms had a general tendency towards diversifying incremental change in their technological profiles even in the presence of strong persistence, as long as they did not undergo substantial institutional restructuring. Whilst diversifying incremental change is suggestive of an increase in the diversity of technological competence within each firm, in itself, it is not an adequate indicator of technological diversification; a stronger indicator is required. This chapter will seek to measure technological diversification directly, its pervasiveness across firms and the strength with which it has been engaged in over time.

5.2 THE EXISTENCE OF DIVERSIFIED FIRMS

The fact that firms are diversified is well documented. Firms have diversified the markets they serve for well over a century now, improvements in transport, infrastructure and communications have facilitated the supply of goods from one geographic market to another. As demand for goods rose, many firms sought out economies of scale in production but also as consumer demands altered and changed, firms exploited economies of scope as they found that they could draw upon certain competencies and resources to produce a greater range of products (Penrose, 1959; Chandler, 1966, 1990a; Rumelt, 1974). The multi-product firm is the contemporary 'norm', and increasingly, medium- to large-sized firms are multinational. Thus, firms have diversified across products, markets (Teece, 1982) and industries (Pearce, 1983) for a long time. By contrast, technological diversification in its own right appears to be the subject of relatively recent debate.[1]

Discussion of diversification in general terms has tended to assume that when market and product diversification are engaged in, technological diversification will also occur as a complementary process, indeed the three are closely related. However, any single firm with an established technological base is able to engage in some market and/or product diversification without necessarily diversifying technologically, and vice versa as time progresses. If the firm is truly regarded as a 'pool of resources' whose products merely reflect the manner in which the firm has chosen to combine its resources at that point in time (Penrose, 1959), then the firm can configure and re-configure its product range to a considerable extent without taking on board any new technologies. The firm would just transfer technology from one application to another (see Granstrand and Sjölander, 1990 for an example of technology transfer in the Swedish auto- and aerospace company Saab-Scania).

There is also the converse argument that a firm can technologically diversify without apparently becoming more diversified in its products and markets. This is particularly the case in the hi-tech industries as demonstrated by Gambardella and Torrisi (1998) in the electronics industry, and by Andersen and Walsh (2000) in the chemical industry. These industry studies support the argument forwarded earlier by Granstrand and various co-authors (Granstrand and Sjölander, 1990; Granstrand and Oskarsson, 1994; Granstrand et al., 1997; Patel and Pavitt, 1997) for the emergence of the multi-technology or 'mul-tech' firm in recent decades.[2] The increasing technological complexity of even once simple artefacts, combined with the increasing inter-relatedness perceived to be growing between technologies (Kodama, 1986, 1992) would imply that most firms must necessarily become multi-technology in order to compete effectively in the current economic climate. This does not automatically mean that their product ranges increase,[3] just that as generations of products proceed, technological transitions have to be made in the competence base of the firm as the products they produce become more technologically complex.[4] Thus whilst technological, product and market diversification can, and probably do, occur together,[5] it is not necessarily the case.

5.3 WHY DO FIRMS DIVERSIFY?

Firms in Japan, Sweden and the US have exhibited, to varying degrees, a trend towards technological diversification (Granstrand et al., 1990). Firms diversify because of competitive pressures, but these pressures are numerous in their forms. Traditional economic theory would provide that firms diversify to exploit economies of scale and scope in order to lower costs of production. They might also interpret product proliferation through a diversified, differentiated range as a means of protecting incumbent firms in an industry from new entrants who are better able to meet consumer demands with respect to the types of products they want and the features and characteristics they wish them to contain (Saviotti and Metcalfe, 1984). One might view this as horizontal integration. Similarly, firms may diversify vertically up- or downstream to protect themselves against, or themselves exert, monopoly or monopsony power in specialized resources or distribution networks. There is also the notion of diversification undertaken to offset risk with respect to dependence upon any single market or to generate financial returns on portfolio investments.

In terms of technology, it would seem that, given the apparent diminishing returns to R&D expenditure caused by the complex nature of technological progress today, and the speed with which it develops, the motivation to exploit economies of scope in the application of a technology to many areas is high (Granstrand et al., 1990). Technological diversification may also be a necessity for the producers of products and artefacts, either because the technology can be employed in the production process and enable the firm to produce more rapidly and efficiently, or because the artefacts themselves need to embody new technology to compete with rival products in existing markets. It may also be that technological diversification is employed strategically: as a hedge against the potential litigation from or opportunistic behaviour of the firm's partners, customers and suppliers (Mowery, 1983 from Pavitt et al., 1987); defensively against the risks associated with being dependent upon a technologically dynamic environment (Hill and Hansen, 1991); or indeed to behave in an opportunistic manner themselves as observed in the rise of patenting in the 1990s for cross-licensing or technology blocking purposes (Jaffe, 2000).

Penrose suggested early on that firms diversify not only because changing conditions present threats to firms, but because they also present new profitable *opportunities* for firms whilst maintaining or even expanding their current lines of production (1959, p. 106). In other words, diversification can be a defensive measure in the face of competitive pressures, but it may also be offensively motivated. It may also arise because potential interdependencies might occur in the firm's technical relationship with its network of partners, etc. – an important factor particularly in the current trend towards outsourcing and linkages between firms and external suppliers (Brusoni et al., 2001). Penrose's alternative view is an accepted stance in contemporary evolutionary and resource-based literature that speaks of the technological opportunities facing firms, although even in these areas the issue was not truly embraced until relatively recently (Klevorick et al., 1995). However, it is still not an issue which is encompassed in neoclassical economic theory because of the latter's failure to perceive technological development as anything other than some exogenous shock – a phenomenon that takes place within a 'black box' (Rosenberg, 1982, 1994). The firm is seen to be forever trying to catch up or maintain pace with the scientific and technological changes taking place in its external environment. But as evolutionary economists and resource-base theorists have recognized, new opportunities are not just related to changes in market conditions, but also to 'special kinds of productive services and knowledge developed within a firm' (Penrose, 1959, p. 106). This fits well with the view taken here of the firm as a repository of competence and a vehicle of stability in a turbulent environment.

Given that firms diversify because of both threats and opportunities, these are likely to differ depending on the principal industrial activity the firm is engaged in. Pavitt (1984) found that firms were likely to diversify upstream into production technologies for scale-intensive and supplier-dominated firms in industrial areas such as mining, vehicles, metals, agriculture, etc.; upstream, downstream and horizontally for chemical firms; and horizontally for mechanical, instrument and electrical/electronic firms. Hence, the issue of diversification will be examined in the light of each of the four industrial groupings.

5.4 THE CONCEPT AND MEASUREMENT OF DIVERSIFICATION

It is important to define diversification. This book considers the notion of technological diversification as the changing degree of diversity in a firm's technological base (Kodama, 1986; Pavitt et al., 1989; Granstrand and Sjölander, 1990; Oskarsson, 1990). However, as Oskarsson (1990) points out, the notion of diversity is generally referred to as a state, and diversification is the process of increasing diversity over time. This implies that to test for the occurrence of diversification I need to examine whether the diversity, or width, of the corporation's technological base has been increasing over time. There are two main problems with this.

The first applies to all studies of diversity and diversification, in that there must be a unit of measurement. Such units are dependent upon the means of classifying categories across which to observe and measure diversity. These are largely subjective, although in some cases such as the Standard Industrial Classifications (SIC) these have become rather more standardized and accepted. Even here though, national systems differ and the classification level itself (e.g. three or four-digit codes) will affect any analysis of industrial diversification by a firm within a national system. With technologies, there is no directly comparable standardized classification of technologies. The nearest proxy is the patent system. Here again though, problems exist associated with their national differentiation with respect to classification and whether analysis is conducted at the level of patent classes or subclasses.

As stated in Chapter 2, this book relies on US patent data drawn from the US Patent and Trademark Office. The reason is simply that the US still provides the world's greatest market and any significant international innovations will most likely apply for and receive a patent there. Also mentioned earlier was the fact that as patent classes evolve, the USPTO fortunately reclassifies all earlier patents accordingly. Hence by using one patent system, I overcome the national differentiation problem. The Reading database classifies all patents within it at various levels (see Chapter 2). I shall continue to use the 56 technological fields level but still filtered to eliminate small number problems on the basis of the pat30>100 criterion. This does mean that a rather specific view of technological diversity will be observed within this dataset. With this restriction we cannot observe diversification across all technological fields, those sectors that initially started off small numbers (less than 100 patents in 1930) will not be picked up as they grow in importance over time. However, at the level of each individual firm, constrained diversification[6] will be picked up in those sectors that were large enough to qualify because the individual firm itself may have had no patents in 1930 in some of the selected sectors. The problem of not encompassing some of the historically small, but more recently significant technologies into which firms may have diversified (e.g. semiconductors) was potentially offset to a degree by the use of the alternative selection criterion of pat60>500, which was particularly useful for capturing rapidly emerging technologies especially in the chemical and electrical/electronic industrial groupings, but this still does not overcome the problem entirely. Therefore, the concept of diversification used in this book is that the firm's profile of technological expertise enters and/or becomes more evenly spread across the selected sectors over time, and thus the firm's activities in fields not previously entered or previously less favoured are rising relative to their activities in previously favoured fields.[7]

Even if all 56 fields were used, there may be problems because an upper bound limits the extent of diversification. For example, if a firm should be actively patenting in 56 technologies at the beginning of any period under study, it cannot demonstrate further diversification in the sense of moving into more technologies and demonstrating increased breadth across the fields. In fact that firm would probably appear to be concentrating in certain technologies unless the proportion of patenting activity devoted to each of the 56 technologies remained constant over time, which is unlikely given that technological opportunities change over time. For this reason, it is prudent to consider not only diversification as measured by changes in technological breadth, but also the actual strength of diversification across the technologies a firm patents in.

5.4.1 Measuring Diversity and the Strength of Diversification

A firm's degree of technological specialization can be measured by the estimated coefficient of variation (CV) of the RTA index across all technological sectors, expressed as a percentage ratio:

$$CV_{RTA} = \sigma_{RTA}/\mu_{RTA} \times 100\% \tag{5.1}$$

This takes into account the possibility of a changing mean RTA value in the firm's technological profile over time. The mean of the RTA index varies because not all technological fields are of equal size in terms of their total patent stock. The mean rises when the firm is specialized in (or moves towards) 'smaller' rather than 'larger' sectors. Since these variations in mean values are an arbitrary result of the sectoral classification scheme, they must be controlled for when measuring diversification. This measure was used earlier in Chapter 3; however, there I was considering the technological *convergence* between the four broadly defined industrial groupings, and the CV was used to measure a decrease in each industrial group's technological concentration. Whilst the CV is a positive measure of concentration, it is also an inverse measure of diversification. Therefore, since diversification is the issue at hand, for ease of exposition, I have chosen to use $(1/\hat{C}V)$, expressed as a percentage, as an indicator of diversification. If $(1/\hat{C}V)$ rises, the firm demonstrates that its technological profile has become more diversified over time, and vice versa. To explore the strength of diversification I employ a simple percentage change measure based on the original observation calculation, which is similar to the measure used by Cantwell and Andersen (1996, p. 227) but applied to the inverse of the CV for the reason identified earlier.

Initially, to establish whether technological diversification is a recent phenomenon or one that occurred historically also, the $(1/\hat{C}V)$ values were compared over the periods 1930–60, 1960–90 and 1930–90 for the 32 firms and corporate groups. The results for the presence of diversification versus concentration are summarized in Tables 5.1–5.5, whilst the strength of diversification is given in Figures 5.1–5.4.

5.5 THE PREVALENCE OF DIVERSIFICATION ACROSS FIRMS

Table 5.1 shows that across all industrial groups, in each subperiod, technological diversification is more widespread than concentration. Moreover, diversification is slightly more widespread across the selected firms in the earlier subperiod. This is a little at odds with the observations of Granstrand, Pavitt and other authors, who have regarded technological diversification as a phenomenon of recent decades due to the growing inter-relatedness between former distinct technologies.

As mentioned above, Pavitt's taxonomy (1984) found that there were very different technological directions in which certain types of firms were likely to diversify. Similarly the timing with which their diversity changes differs across industrial groups. Looking broadly at the individual industry patterns it can be seen that more firms in the electrical/electronics, mechanical and transport groups experienced diversification in 1930–60, whereas chemical firms generally experience diversification that becomes more widespread from one subperiod to the other. Over the entire 60-year period, significant proportions of the chemical, electrical/electronic and mechanical groups reveal firms showing diversification in their technological competencies whilst the transport group was evenly split between diversification and concentration.

Table 5.1   Evidence of diversification – all firms

1930–60 (pat30>100)	
Diversified	*Concentrated*
4C 6E 9M 4T	2C 3E 2M 2T
(23)	(9)

1960–90a (pat30>100)	
Diversified	*Concentrated*
5C 3E 8M 2T	1C 4E 3M 4T
(18)	(12)

1960–90b (pat60>500)	
Diversified	*Concentrated*
6C 4E 7M 3T	0C 3E 4M 3T
(20)	(10)

1930–90 (pat30>100)	
Diversified	*Concentrated*
4C 6E 10M 3T	2C 1E 1M 3T
(23)	(7)

Note: Sperry and Burroughs merged in 1984 to form Unisys, so the analysis of 1960–90 was not possible for these firms, and the number of electrical firms drops in total from nine to seven between the two intervals.

In the next section, I consider intra-industry outcomes. As a point of general comparison, it is interesting to note that the outcomes of this more direct measure of diversification generate markedly different outcomes for each of the firms than the indicator for diversifying incremental change used in Chapter 4 (see Tables 4.2–4.5). This suggests that there is considerable movement in the mean RTA values over time, making the changes in the $1/\hat{C}V$ measure a more reliable indicator of diversification than the balance of regression and mobility effects.

5.5.1 Chemical

From Table 5.2, there is a notable difference in behaviour between American and European firms. All the American companies diversified constantly over the period (except Allied Chalmers, which was explained in the previous chapter). The two European firms have quite different behaviour despite having the common origin of coal-based dye production. The IG Farben group appears to diversify over 1930–90[8] while the Swiss IG group on the other hand appears to concentrate continuously over the period.[9]

In the inter-war period, IG Farben benefited from its close association with the Nazis, who encouraged them to develop technologies useful to the military economy, including synthetic oil, synthetic rubber, nitrates, explosives, dyestuffs and much more. Post-World War Two, the group was dissolved into three separate companies again and their patents were removed from their ownership as a means of post-war retribution. However, this spurred all three companies towards strong diversification in the late 1950s and beyond. Bayer reverted to dyestuffs, pharmacology and photographics, developed new insecticides, fibres, and new raw and plastic finished materials, and in the 1980s committed itself to pharmaceutical and agricultural chemicals. Hoechst reverted to dyestuffs, fibre manufacturing and pharmaceuticals, and although it later also moved into plastics and agricultural chemicals, its primary interests in the 1980s and 1990s were in pharmaceuticals. BASF initially reverted back to dyestuffs, nylons and inorganic chemicals, but switched emphasis in the 1960s into oil-based products, enabling it to become a leader in plastics and synthetic fibres. By the 1990s BASF had six diversified business sectors: health and nutrition, colorants and finishing products, chemicals, plastics and fibres, oil and gas and other interests (Borkin, 1979; *International Directory of Company Histories, 1988–1992*). Hence, the empirical pattern in the data supports qualitative accounts of the company's behaviour.

The same can be said for Swiss IG. The Swiss firms remained politically neutral during World War Two but formed the cartel Swiss IG because of the strength of German competition. Together the three companies brought competencies relating to pharmaceuticals, inorganic, organic and synthetic dyes. Not a great deal is known about the Swiss group's activities during the war, but their neutrality may have meant that they were not so disrupted in their technological activities in that period. Even though their access to raw materials

Table 5.2   Chemical group

1930–60 (pat30>100)	
Diversified	*Concentrated*
Union Carbide	Allied Chemical
Standard Oil	Swiss IG/Ciba/Geigy/Sandoz
Du Pont	
IG Farben/Bayer/BASF/Hoechst	

1960–90a (pat30>100)	
Diversified	*Concentrated*
Union Carbide	Allied Chemical
Standard Oil	
Du Pont	
IG Farben/Bayer/BASF/Hoechst	
Swiss IG/Ciba/Geigy/Sandoz	

1960–90b (pat60>500)	
Diversified	*Concentrated*
Union Carbide	
Standard Oil	
Du Pont	
IG Farben/Bayer/BASF/Hoechst	
Allied Chemical	
Swiss IG/Ciba/Geigy/Sandoz	

1930–90 (pat30>100)	
Diversified	*Concentrated*
Union Carbide	Allied Chemical
Standard Oil	Swiss IG/Ciba/Geigy/Sandoz
Du Pont	
IG Farben/Bayer/BASF/Hoechst	

from Germany was curtailed, they managed to gain some supplies from Great Britain and the United States, and all three firms benefited from their collaborations into broader chemical interests whilst part of Swiss IG. However, whilst the Swiss firms as individual entities after WWII did grow and diversify, they deliberately embarked on a highly focused diversification strategy, continuing in pharmaceuticals, dyes, plastics, textile auxiliaries, agricultural and speciality chemicals (the overlap of interests lay behind the Ciba-Geigy merger in 1970, and the merger with Sandoz to form Novartis in the 1990s was also logical given its diversification into dyes, chemicals and pharmaceuticals). Hence the technological diversification evident in Table 5.2 appears to reflect a parallel development to this more qualitative account of product diversification.

In Figure 5.1, it is clear that the strength of diversification was greater (or at least, concentration was weaker) in 1960–90 than 1930–60 for all firms except Standard Oil (NJ). Indeed, in 1930–60 Standard Oil experienced much product diversification (from kerosene to gasoline and also into residual fuel oils that were used as coal substitutes) and this appears to be accompanied by technological diversification. The strength of diversification in the later subperiod (on

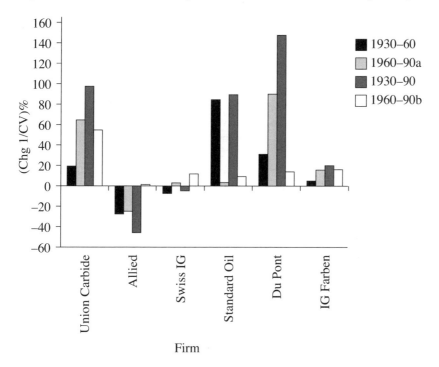

Figure 5.1   Strength of diversification – chemical

either set of criteria) is due to the technological opportunities provided to scale-intensive, scientific-based firms such as these, through diversifying upstream, downstream and horizontally, as in Pavitt's taxonomy (Pavitt et al., 1989).

5.5.2 Electrical/Electronic

In the early subperiod the electrical/electronic grouping is split favourably on the side of diversification (Table 5.3) and, whilst most firms display diversification over the entire 60-year period, a number of firms experienced concentration.

In 1930–60, Singer became more concentrated because the company basically remained a one-product firm until the 1960s (Stopford, 1992, p. 1173). Westinghouse's experience in the same subperiod can be accounted for by a lack of expansion in the 1930s and strong, military-motivated diversification during WWII, leading to phenomenal growth but in highly focused technological areas. Post-war, the company failed to move into other areas of opportunity and was dogged by labour and competitive problems. By 1963 Fortune wrote that Westinghouse had 'reached a low ebb in its corporate life' (*International Directory of Company Histories*, p. 121). In 1960–90 AEG, AT&T and RCA all became more technologically concentrated in both sets of technologies, but it seems that all three suffered considerable problems and endured radical organizational rationalization in this period, with AT&T being forced to break up into the American Bell Systems in 1984, AEG being bought by Daimler-Benz in 1985, and RCA being acquired by General Electric in 1986.

One outstanding result here is the continuous concentration of General Electric. This is currently one of the world's largest companies, and a highly diversified company with 12 major businesses.[10] This is, therefore, a peculiar and unexpected outcome.

It is likely that the observed concentration in this case is an empirical phenomenon brought about by the limitation of observing the behaviour of the company in only 21 (24 on pat60>500 basis) broadly defined technological fields, whereas the company has actively patented in almost all 56, thus highlighting the shortcomings of using technologies selected on their historical significance at two points in time. However, General Electric is a unique firm in the magnitude and extent of its interests. Given the long-term perspective of this study, it is felt that the trade-off in the results for this single firm is more than offset by the more reliable results obtained across the other firms as a result of imposing the selection criteria on the technologies to overcome small number problems in the historical data.

The other company of note for the consistency of its behaviour is Siemens. This company has continuously diversified across the selected technological sectors. In the inter-war period this was probably through military-led research

Table 5.3   Electrical/electronic group

1930–60 (pat30>100)

Diversified	Concentrated
Siemens	General Electric
AEG-Telefunken	Westinghouse Electric
Sperry	Singer
Burroughs	
AT&T	
RCA	

1960–90a (pat30>100)

Diversified	Concentrated
Westinghouse Electric	General Electric
Singer	AEG-Telefunken
Siemens	AT&T
	RCA

1960–90b (pat60>500)

Diversified	Concentrated
General Electric	AEG-Telefunken
Westinghouse Electric	AT&T
Singer	RCA
Siemens	

1930–90 (pat30>100)

Diversified	Concentrated
Westinghouse Electric	General Electric
Singer	
Siemens	
AEG-Telefunken	
AT&T	
RCA	

Note: See Table 5.1 on Sperry and Burroughs.

into electrical systems for armaments and, although badly affected by bombings, through considerable restructuring, the company was once again producing railroad, medical, telephone, power-generating equipment and consumer electronic products by the early 1950s. Thereafter, Siemens experienced tremendous growth and diversification in products and technology to the extent that by 1978 it had replaced Westinghouse Electric as General Electric's major global competitor and it had also become a competitive force against IBM in West Germany. In the 1980s the company continued to pursue a long-term programme of acquisitions and intensive R&D to make itself into a high-technology world leader (*International Directory of Company Histories*, Vol. 2, pp. 97–100).

For the electrical/electronic firms diversification was very strong in 1930–60 for Sperry, Burroughs and RCA (Figure 5.2) due to the electrification of type-writers, calculators, counting machines and other previously mechanically based office equipment and their development into computers and computing systems. On the other hand, GE, Westinghouse and Singer experienced stronger

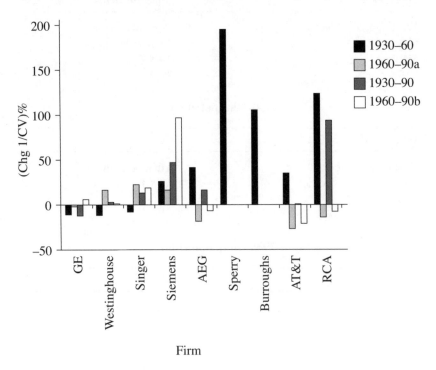

Note: Sperry and Burroughs merged in 1984 to form Unisys, so the analysis of 1960–90 was not possible for these firms.

Figure 5.2   Strength of diversification – electrical/electronic

diversification (or weaker concentration) in 1960–90 (pat30>100 basis – add Siemens on the alternative criterion). This is associated with the emergence of semiconductor activity, whose technological trajectory provided an abundance of technological opportunities to electrical firms in the late 1950s and early 1960s (Pavitt, 1986) – a time when the above electrical firms started to move into electronics technologies and product areas.

5.5.3 Mechanical

Among the mechanical industrial group most firms experienced diversification and, when combined with the results for persistence from the previous chapter, conform quite well to the view that corporate profiles of technological competencies are path-dependent and cumulative in nature, but at the same time may diversify incrementally over time (Table 5.4). The prevalence of diversification among this group of firms is not surprising given the earlier caveat of their heterogeneity and when set in the context of the pervasiveness of general purpose technologies (Chapter 3). A small number of firms experienced concentration in one subperiod, but again these appear to mirror more qualitative accounts of their histories that relate to various problems: labour disputes (Deere), economic pressures (Westinghouse Air Brake, Deere and International Harvester), competitive pressures and antitrust lawsuits (Eastman Kodak), failed attempts to break into overseas markets (Deere) and organizational and ownership instability (Vickers). Although none of these deal with technologies directly, it is inferred here that these 'other' problems are likely to have diverted resources from being directed at technological diversification.

Only Emhart experienced concentration strong enough to reveal itself over the entire period. The company engaged in horizontal integration to become a major manufacturer of builders' hardware from 1902 to the 1950s (Stopford, 1992, pp. 442–4); but it looks as if this involved the more concentrated use of certain technologies to do so, emphasizing the point made in an earlier section that product diversification and technological diversification need not happen concurrently. There was moderate diversification in the late 1950s–60s and throughout the 1970s business activities were largely geared towards the eventual merger of Emhart Industries Inc. with USM Corporation, which was eventually completed in 1987 (ibid.).

With respect to the strength of technological diversification in Figure 5.3, amongst the mechanical firms only four firms (Bethlehem Steel, Krupp, Emhart and Westinghouse Air Brake) diversify more strongly in the later subperiod than the earlier one (substitute US Steel for Bethlehem Steel for the pat60>500 criterion). In this grouping therefore, it seems that diversification was not only more widespread across firms but also stronger within firms in 1930–60 than in 1960–90.

Table 5.4　Mechanical group

1930–60 (pat30>100)	
Diversified	*Concentrated*
US Steel	Emhart
Bethlehem Steel	Westinghouse Air Brake
American Can	
Krupp	
International Harvester	
Deere	
Allis Chalmers	
Vickers	
Eastman Kodak	

1960–90a (pat30>100)	
Diversified	*Concentrated*
US Steel	Emhart
Bethlehem Steel	
American Can	
Krupp	
International Harvester	
Deere	
Allis Chalmers	
Vickers	
Eastman Kodak	
Westinghouse Air Brake	

1960–90b (pat60>500)	
Diversified	*Concentrated*
US Steel	International Harvester
Bethlehem Steel	Deere
American Can	Eastman Kodak
Krupp	Vickers
Allis Chalmers	
Emhart	
Westinghouse Air Brake	

Table 5.4   continued

1930–90 (pat30>100)

Diversified	Concentrated
US Steel	Emhart
Bethlehem Steel	
American Can	
Krupp	
International Harvester	
Deere	
Allis Chalmers	
Vickers	
Eastman Kodak	
Westinghouse Air Brake	

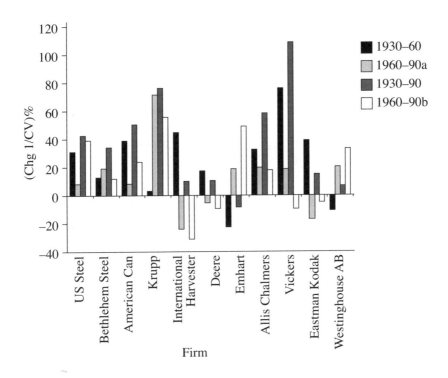

Figure 5.3   Strength of diversification – mechanical

5.5.4   Transport

In the 1930–90 period, the split of the behaviour between the automotive and tyre firms in Table 5.5 is very pronounced, with the automotive companies technologically diversifying and the tyre companies concentrating. The behaviour of General Motors is probably to be expected, since automotive production has become increasingly sophisticated through automation and computerization pervading many activities from the design to manufacturing.

Table 5.5   Transport group

1930–60 (pat30>100)	
Diversified	*Concentrated*
General Motors	Firestone Tire & Rubber
Bendix	BF Goodrich
United Aircraft	
Goodyear Tire & Rubber	

1960–90a(pat30>100)	
Diversified	*Concentrated*
Bendix	General Motors
United Aircraft	Goodyear Tire & Rubber
	Firestone Tire & Rubber
	BF Goodrich

1960–90b (pat60>500)	
Diversified	*Concentrated*
General Motors	Goodyear Tire & Rubber
Bendix	Firestone Tire & Rubber
United Aircraft	BF Goodrich

1930–90 (pat30>100)	
Diversified	*Concentrated*
General Motors	Goodyear Tire & Rubber
Bendix	Firestone Tire & Rubber
United Aircraft	BF Goodrich

At the same time automotives themselves as artefacts have embodied knowledge drawn from an increasingly wide range of technologies. For United Aircraft, this diversification is not unexpected. As noted in the previous chapter, United Aircraft diversified to such an extent from the 1960s onwards that they renamed themselves United Technologies.

Bendix by 1930 was already diversified into automotives and aeronautic systems and diversified into defence systems during the war and post-war period. By the 1960s it was manufacturing products for use in a wide variety of industries and continued to pursue deliberate diversification away from the less stable automotive and defence-related businesses. However, in the late 1970s to early 1980s, much wrangling at the executive board level and potential threats of hostile acquisition left the company vulnerable. It was acquired by the Allied Corporation in 1982 as a subsidiary and fully assimilated into Allied-Signal's operations in 1985, although Bendix remained a brand name (*International Directory of Company Histories*, Vol. 1, pp. 141–3). An interesting feature from Figure 5.4 is that none of the selected firms experience stronger diversification in 1960–90, when technological inter-relatedness is perceived to be of greater importance, not even the automotive firms which have a greater dependence on systems of technology.

In contrast to the automotive firms, the tyre companies remain relatively focused upon tyre production, albeit for a variety of uses, despite competitive pressure from Europe and Japan and more general economic pressures. For instance, although US tyre companies suffered from the stagnation of a previously buoyant automobile market in the 1930s, they managed via the considerable redirection of R&D to enter the steadily growing markets for pneumatic tyres for tractors, earth-moving equipment, aircraft, etc. The wartime development of synthetic rubber enabled the development and production of lighter, more resilient and cheaper tyres post-WWII, but the challenge of Michelin's innovative radial tyre in 1948 was too great. The radial tyre improved vehicle wear, road handling and fuel consumption, but also required a different configuration of the vehicle's suspension to the traditional bias tyres. US tyre producers were reluctant to make this technological switch, because of both the potentially very large costs that would be incurred through heavy capital expenditure on new machinery plus the implications for US automobiles themselves. However, the oil crisis in 1973 fuelled the demand for radial tyres because of their greater fuel efficiency and also led to the import of more efficient and cheaper Japanese automobile imports, whose tyres were supplied by the Japanese manufacturer, Bridgestone.

As a result, the US tyre industry's output, capacity and employment contracted between 1973–87. Attempts to diversify into farm machinery and motor bikes could not ease the hardship and, although niche areas like semi-pneumatic and solid tyres for industrial equipment, tyres for trailers, mobile

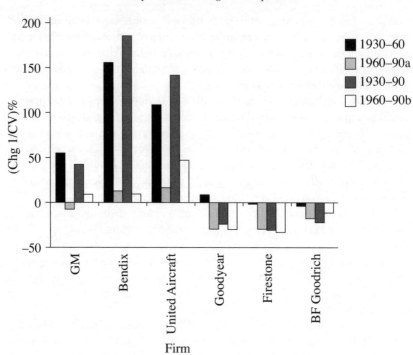

Figure 5.4   Strength of diversification – transport

homes, antique and classic cars emerged, they were not regarded highly by
large tyre firms. As a result Goodrich divested its tyre interests entirely in the
late 1980s and Bridgestone acquired Firestone in 1988. Goodyear attempted
some diversification into non-tyre areas in the early 1980s and survived well
enough so that by 1990 it remained the only major domestic tyre manufacturer
in the US (Chandler, 1990a; French, 1991; *International Directory of Company
Histories*, Vol. 5, pp. 231–3, 234–5, 244–8). Hence it is not altogether surprising
that the US tyre companies experienced concentration in their technological
profiles, especially in the 1960s-90s.

5.6   CONCLUSIONS

With the exception of the group of chemical firms, there is no doubt that diversification truly was a greater phenomenon both in its pervasiveness across firms
and the strength with which it occurred within firms in the 1930–60 period than
in 1960–90. This is perhaps a little strange given that the observations of

Granstrand and Sjölander (1990), Patel and Pavitt (1994a) and other authors seem to imply that it is a phenomenon of recent decades due to the growing inter-relatedness between former distinct technologies. However, studies on technological diversification have largely tended to consider only the activities of the 1970s and 1980s. Pavitt et al. (1989) are the exception in considering 1945–83. However, they examine the diversification activities of UK companies only, focusing mostly on the industrial differences in the directions of techno-logical diversification (upstream, downstream and horizontally), whereas I am dealing largely with American (and to a lesser extent European) firms, whose dominance in the twentieth century may affect at least the timing if not the outcome of observations on technological diversification.[11] Thus, the apparently anomalous results obtained here may merely be a function of the length of time analysed. If this is the case, it is well known from Chandler's work that diver-sification in the early part of the twentieth century was closely associated with increases in firm size through the exploitation of both scale and scope, and this may imply that the nature of diversification in the earlier subperiod was of a different nature to that occurring in recent times. In fact over the 60-year period, a number of organizational changes have taken place that may have implica-tions for the type and extent of technological diversification the large firms studied here engage in.

Another reason for the results could lie with the level of analysis of the phenomenon of technological diversification. Up to this point, I have only regarded the evolution of technological competencies in large firms at the aggregated level of 56 technological fields. It could well be the case that tech-nological complexity in recent times is such that analysis at a more disaggregated level is required in order to pick up on any of the more subtle changes that might be occurring.

As a result of both these conjectures, the issue of technological diversifica-tion warrants a more detailed investigation. Consequently, I shall examine technological diversification with respect to the Chandlerian argument that diversification is a function of increases in firm size in Chapter 6, and consider the more subtle nature of technological changes at the more disaggregated level of the 399 technological classes in Chapter 7.

NOTES

1. For an overview of the analytical traditions that have contributed to the understanding of the role of technology in firm behaviour, see Pavitt et al. (1989).
2. Granstrand and Oskarsson (1994) define a multi-technology corporation as one which operates in at least three different technologies, where technologies are defined roughly at the level of coherent textbooks, chairs in academic departments or the specialization of scientists and

engineers. The authors also admit that the number of technologies is dependent upon the level of abstraction used.

3. In fact, Pavitt et al. (1989) found more technological diversity across SIC classes than diversity across principal sectors of the firms' output. Similarly, Granstrand and Sjölander (1990) found that between 1974–85, many Swedish companies narrowed their product specialization, whilst simultaneously engaging in technological diversification. Gambardella and Torrisi (1998) and Andersen and Walsh (2000) both find that technological diversity increases whilst product diversity decreases.

4. Of course, technological and product diversification can increase for the firm if the older 'models' are kept in production for a time as new models are introduced and phased in. For examples of technological transition in telecommunication cables, cellular phones and refrigeration see Oskarsson (1990).

5. Rycroft and Kash (1999) find that in a simple process/product, complex process/product matrix, no simple processes lead to complex products, and furthermore, the complexity of products and the proportion of total value represented by complex products has increased markedly over the 1970s–90s (p. 57).

6. I wish to emphasize that this notion of constrained diversification is different to Rumelt's use of the term in his 1974 thesis.

7. It is assumed that the evolutionary perspective means the firm is unable to directly substitute currently favoured technologies for historically favoured technologies. If this were the case, diversification may not be observed at all if the number of technologies and effort devoted to each remained constant. Path-dependence and incremental, cumulative change means that firms will retain older technologies as they move into new ones and only move out of the older technologies more slowly.

8. The latter subperiod should be interpreted with care, as it is an empirical amalgam of the three individual firms whereas IG Farben itself consisted of these main three plus four other minor firms (Borkin, 1979, p. 42). When the analysis of diversification was conducted for the three individual firms in the 1960–90 period, each did show that they had diversified over the period.

9. The same caution must be employed when considering the Swiss IG as a single empirical entity as with the IG Farben cartel. Closer analysis not reported here showed that whilst Ciba (later Ciba-Geigy) diversified in 1960–90, Sandoz concentrated its technological activities marginally.

10. General Electric's 12 businesses include: aerospace, aircraft engines, appliances, communication services, electrical distribution & control, financial services, industrial & power systems, lighting, medical systems, motors, plastics, transportation systems, NBC and support operations (GE, 1996).

11. It is well known that the Europeans, in general terms, lagged behind America technologically in most sectors in the twentieth century. Those European firms that were as technologically advanced as the American firms historically have already been picked up in the few German, Swiss and British firms represented here. Over time, there has been a degree of general technological convergence between American, Japanese and European firms in terms of levels of technological complexity (Freeman and Hagedoorn, 1995) although the sectors of specialization for the triad of nations (indeed each country within Europe) remain distinct and are even divergent (Patel and Pavitt, 1995). Nevertheless for the most part, in general terms, the Europeans are still regarded as somewhat technologically backward relative to the US and Japan.

6. Scale and scope in technology: influences on diversification[1]

6.1 INTRODUCTION

I suggested in Chapter 5 that one of the reasons why taking a longer historical view of technological diversification is suggestive of more widespread activity pre-1960 than post-1960 could be the closer association between increases in firm size and technological diversification historically. The relationship between the size of firms and their internal diversity is one that has been considered in many dimensions in the literature of economics, economic and business history, and management studies (e.g. Rumelt, 1974; Pavitt et al., 1987). The notion of economies of scale has a long history, but this has been added to during the past three decades by the increasing attention being given to economies of scope. The inter-linking of scale and scope was epitomized in the title of the business historian Alfred Chandler in 1990: *Scale and Scope: The Dynamics of Industrial Capitalism.*

A simple reading of such works strongly implies that economies of scale and economies of scope are mutually reinforcing. Yet, with limited resources, if economies of scale do exist, one would expect any diversification (to achieve economies of scope), ceteris paribus, to be at the expense of advantages of specialization obtainable from economies of scale, at least to some degree. If this is true then perhaps scale and scope follow one another in a stepwise fashion. For example, market opportunities might lead to economies of scale in production, but exposure to these new markets might then lead to demand for new products and economies of scope might arise. Of course, if the firm is experiencing strong growth in its resources it may well engage in both increases in scale and scope simultaneously.

Another complicating factor is that scale and scope economies arise at various functional levels within firms.[2] Scale economies are normally thought of as arising in production processes, e.g. via mass production on assembly lines, and scope economies as coming from product inter-relationships, e.g. the classic example of using sheep to produce both meat and wool. If scale and scope operate at different functional levels, such as in processes versus products, then conceivably both could be valid (e.g. mass production of genetically modified sheep for both meat and wool production). However, the business literature demonstrates countless examples of *both* economies of scale and of scope that arise simultaneously within the various functions of the firm. Scale and scope in practice have been simultaneously reaped in processes, in products, in finance and in technology, as the generic functions of a firm (see Athreye and von Tunzelmann, 1997 for a fuller typology). In the light of these considerations, care needs to be taken in assuming that scale and scope will always go together, and if so in which circumstances.

In this chapter I particularly address economies of scale and scope in *technology*. My interest in technology stems from the recognition in the literature that firms are increasingly 'multi-technology' (Granstrand and Sjölander, 1990) and that they are operating in an era of growing technological inter-relatedness (Patel and Pavitt, 1997) and technological fusion (Kodama, 1986, 1992). Recent empirical evidence has also shown that a reduction in product scope can be accompanied by an increase in technological scope, at least within certain industries (Gambardella and Torrisi, 1998; Andersen and Walsh, 2000). This suggests that although we tend to make implicit assumptions about technological scale and scope when faced with descriptions about scale and scope at the level of products, our assumptions may need re-evaluating. In this light, it is necessary to re-examine scale and scope specifically at the technological level.

Scale and/or scope economies in technology might be thought of as occurring in the *use* of technology, or alternatively in the *production* of technology (Fai and von Tunzelmann, 2001a). Therefore our interpretation of technology here is broad and encompasses all technological changes that pervade across production processes (encouraging the use of existing and production of new technological areas) as well as those embedded within products (embodying existing and new technological competencies).

Suppose there are just two technologies: T_1 = mechanical equipment (say) and T_2 = information technology. Then by the standard properties of scale and scope economies, a scale economy can be said to arise in the use of technology when the productivity of two or more units of T_1 (or T_2) used together in a plant i is greater than using single units in more than one plant:

$$Q_i(T_1) + Q_j(T_1) < Q_i(T_1 + T_1) \qquad (6.1)$$

Equivalently, the dual cost for economies of scale is:

$$C_i(T_1) + C_j(T_1) > C_i(T_1 + T_1) \qquad (6.2)$$

Similarly, a scope economy arises in technology when:

$$Q_i(T_1) + Q_j(T_2) < Q_i(T_1 + T_2) \tag{6.3}$$

or in cost terms when:

$$C_i(T_1) + C_j(T_2) > C_i(T_1 + T_2) \tag{6.4}$$

Fisher and Temin (1973, 1979) assessed scale economies in technology production. They argued that, if such scale economies arose, then for a given R&D intensity, the R&D carried out in a large firm ought to be more productive (or cheaper) than equivalent R&D executed in several smaller firms. They termed this the Schumpeterian hypothesis, and argued that it had rarely, if ever, been formally tested.[3] Similarly, scope economies in technology creation would arise if bringing together two or more technologies for development in one laboratory or firm were more productive or cheaper than developing them in separate labs or firms. More recent empirical evidence, however, has undermined the Schumpeterian suggestion that the 'formally organized R&D labs administered by large corporations are the source of most innovation in a modern capitalist society' (Cohen and Levinthal, 1989, p. 1071).[4] Whilst stimuli for innovation can come from the conventional science-push, demand-pull sources as well as the formal R&D function within firms, they also arise from learning in production in interaction with these other stimuli (Cantwell and Fai, 1999) and through interactions between firms.

A firm's products and processes can relate to its mix of technological capabilities in a variety of different ways (von Tunzelmann, 1995a; Piscitello, 2000). The implication of this is that, when examining changes in firm scale and scope, one must clarify the functional basis on which the scale and scope is being measured. We interpret increases in technological scale as the proliferated use of a technology within or across product categories (hence technological scale may or may not be accompanied by an increase in product scope). Similarly, technological scope is interpreted as the range of technological areas the firm is active in (as per the notion of diversity in Chapter 5). These may be combined to produce one complex product, or a number of relatively simple products each based on just a few, but different technologies. Hence, technological scale and scope can occur together or independently of one another and both may or may not be accompanied by corresponding activity at the product level.[5]

The primary objective is to show that the nature of corporate technological diversification has changed over time. Whereas historically, changes in technological scale and scope were assumed to be more directly linked to corresponding changes in scale and scope across markets and products (as in Chandler's accounts), in recent times, the prominence of technology as an important factor has meant that changes in technological scale and scope have been more deliberate and distinct from those occurring in other functions. We attribute this change to the pressures arising from the aforementioned increasing degrees of inter-relatedness between formerly distinct fields of technology, etc. In other words, we attempt to chart the purposeful switch towards increased technological diversification as a strategy in its own right through a reaction to technological opportunities. This is opposed to technological diversification occurring due to some 'drift' effect that arises as a by-product of strategies more directly concerned with increasing firm size and market shares. The patterns that emerge, however, show some significant differences between the main industrial sectors. Such differences are found to be associated with underlying patterns of long-term technological change. In the following sections, we outline the background to scale and scope discussions more fully, and describe the qualitative patterns of scale and scope as documented by the economic and business history literature. This then provides a backdrop against which we may consider the empirical patterns of specifically technological scale and scope.

6.2   HISTORICAL BACKGROUND

6.2.1   Production, Products and Technologies

Ceteris paribus, one would expect large firms to be more technologically diversified in their capabilities than smaller ones. Large size is advantageous for firms, as the variety of skills and specialized knowledge available through the greater division of labour can generate more innovative activity in ways that smaller firms are simply unable to achieve (Loasby, 1996). Indeed, Chandler (1990a) illustrated that historically, increases in firm scale and scope were simultaneously achieved through growth over time. However, a possible disadvantage is the onset of the co-ordinative bureaucracy (Hill and Hansen, 1991) that a large, more diversified and hence complex organization may bring. As such, the probability that the organizational coherence of the firm may be disturbed increases (Teece et al., 1997).

Over the twentieth century many of the firms, which were large even at the beginning of the century, have continued to experience growth. Whether they have become increasingly diversified and in what ways is less self-evident. Certainly they tend to operate across a greater geographical spread of markets, but whether they have also been diversifying their range of products and technologies is not so obvious (Granstrand and Sjölander, 1990; Oskarsson, 1990; Granstrand et al., 1997; Patel and Pavitt, 1997). Part of this lack of clarity lies in the fact that firm diversification across products was rarely recognized as distinct from that of diversification across technologies. In much early work, e.g. that of Chandler, these were conflated and were only attributed a secondary role in firm formation (Granstrand, 1999). However, subsequent writers have drawn sharper distinctions between product diversification and technological diversification (Patel and Pavitt, 1997; Piscitello, 2000).[6] Gambardella and Torrisi (1998) in their study of the electronics industry found that in recent years, numerous firms have reduced the diversity of their product offerings, whilst simultaneously increasing their portfolio of technological activity. Andersen and Walsh (2000) found similar results in the chemical industry. It is now recognized that product diversity can be, but is not necessarily, associated with technological diversity and vice versa.

Relatedness in a firm's product mix is distinct from the relatedness in its technological capabilities. Given the greater distinction between products and technologies, one cannot necessarily infer that as a result of product diversification, the firm has automatically diversified technologically at the same time. Rycroft and Kash (1999) found that, in the late twentieth century, whilst complex technologies could produce complex or simple products, no complex products were produced by simple technologies. Hence, the assumed direct relationship between increases in scale and scope in product markets and technologies, which is implicit in Chandler's historical accounts, has become decoupled more recently.

6.2.2   Technological Scale and Scope

Chandler (1977) defined 'big business' in the late nineteenth century as the combination of mass production and mass distribution. Such firms benefited from scale economies. As such, we might expect greater technological scale and technological scope to appear as firms developed mass-production techniques to serve more numerous geographic markets.

In the early part of the twentieth century, by making simultaneous three-way investments in manufacturing, management and marketing (distribution), large firms were also able to exploit economies of scope in order to produce new products (Chandler, 1990a). As such, in the 1930s and 1940s multi-product firms with suitable multi-divisional organizational structures established themselves as 'modern industrial enterprises'. On these grounds, we speculate here that: any observable increases in technological scale or scope at this time are likely to be in response to the demands of new product market entry.

As greater numbers of technologies emerged in the 1950s and 1960s, they proliferated and often cut across product divisional boundaries. However, the multi-divisional form delegated the majority of R&D into the product divisions and often curtailed the possibilities for spillovers across divisional boundaries (Mowery et al., 1995; von Tunzelmann, 1995b). The multi-divisional structure, in sacrificing opportunities to strengthen underlying, firm-specific competencies across divisions, also sacrificed much of the possibility of technological scale through its use across divisions. Additionally, despite the access to new sources of innovation that these divisions gave them, the degree of separatism between divisions meant that the firms were largely unable to build up further potential firm-specific competencies, and the opportunity to reap scope economies across technologies was undermined. At this time, it was also the vogue to use acquisition and merger (A&M) activity to gain access to new businesses and markets (Chandler, 1990a, 1994). So whilst scale and scope at the product level continued to increase in the 1950s and 1960s, we propose that: the increase in the scale and scope of the underlying technological competencies of the firm in this period was limited.

The diversity of product markets entered during the 1950s and 1960s had serious implications for organizational cohesiveness and coherence in the 1970s. The state of the global economy at that time also created economic hardship for many firms and a subsequent wave of divestitures took place (Chandler, 1990a). Many firms shrank in terms of product scale and scope. However the environment appears to have spurred firms on to look for new avenues in terms of products, or new more efficient means of production. Andersen (2001) demonstrates that US patent stocks in the 1970s rose in all five of the technological groups (CEMTO). The implication for technological scope is uncertain, although scale would appear to have increased significantly.

In the 1980s firms found A&M activity and divestitures to be financially lucrative. However, astute firms also used the activity to engage in 'corporate refocusing'[7] or 'dis-integration'[8] to regain some of their lost coherence. The resulting firms were organizationally leaner and relied more greatly on networks of relationships with subcontractors, etc., as witnessed in industries such as computing and automobiles. Consequently, they became more focused in their product offerings. These firms were also much more aware of the increasingly complex technological environment and the subsequent technological demands made of them to produce these products competitively. Hence, we propose that: firms in the 1980s engaged in technological scale and scope not so much in the pursuit of production scale and product scope,[9] but more deliberately to ensure their continued participation in a competitive environment that was increasingly dependent upon technological advance.

Given this, it would appear that the nature of technological diversification has changed over time. I propose that firms are no longer experiencing technological diversification primarily as a 'by-product' of firm growth through the exploitation of economies of scale and scope across different geographic and product markets. Instead, at least some large firms are deliberately becoming more technologically diversified as a purposive route to enhance further firm development and growth (Montgomery and Hariharan, 1991; Granstrand, 1999; Cantwell and Santangelo, 2000). Moreover, such behaviour might be expected to continue because opportunities created on the basis of technologies are not depleted but are continually replenished, since technologies continually progress incrementally forward, even if occasionally bottlenecks might appear (Klevorick et al., 1995).

6.3   METHODOLOGY

To examine whether technological scale and scope follow the broader patterns detailed in business history I used total accumulated patent stocks as a proxy for scale ($\Sigma_i P_{ij}$).[10] The measurement of a firm's technological efforts has been shown to be best related to measures based on technology, e.g. R&D expenditure, R&D programmes or patents, rather than employees, sales or output (Archibugi and Pianta, 1992; Freeman and Soete, 1997). However, the growth of a firm's scale does not occur in a linear fashion so I measure it logarithmically.

Since technological scope is essentially diversity, the inverse of the coefficient of variation about the intra-industry RTA used previously is used once more – when the value of 1/CV rises, the firm becomes more technologically diversified and hence increases its technological scope.

The above measures were then employed in the following simple linear regression to examine the changes in the relationship between a firm's technological scale and its technological scope:

$$1/CV_t = \alpha + \beta \ln(\Sigma_i P_{ij})t + \varepsilon_t \qquad (6.5)$$

where ε_t is the residual, assumed to be IID.

To overcome the effects of small numbers of observations within each subsample, panel-data methods were adopted to estimate the coefficients and standard errors. In contrast to usual panel-data approaches, with dummy intercepts, both intercepts and slopes and their interaction by sector in each time period were dummied. This yields the same coefficients as simple regressions on each individual subsample, but with standard errors that are based on large rather than small numbers of degrees of freedom. The resulting intercept and slope coefficients are displayed in Tables 6.1 and 6.3 (columns iii and iv). Significant results were achieved in the majority of the industrial groups as well as across groups.

In Table 6.3, the chemical and electrical/electronic groups are reported twice. In both groupings certain firms experienced extensive de-merger activity (IG Farben and Swiss IG into Bayer, BASF, Hoechst and Ciba, Geigy, Sandoz respectively), or mergers (Sperry and Burroughs to form Unisys). Their inclusion would obviously affect the results as the firms radically altered their structure over time. Accordingly, the first set of results in Table 6.3 omits these firms entirely, the second set includes all firms in whatever form they existed during the particular year under observation for a fuller (if more dubious) set of results. In fact, the full set of results generates only slightly weaker or comparable coefficients of significance. The overall adjusted R-squared is 0.788 for the abbreviated sample ($F = 14.14$, df $= 140$) and 0.649 for the full sample ($F = 8.82$, df $= 178$).

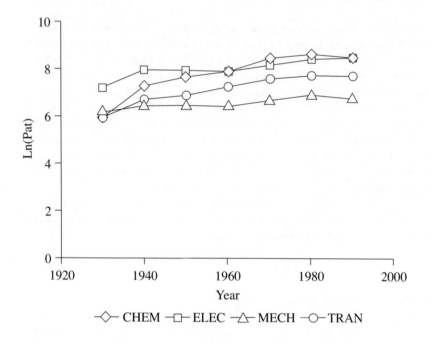

Figure 6.1   Average size by sector, large firms 1930–90

The upward drift over time in both average technological scale and scope (columns v and vi) suggests that the two series are likely to be co-integrated. Figure 6.1 graphs the average size of firm in each industrial grouping, Figure 6.2 similarly graphs the average diversity (scope) and on inspection it appears that co-integration is not always the case. However, their similarity or divergence in time patterns is central to the analysis, so I proceed on the basis of these results into shift-share analyses of the relationships.

Generally, successful firms grow larger over time and enter new product and geographic markets. Similarly, empirical observation shows that successful firms have become more technologically diversified over time. However, we do not know the extent to which technological diversification arises because

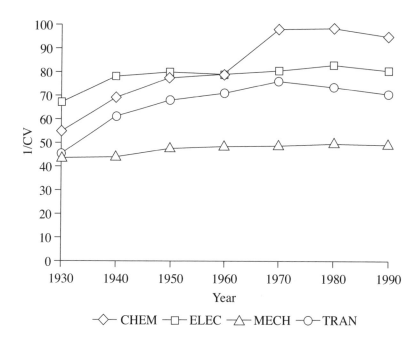

Figure 6.2   Average diversification by sector, large firms 1930–90

of the growth opportunities relating to the market as opposed to other factors (such as technological opportunity or necessity to survive in an increasingly complex and inter-related technological environment). Plots of scope (1/CV) against scale (ln $\Sigma_i P_{ij}$) merely demonstrate that, in each decade, a positive relationship holds to a greater or lesser extent over time, within each industrial group. However, as Figure 6.3 indicates, through such a graphical representation, the compound effects of scale and scope make it appear that the lines rotate across decades. This is true also at the level of the individual industrial groups (not shown).

Shift-share analysis enables us to identify, over successive periods, the extent to which any observed change in technological scope is accounted for by 'drift' effects associated with an increase in technological scale (a simple movement along the regression trend line, showing how much technological diversity there 'should be' based on the previous decade's relationship with size). It also allows us to identify that portion of the observed increase in technological scope accounted for by 'other' effects like necessity or opportunity – the residual effects (through the upward shift of the line itself). A worked example of how

Diversity (1/CV)

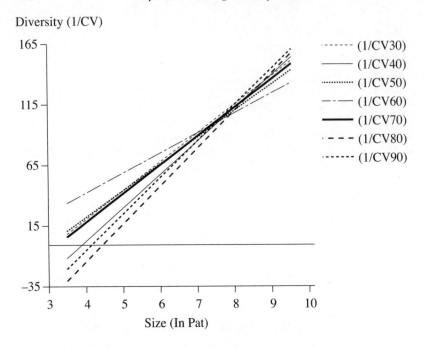

Figure 6.3   Regression trend lines – all firms

the values for 'drift' and 'other' effects are calculated in the columns within Tables 6.1 and 6.3 is given in the Appendix, in conjunction with a graphical representation of the shift-share analysis (Figure A6.1).

The notion that these 'other' effects are associated with technological opportunity or necessity is a crucial assumption. With the advent of new opportunities (or indeed threats), in the guise of emerging technological paradigms and the pervasiveness of GPTs, firms may extend their patenting into these fields and relatively diminish that in their old areas of strength. In such cases, the technological scope of a firm may increase without any necessary change in technological scale (Table 6.1). On the other hand, if the technological opportunities of a rising paradigm were exploited in the extreme, it might appear that technological concentration occurs within that paradigm, again with uncertain impacts upon technological scale.

Therefore, in line with the findings from Chapter 3, if the new paradigms arose within a sector's traditional domain, they would at first induce technological scope (diversity) as more firms in the industry developed the competencies associated with this paradigm, followed by a concentration of the patent portfolio at the industry level as it gradually moves away from older technologies with diminished opportunities. This movement may be accom-

Table 6.1   Effects encouraging increased technological scope

Sector i	Year ii	Intercept iii	Slope iv	Av. LPAT v	Av. 1/CV vi	Chg LPAT vii	Chg 1/CV viii	Est. 1/CV ix	Drift x	Other xi
CEMTIND	1930	−76.30 *	23.93 ***	6.39	76.54					
	1940	−106.45 **	27.37 ***	7.01	85.42	0.62	8.89	91.94	15.41	−6.52
	1950	−66.04 *	22.03 ***	7.05	89.63	0.04	4.21	86.59	1.17	3.04
	1960	−24.11	16.61 ***	7.14	94.58	0.10	4.95	91.99	2.26	2.70
	1970	−75.74	23.68 ***	7.43	100.80	0.29	6.22	99.26	4.68	1.54
	1980	−139.29 **	31.24 ***	7.63	100.04	0.20	−0.75	105.08	4.29	−5.04
	1990	−123.81 *	29.84 ***	7.55	102.06	−0.08	2.02	96.23	−3.81	5.83

Key:
LPAT = logarithm of patent stock (measure of size).
1/CV = inverse of coefficient of variation (measure of technological diversification).
Est. 1/CV = estimate of 1/CV from shift-share analysis (see Appendix).
Drift = change in diversity due to change in size effect.
Other = change in diversity due to other effects (technological opportunity).
Significance levels: * = 0.10, ** = 0.5, *** = 0.01.

panied by either an increase or decrease in technological scale at the firm level. Obvious examples include semiconductors for the electrical industry or pharmaceuticals for the chemical industry. Conversely, if they arose outside the sector, they might still bring change as firms from within the sector try to incorporate them into their portfolios (probably later than in the previous case), thus inducing diversification and increased technological scope, again with uncertain impacts on technological scale at the firm level.

6.4   RESULTS

6.4.1   All Industrial Groups

There are a number of broad results. Firstly, over the period 1930/90, both the average scale of large firms and the extent of their technological scope have increased (Table 6.1, columns v and vi). However, the increases in these variables do not occur evenly across decades. In line with the literature on scale and scope more generally, changes in technological scale and scope sometimes move together in the same direction, at other times they work independently and in opposite directions.

The influences of the 'drift' and 'other' effects are summarized in Table 6.2 and presented graphically in Figure 6.4. These indicate that changes in technological diversity, for reasons such as technological opportunity and necessity associated with changing paradigms or growing technological relatedness, occur a little less frequently than diversity associated with the drift accompanying increases in scale. Perhaps this is because the paradigms themselves change infrequently. However the results for the 1970s/80s and 1980s/90s lend some support to the proposition that technological scope has become less associated with increases in scale over the twentieth century.

Table 6.2   Effects encouraging increased technological scope – all industrial groups

Sector	1930/40	1940/50	1950/60	1960/70	1970/80	1980/90
CEMTIND	drift(s)	drift & other	drift & other	drift & other	drift	other

Note: (w) = particularly weak effect, value <1; (s) = particularly strong effect, value >10.

Turning to look across the results at the disaggregated industrial group level, an interesting broad feature that emerges from Table 6.3 is the interactive

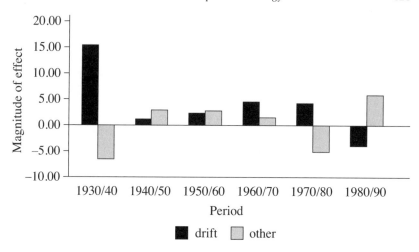

Figure 6.4   Graphical representation of 'drift' and 'other' effects – all industries

pattern, which emerges between the 'drift' and the 'other' effects in each industrial group. It has been established that technological paradigms tend to follow 'S-shaped' curves of progression (Andersen, 1999, 2001). When an industry (through a single, or few, firms) first enters a new technological paradigm, there will be few innovations and relatively little patenting. Beyond a certain point, clusters of innovations built on and around the initial innovation(s) follow.

What this means for technological scope is that, at the start of a new paradigm, when the firms in an industry are presented with entirely new technological opportunities, the 'other' effect will be strong and positive. Firms are likely to enter the new paradigm with a few innovations and hence patents. However, when the paradigm's path turns sharply upwards, further innovations *within* this paradigm are made. Hence, technological opportunities, whilst abundant, appear to become concentrated in this particular paradigm at the industry level. This accounts for falling and even negative 'other' effects. Nevertheless, because firms will do more patenting within this existing paradigm, there will be strong scale effects, and these will cause the firm to experience a strong and positive 'drift' effect through which technological diversity will be projected.

Whilst all the above activity is associated with entering a new technological paradigm, we must remember that the firm also has existing areas of techno-logical activity. Entering new technological areas is costly and requires large amounts of resources. If these resources are limited, it may be that the firm has to forego technological activity in other existing technological fields associated

Table 6.3 Panel data regression and shift-share results, by industrial group

Sector i	Year ii	Intercept iii	Slope iv	Av. LPAT v	Av. 1/CV vi	Chg LPAT vii	Chg 1/CV viii	Est. 1/CV ix	Drift x	Other xi
Chemical	1930	-103.58	26.14	6.06	54.92					
	1940	-174.39	33.39 **	7.29	69.18	1.23	14.26	87.10	32.18	-17.91
	1950	-158.31 *	30.84 ***	7.65	77.60	0.35	8.42	81.02	11.83	-3.41
	1960	-95.38	22.11 **	7.88	78.73	0.23	1.13	84.60	6.99	-5.87
	1970	-360.31 ***	54.76 ***	8.37	98.31	0.50	19.58	89.77	11.04	8.54
	1980	-668.32 ***	90.40 ***	8.48	98.70	0.11	0.39	104.31	6.00	-5.61
	1990	-691.92 ***	93.40 ***	8.43	95.02	-0.06	-3.68	93.30	-5.39	1.72
Electrical/ electronic	1930	-151.19 ***	30.61 ***	7.15	67.62					
	1940	-223.19 ***	37.87 ***	7.96	78.32	0.81	10.69	92.49	24.86	-14.17
	1950	-135.56 **	27.17 ***	7.93	79.99	-0.03	1.67	77.27	-1.05	2.72
	1960	-101.22 *	22.93 ***	7.85	78.73	-0.09	-1.26	77.66	-2.33	1.07
	1970	-156.71 ***	29.30 ***	8.10	80.51	0.25	1.77	84.44	5.71	-3.94
	1980	-183.81 ***	31.91 ***	8.36	82.87	0.26	2.36	88.17	7.67	-5.30
	1990	-127.97 **	25.04 ***	8.33	80.54	-0.03	-2.33	81.92	-0.95	-1.38
Mechanical	1930	40.34	0.58	6.32	43.98					
	1940	42.49	0.32	6.55	44.58	0.23	0.59	44.11	0.13	0.46
	1950	28.56	3.03	6.45	48.10	-0.10	3.53	44.54	-0.03	3.56
	1960	17.68	4.88	6.42	48.99	-0.04	0.89	48.00	-0.11	1.00
	1970	-12.46	9.22	6.67	49.01	0.25	0.02	50.21	1.22	-1.20
	1980	4.16	6.64	6.91	50.04	0.24	1.03	51.22	2.22	-1.18
	1990	13.28	5.37	6.76	49.56	-0.15	-0.48	49.07	-0.97	0.49

		LPAT	Drift	Est. 1/CV	Other	1/CV	
Transport	1930	-139.02	30.60 *	6.01	44.90	0.68	16.24	65.70	20.80	-4.56
	1940	-55.48	17.43 **	6.69	61.14	0.15	7.11	63.70	2.56	4.55
	1950	-37.13	15.41 **	6.84	68.25	0.39	3.01	74.23	5.97	-2.97
	1960	-108.29 *	24.85 ***	7.23	71.26	0.32	4.78	79.11	7.86	-3.07
	1970	-86.40	21.54 ***	7.54	76.04	0.32	4.78	79.11	7.86	-3.07
	1980	-81.61	20.22 **	7.68	73.73	0.14	-2.31	79.09	3.05	-5.36
	1990	-76.32	19.40 **	7.59	70.93	-0.09	-2.80	71.81	-1.92	-0.88
Chemical#	1930	-17.83	11.30	6.21	52.36	1.17	12.91	65.58	13.22	-0.31
	1940	-72.57	18.68	7.38	65.27	0.22	4.39	69.32	4.05	0.33
	1950	-173.79 *	32.04 **	7.60	69.66	-0.74	-16.01	45.95	-23.71	7.70
	1960	-85.31	20.26 **	6.86	53.65	0.96	18.47	73.18	19.53	-1.06
	1970	-202.34 ***	35.09 ***	7.82	72.11	0.52	6.24	90.45	18.34	-12.10
	1980	-228.00 **	36.73 ***	8.34	78.35	0.09	0.44	81.70	3.35	-2.91
	1990	-150.11	27.15 **	8.43	78.79					
Electrical/	1930	-130.26 **	27.73 ***	6.83	59.23	0.70	9.42	78.73	19.50	-10.08
electronic#	1940	-147.01 **	28.62 ***	7.54	68.65	0.01	3.15	68.85	0.20	2.95
	1950	-102.76 *	23.14 ***	7.54	71.80	0.11	-0.22	74.27	2.47	-2.69
	1960	-107.21 *	23.37 ***	7.65	71.58	0.49	6.45	83.03	11.50	-5.05
	1970	-150.96 **	28.12 ***	8.14	78.02	0.23	1.26	84.56	6.53	-5.27
	1980	-183.21 ***	31.34 ***	8.37	79.29	-0.06	-3.25	77.44	-1.85	-1.40
	1990	-135.05 *	25.38 ***	8.32	76.04					

Key:
LPAT = logarithm of patent stock (measure of size).
1/CV = inverse of coefficient of variation (measure of technological diversification).
Est. 1/CV = estimate of 1/CV from shift-share analysis (see Appendix).
Drift = change in diversity due to change in size effect.
Other = change in diversity due to other effects (technological opportunity).
# Indicates the full set of firms in decade was used.
Significance levels: * = 0.10, ** = 0.5, *** = 0.01.

with older or more mature paradigms. Hence, the observed scale may rise more slowly, or even decrease, and technological scale and scope will work in opposite directions. On the other hand, if resources are plentiful the firm may gain increases in scale, in which case technological scale and scope will work together in the same (positive) direction.

Looking at columns vii and xi in Table 6.3, we see that whenever a series of positive 'other' effects arises (column xi), in the decade that immediately follows, the change in observed scale (column vii) demonstrates a strong increase in scale. This suggests that the explanation above regarding entirely new paradigms, their S-shaped paths of progression and their effects on scale, scope and the impact 'drift' and 'other' effects have on these is highly plausible. However, broadly applicable, cross-industrial group results, as one might expect, are limited, and finer details are only observable on a group-by-group analysis.

6.4.2   Chemical

Recall the earlier account of the expected relationship between scale and scope and technological change over the twentieth century. With this in mind we can interpret the results of our technological scale and scope analysis.

In the chemical industrial group, the general technological scale and scope effects concur with Chandler's broader story in each decade to 1980 and also the movement towards greater focus in the decade 1980/90 (Table 6.3, columns v and vi).

However the magnitude of the change in scale or in scope is not even across decades. The largest increases in technological scale and scope take place between 1930 to 1940 and 1960 to 1970 (vii and viii). These are clearly illustrated in Figure 6.5 in the graphical representation of scale and scope.

The explanation of the role and timing of the 'other' effect in observed increases in technological scope fits well here. Heavy chemicals dominated in the late nineteenth century, and organic chemistry and synthetics were the new chemical paradigms at the cusp of the twentieth. I speculate that for the intervals between 1930 and 1960, chemical firms were in the process of fully encompassing such technologies and exploiting these to their greatest extent.

In fact, reference to Chapter 3, Table 3.4 shows coal and petroleum and synthetics as the two fastest growing technologies for the chemical industry in 1930/45 and 1945/60 respectively. Hence, although both observed scale and scope (Table 6.3, columns v and vi) continually increased until 1960, it would seem that much of the scope effect was due to exploiting innovations in these established paradigms. Their exploitation enabled technological scale to increase and the 'drift' associated with scale was large and positive. The scope induced by the emergence of entirely new paradigms represented by 'other' is, by way

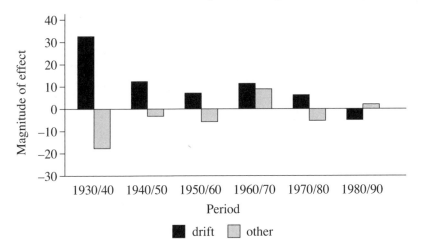

Figure 6.5   Drift and other effects – chemical

of contrast, negative. Another interesting point is that it would appear that economies of both technological scale and scope in these established paradigms were experiencing diminishing returns over this period (values in columns vii and viii get smaller). This would seem to fit well with the final part of the technological S-curve, where patenting and innovations become fewer.

In the period 1960/70, 'other' makes a positive contribution to the observed increase in technological scope (value of 8.54). Again, referring back to Table 3.4, it seems that the rise of the pharmaceutical and biotechnology paradigm is the source of these new technological opportunities. A large increase in technological scale makes a positive contribution through 'drift' to increasing observed technological scope. In 1970/80 scale increases further and 'drift' is responsible for further increases in technological scope. Finally, in 1980/90 both observed scale and scope fall, despite the fact that 'other' effects indicate that opportunities associated with new paradigms were available. These paradigms are probably related to the continuing strength of biotechnology and the rise of agricultural chemicals (Table 3.4). However, as mentioned earlier, the 1980/90 period was one in which firms sought more focus through dis-integrating and flattening organizational structures.

6.4.3   Electrical/Electronic

Broadly, this group's pattern of observed changes in scale and scope concurs with that set out in the business history literature, but there is a deviation in that the scale of the average electrical firm fell in 1940/60.

   The influence of the 'drift' and the 'other' effects however holds as strongly
in this industrial group as it did for chemicals (Figure 6.6). Increases in scope
in 1930/40 are due to large drift effects associated with the increase in technological scale. Results for 1940/50 and 1950/60 indicate that the opportunities
afforded by new paradigms such as semiconductors and data-processing systems
led to further scope (column xi is positive in Table 6.3). However, the observed
scope was smaller than it might otherwise have been, due to the decreases in
technological scale. I tentatively suggest that semiconductor technology in
particular (by involving a movement into electronics) was sufficiently different
from the previous electrical paradigm that it took a large amount of limited
resources to truly establish competencies in this area. This would mean that the
fall in scale associated with a movement away from the previous paradigm was
not fully compensated for by an increase in technological scale in the new
paradigm (hence increased scope in the absence of increased scale). This com-
pensation of increases in scale in the newer paradigm only fully emerges in the
post-1960 period (as opportunities become concentrated). Once again the scale
and scope effects are negatively affected by organizational restructuring in the
1980/90 interval.

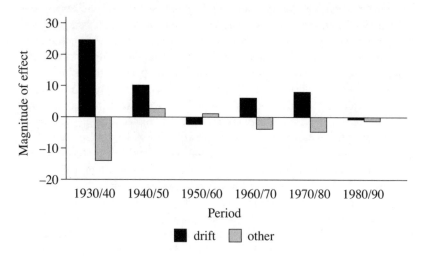

Figure 6.6   Drift and other effects – electrical/electronic

6.4.4 Mechanical

This industrial grouping has to be interpreted with caution as the linear model
of the relationship between size and technological diversity is poor here (the
regression gives slope coefficients not significantly different from zero in each

decade). The heterogeneity of the firms selected may give the appearance that mechanical firms are less diversified because each individual firm will appear to operate in a more specialized, and hence narrower, range of technological fields (e.g. compare Kodak against Deere). A finer level of disaggregation in mechanical industries may have yielded more significant results, but this was not possible given the selection criteria imposed upon the firms and the structure of the original Reading database. Comparisons with the other industrial groups also show the sample of mechanical firms to be smaller in size compared to the other industrial groups.

Given these caveats, the general increase in both technological scale and scope in 1930/80 with a decrease in 1980 and 1990 still mirrors some of the broader notions of scale and scope (Figure 6.7). In the 1930 to 1960 period the 'other' effects contributed towards technological scope, quite considerably in 1940/50 in fact. This is difficult to interpret given this industry's heterogeneity. The 'other' effects may be associated with new paradigms emerging in the areas of photographic chemistry, building materials or synthetics (Table 3.4) that provided new opportunities for some subsets of the mechanical industrial group. The pattern of 'drift' effects associated with scale replace 'other' effects in their contribution to technological scope, immediately after the period in which the latter was dominant.

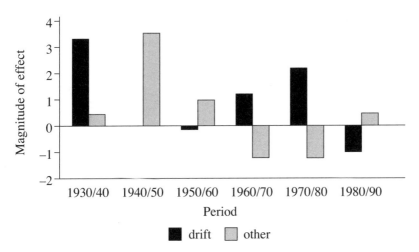

Figure 6.7   Drift and other effects – mechanical

6.4.5   Transport

The transport industrial group pattern of technological scale and scope also follows the broader accounts, but the decrease in technological scope starts earlier – in 1970/80 rather than 1980/90. This 'medium-tech' industry experienced organizational restructuring and rationalization earlier than many other manufacturing industries and established networks of component suppliers built up of many tiers.

However, the pattern of positive 'other' effects leading to scope, followed by a substantial increase in scale in the subsequent interval, continues to apply (Figure 6.8). Thereafter, technological opportunities offered by new paradigms apparently become more limited because the opportunities concentrate in the paradigm that emerged in or prior to 1940/50. Hence technological scale continues to rise and scope increases through 'drift'. The paradigm shift in 1940/50 is difficult to identify in this industrial group, but observations drawn from the fastest growing technological fields (Table 3.4) suggest that data processing makes a sustained contribution. This technological field includes patent classes not only in information storage and retrieval, but error/fault detection and recovery, and certainly the use of such electronic systems in both automotives and in transport-related production processes has proliferated in the latter half of the twentieth century.

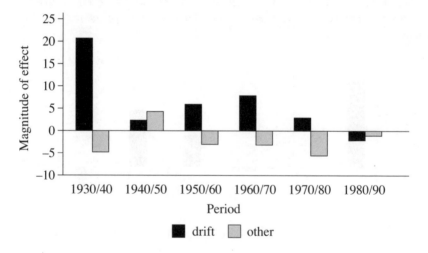

Figure 6.8   Drift and other effects – transport

6.5   CONCLUSIONS

Notions of scale and scope can be applied to the arena of technologies, just as they can to other – often more widely recognized – functions such as production processes or products. However, despite the similarity in the definitions of scale and scope themselves (see the Introduction section above), these refer to rather different things and will not necessarily arise in parallel fashion at the same time and place. Nevertheless, the story that emerges from the specifically technological economies of scale and scope are in keeping with the more general picture from business history and other sources.

Another of our findings is that 'bursts' of technological scale and scope have apparently occurred in two distinct phases: one large burst from 1930/40 to 1960 and a smaller one from 1960/70 to at least 1990. In the former, 'scale' seems to have been the driving force. Larger scale brought about by the development of new product markets brought increases in technological scale and scope as a consequence. However in the latter period, 'scope' was perhaps the more dominant force. Diversity rose because of the emergence of new technological paradigms, applied both within industrial sectors and as spillovers across industrial sectors. However, in the later years of this second phase, technological scale contracted in several key sectors, often as deliberate managerial strategy (note the rotation of the curves in Figure 6.3).

Scale and scope in technologies are thus differently aligned according to historical context. There is a general upward progression which no doubt reflects secular patterns of the increasing science base of industrial activity and increasing technological complexity. Imposed on this are matters of corporate strategy and choice, which do not always drive scale and scope in the same direction. Future research should therefore have a greater awareness not just of the independence and interdependence between products, processes and technologies, but triangulate their interplay with organizational considerations. The new organizational structures appearing in the final decades of the twentieth century (Loasby, 1998) partially reflect a response to the sustained long-term rise in technological diversity, especially in conjunction with new technological paradigms. Time will tell whether the long-term positive correspondence between technological scale and technological scope at the intra-organizational level has finally broken down.

NOTES

1. This chapter is based on Fai and Cantwell (1999, pp. 113–37), with permission from Edward Elgar publishers and Fai and von Tunzelman (2001b), with permission from Taylor-Francis Ltd.
2. For simplicity, we exclude here the large literature on scale and scope economies *external* to firms.
3. See also Kohn and Scott (1982, 1985). von Tunzelmann (1995a, p. 80) claims that the hypothesis is much more explicit in the work of Alfred Marshall (1919, pp. 242–3) than in that of Joseph Schumpeter.
4. See Symeonidis (1996) for a review and discussion of this literature.

5. Granstrand (1999, p. 126) suggests a somewhat broader definition of technological scale economies and a correspondingly narrower one of technological scope economies. Our subsequent results are, however, straightforward to reconcile with his definitions.
6. Piscitello (2000, pp. 295–315) has obtained both product and technology data for many large firms and compared their relative shifts in recent times. Ideally the present book would also compare sales data with the technology data in similar fashion, but we do not have such sales data (disaggregated by products) for our group of large firms over the much longer time period considered here.
7. Corporate refocusing is defined as 'the voluntary or involuntary reduction in the diversification of U.S. firms – usually, but not necessarily, achieved through major divestitures' (Markides, 1995, p. 101).
8. Malerba et al. (1999) draw a distinction between 'disintegration', which has connotations of falling apart, and 'dis-integration' which they use to mean taking apart processes involved when building an integrated firm.
9. In fact we speculate that this proposed relationship continued into the 1990s, although the present study stops at 1990 due to the limitations of the database at the time of writing.
10. Scazzieri (1993) argues strongly against equating scale with size, and instead relates scale to the number of what he terms 'elementary processes'. However our unit of analysis in the technological field can reasonably be compared with an 'elementary process' in Scazzieri's sense, so our definition is also compatible with his. Similar comments relate to equating scope with variety.

7. Technological inter-relatedness and complex diversification

7.1 INTRODUCTION

This chapter considers the notion of inter-relatedness between technologies in the process of diversification. So far this book has analysed diversification at the level of 56 distinct, broadly defined technological fields. However, if relatedness between two technologies lies with their use of a common set of underlying scientific and engineering principles (Breschi et al., 1998) it could be that diversification in more recent decades has been occurring more subtly at a lower level of aggregation. Contemporary technological diversification may involve more depth than breadth. This is intuitively logical given the rising costs of R&D and the desire to reap economies of scope in the application of technologies and competences generated in many industries (Fisher and Temin, 1973, 1979). In other words, in recent times, diversification may be occurring across the classes *within* the 56 technological fields rather than across the fields themselves. I develop this here by examining the nature of diversification both at the broadly defined technological field level and at the more narrowly defined technological class level. I investigate whether the nature of technological diversification across these two levels has altered over time.

The current technological environment and that of the recent past is an increasingly complex one in which greater technological complexity in products and production processes has led to the emergence of the multi-technology or 'mul-tech' firm (Grandstrand and Sjölander, 1990; Patel and Pavitt, 1997). von Tunzelmann (von Tunzelmann and Wang, 1997; Wang and von Tunzelmann, 2000) has questioned what is meant by technological complexity and perceives that it can be interpreted in two ways. The more widely accepted interpretation is that technological complexity implies the need to draw upon a broader *range* of technologies to produce, or further develop, the product range of a firm. This was the interpretation that underlay Chapters 5 and 6. For example, it is quite feasible for any single firm to be diversified across the broadly defined technological fields, whilst specializing in a few classes within each of these. An extreme hypothetical example would be that firm Z is active in one class in each of the 56 technological fields and is complementary to the notion of technological complexity through breadth.

The perhaps unexpected result of the previous chapters however requires us to consider more closely the alternative interpretation, that the *depth* of knowledge required in a specific technological area has become greater in modern times. That is to say, any single firm might become less diversified across the fields in order to focus upon diversifying across the technological classes within each of them. Again, an extreme hypothetical example might be that firm Z is active in 20 classes within one technological field. The two are alternative (but not mutually exclusive) technological strategies: 'Diversification may take place within a firm's existing areas of specialization or it may result in the firm going into new areas' (Penrose, 1959, p. 109). Similarly, 'Technological capabilities, often the wellsprings for future products, can be broadened by pursuing complementary R&D or deepened by further specialization in R&D' (Argyres, 1996, p. 408). A possible consequence of these two alternatives is that at some point, firms may have to trade off increasing technological breadth against relatively greater technological depth. This distinction might account for the results of Chapter 5, which appear anomalous in the light of other recent work on technological diversification. In Chapter 5, the analysis was conducted at the level of the selected technological fields. However, it is possible that large firms engaged in broad diversification strategies across fields historically, but have engaged in relatively more subtle and focused diversification across the technological *classes* in more recent decades.

The possible configurations for diversification at the levels of technological fields and classes together can be highly complex. For example, Figure 7.1 presents a matrix of combinations between diversification and concentration at the class and the field level. There are four possible outcomes.

| | | Classes (399) | |
		Div	Con
Fields	Div	1	2
(56)	Con	3	4

Figure 7.1   Diversification combinations at field and class level

To illustrate, say that firm Z is active in three technological fields and within a number of technological classes within each of these:

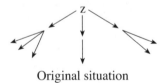

Original situation

Z may decide to engage in any of the modes 1–4:

1. Diversification across fields and across classes within fields

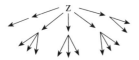

2. Diversification across fields, concentration across classes within fields

3. Concentration across fields, diversification across classes within fields

4. Concentration across both fields and classes within fields

Despite the acknowledgement that inter-relatedness has increased between formerly distinct fields of technology, it is not clear quite how distinct this distinctiveness is, or what inter-relatedness – especially with respect to technology – really means. Studies examining relatedness have used different databases and definitions and applied them to different levels (Granstrand and Sjölander, 1990; Dosi et al., 1992; Markides and Williamson, 1994; Patel and Pavitt, 1994a; Teece et al., 1994). For Markides and Williamson (1994) relatedness is exclusively associated with the inherent properties of the sectors in which firms are operating, and the firm can know, a priori, which sectors are related and exploit this for competitive advantage (Piscitello, 2000). Dosi et al. (1992) and Teece et al. (1994), however, suggest that relatedness is also partially firm-specific and that what is related is not known prior to experimentation. Firms can 'learn' what is or is not related after the event.

Thus in a technology-specific context, Breschi et al. (1998) perceive technological relatedness as a reflection of 'knowledge proximity'. When the two technologies rely upon the same scientific/engineering principles the technological gap between them is smaller. Hence by extending the Markides and Williamson definition to the technological context of Breschi et al., we might be able to estimate relatedness between technologies a priori. By contrast, Piscitello (2000) has drawn upon the Teece et al. perspective by considering measures of the co-patenting incidents of technological pairs by firms – an ex post measure. This means that we cannot anticipate relatedness between technologies a priori by looking at their underlying scientific/engineering principles, as these combinations are partially industry- and firm-specific.

Within the Reading database, the technological classes are distinct from one another but have been allocated to the same technological field on the basis of the underlying scientific/engineering knowledge perceived[1] to exist between them (i.e. using the Breschi et al. notion of relatedness). Given this, when looking at the actual classes and fields (refer back to Chapter 2), it is reasonable to assume that the technological gap between classes in the same field is smaller than that between classes in different fields. However, Zander (1997), drawing upon the same database, has recognized that 'this level of aggregation [i.e. patent classes] ... provides information about technologies which could be used together to create final products or complex systems' (p. 213). Thus it is also possible that technological relatedness might also arise between classes (and indeed technological fields) through use in production (i.e. in the Piscitello sense of relatedness). In fact, both types of technological complexity are potentially observable using the database: increasing technological breadth will be captured by diversification across the 56 fields, whilst increasing technological depth will be captured by diversification across the classes within a field. In parallel, if the nature of technological relatedness lies with the underlying scientific or engineering knowledge required we might expect to see more technological depth across classes within fewer technological fields in recent years. On the other hand, relatedness in the use of technologies in production may include the combination of quite different technological areas and would be revealed by technological diversification across the broader fields. This chapter will examine which type of relatedness dominates the diversification patterns of the selected firms in the industrial groups presented here. Additionally, given the consideration in Chapter 6 of the separate contribution of scale and other effects to increases/decreases in technological diversity, the final part of this chapter will examine whether diversification at one level (field or class) is primarily motivated by one contributory factor or the other (drift via scale effects or other effects such as relatedness), in an attempt to draw the influences of size and diversification at various technological levels together.

7.2 THE BALANCE OF TECHNOLOGICAL BREADTH AND DEPTH OVER TIME (Broad versus Focused Diversification)

7.2.1 Average Diversity in the Industrial Groupings

Table 7.1 presents, for each industrial group, the average diversity in technological activity, its variance and changes in diversity, at both the broad field and more focused class levels. They are also represented graphically in Figures 7.2 to 7.4. The details at the class level are calculated for those classes within the fields that arose under the pat30>100 selection criterion; however, a class level selection criterion was applied in addition to that applied at the field level.

Hence, within the fields that met the pat30>100 criterion for each of the industrial groupings, only those classes which had 10 or more patents in 1930 (pat30>10)[2] were included, otherwise small number problems in the calculation of the RTA index at the class level would have driven the subsequent analysis.

Table 7.1 Comparison of levels of diversity for the average firm in each industrial grouping, at the field and class level of analysis, 1930–90

Chemical	mean 1/cv		Variance		chg. 1/CV		Pattern
Year	(56)	(399)	(56)	(399)	(56)	(399)	(56): (399)
1930	100.46	82.64	1545.21	923.26			
					18.90	12.20	D>D
1940	119.36	94.84	2418.51	1960.83			
					–5.26	–18.47	C<C
1950	114.10	76.37	2139.50	1584.14			
					–1.52	5.96	C<D
1960	112.58	82.33	1590.14	1131.80			
					38.83	17.08	D>D
1970	151.41	99.41	3263.63	1542.60			
					–1.83	12.92	C<D
1980	149.57	112.33	5263.08	2733.70			
					3.81	2.62	D>D
1990	153.38	114.94	10740.98	3644.90			

Electrical	mean 1/cv		Variance		chg. 1/CV		Pattern
Year	(56)	(399)	(56)	(399)	(56)	(399)	(56):(399)
1930	84.67	71.25	3372.14	2948.23			
					6.37	3.62	D>D
1940	91.04	74.87	2924.20	2281.32			
					8.47	2.97	D>D
1950	99.51	77.85	2794.70	2000.46			
					9.19	0.99	D>D
1960	108.70	78.84	2306.69	1499.98			
					1.80	5.22	D<D
1970	110.50	84.06	2876.80	1718.41			
					–1.47	0.23	C>D
1980	109.03	84.29	2629.69	1144.15			
					2.80	1.63	D>D
1990	111.83	85.92	3108.91	1227.24			

Corporate technological competence

Table 7.1   continued

Mechanical Year	mean 1/cv (56)	(399)	Variance (56)	(399)	chg. 1/CV (56)	(399)	Pattern (56): (399)
1930	54.83	51.00	232.33	76.70			
					0.76	3.06	D<D
1940	55.59	54.06	254.27	123.51			
					3.08	3.42	D<D
1950	58.67	57.48	216.89	135.06			
					7.09	0.68	D>D
1960	65.76	58.16	262.76	217.56			
					2.99	−0.07	D>C
1970	68.75	58.09	326.36	293.13			
					3.03	−1.25	D>C
1980	71.78	56.85	742.97	216.74			
					3.41	−0.06	D>C
1990	75.20	56.79	881.62	238.36			

Transport Year	mean 1/cv (56)	(399)	Variance (56)	(399)	chg. 1/CV (56)	(399)	Pattern (56): (399)
1930	80.20	69.41	776.02	669.20			
					17.54	9.99	D>D
1940	97.75	79.41	1295.94	845.17			
					9.33	11.12	D<D
1950	107.08	90.52	981.02	1079.85			
					7.15	2.70	D>D
1960	114.23	93.22	1908.73	1790.47			
					0.25	7.28	D<D
1970	114.48	100.50	2971.49	1935.36			
					−6.13	−8.66	C<C
1980	108.35	91.84	2903.84	1428.02			
					−2.67	−6.62	C<C
1990	105.68	85.22	2625.06	1221.91			

Note: The variances are large because 1/CV values are expressed in percentages.

From Table 7.1 and Figure 7.2 we can see that in agreement with Zander's (1997) study of Swedish firms, the average diversity experienced by the firms from each industrial group has been greater at the broad technological field (56) level than at the narrower class (399) level. Looking at the average level

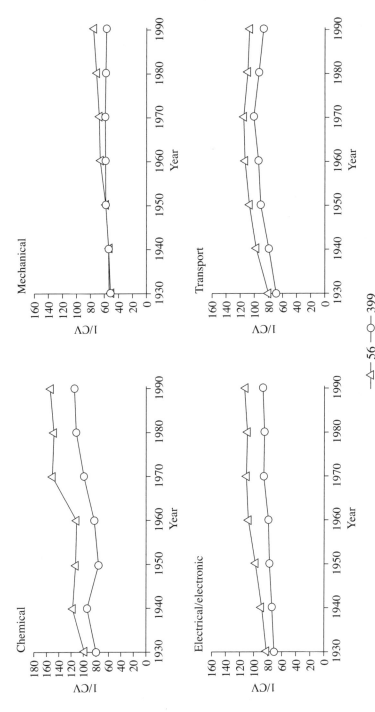

Figure 7.2   Average diversity

of diversity in Figure 7.1, the diversity of the mechanical group is considerably smaller than that of the other industrial groups across both fields and classes – it was comparatively technologically specialized. This goes back to the heterogeneity problem emphasized throughout this book, so the result here is unsurprising. However, the pattern observed suggests that large mechanical firms have been, in recent decades, relatively more concerned with increasing their technological breadth than depth.

The average levels of diversity across the electrical/electronic and transport groups over time are similar at least until 1970. However, post-1970 diversity changes at a greater rate in transport than in the electrical/electronic group but within the electrical/electronic industrial group, diversity across the fields increases faster than across classes. This suggests that technological breadth and depth were of equal importance for the large transport firms between 1930–70; but beyond 1970, the transport group's average diversity declines with that across classes being marginally steeper, suggesting that they have lost technological depth within fields. In comparison, the largest electrical/electronic firms became increasingly concerned with gaining technological breadth over time, but after 1970, the average diversity in the electrical/electronic industrial grouping remains fairly constant with respect to depth and breadth.

The behaviour of the chemical group (C) is far more erratic than that of E, M or T. The chemical group's average diversity across fields is greater than the other three industrial groupings even in 1930, whereas their diversity across the classes starts at approximately the same level. There was a pronounced increase in diversity at both levels between 1930–40 but a loss of technological breadth and particularly depth in 1940–50, probably due to the impact of the war. In 1950–60 it appears that large chemical firms were concerned with technological depth, but in 1960–70 there was a spectacularly large increase in technological breadth that coincided with a continuing steady effort to increase their extent of technological understanding. This large jump in breadth appears to relate to a rapid growth in patenting in synthetics, pharmaceuticals and biotechnology, building materials and photographic chemicals (see Table 3.4). Furthermore, whilst the endeavour for technological depth continued to 1990, the breadth of diversity among these large chemical firms remained fairly stable after its dramatic increase in 1960–70.

7.2.2 Variance in Diversity across Firms

Table 7.1 (second set of columns) and Figure 7.3 show that the variance in diversity across firms at the class level is slightly lower than that at the level of the technological fields, although the differential gradually increases. This suggests that whilst the firms from the same industrial grouping are more or

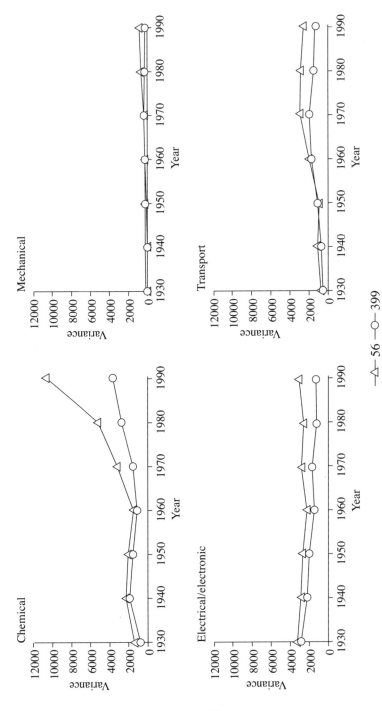

Figure 7.3   Variance of technological diversity (1/CV)

less similar in the depth of their technological understanding, they place different and increasingly different emphasis on the need to be technologically broad as time progresses. This is interesting because it shows that whilst relatedness through depth exists, relatedness through breadth in a firm- or industry-specific manner seems to get stronger over time.

The mechanical group's variance in diversity is very small at both levels of analysis. Combined with the earlier comments on low average levels of diversity, this implies that each individual mechanical firm in the sample is as relatively highly specialized as another, each possessing only a few areas of technological competence which makes them very distinct[3] (e.g. Eastman Kodak will specialize in very different areas from Deere or Bethlehem Steel). This continues to reinforce the heterogeneity argument.

Whilst the average diversity displayed by the electrical/electronic and transport groupings was similar in Figure 7.1, their variance in diversity is quite different. Electrical/electronics starts off relatively high but experiences a slight decline across the fields, and a sharper decline across the classes during 1930–90. This suggests that this group of firms becomes more similar with respect to their depth of technological diversity over time. In fact, Gambardella and Torrisi (1998) found that leading electronics firms were all technologically diversified to the same extent in the 1980s–90s, despite being product-diversified to different extents.

The transport group, on the other hand, starts with fairly low variance in diversity for both the technological fields and classes but this increases, especially during 1950–70, probably reflecting the divergent behaviours of the automotive and tyre companies. In many respects this is not surprising as the technological interests of tyre companies are more likely to be fairly focused upon areas such as artificial fibres, synthetic rubber and tyre design, whereas the automotive companies are more likely to require an understanding of a broader range of technologies that interact with one another in a system, e.g. various sectors of mechanical, chemical and electrical/electronic technologies.

The behaviour of chemicals is again outstanding among the four industrial groups. Its initial variance in 1930 and pattern of behaviour until 1960 are not so dissimilar to those of the other industrial groupings, and the variance across fields and classes rises and falls in tandem. However, in 1960–90, whilst the variance in diversity increases at both levels, that which occurs at the level of the field is rather dramatic. A closer inspection of the data at the firm level revealed this to be due to the very different behaviour of Du Pont and Allied Chemical – Du Pont became increasingly diversified and Allied increasingly concentrated, hence the variance in diversity becomes increasingly large across the selected groups of chemical firms.

7.2.3 Changes in Diversity

The last three columns in Table 7.1 indicate whether the *changes* in technological diversity have been stronger at the field or class level. The results are
represented graphically in Figure 7.4. The final column of Table 7.1 shows that
in the electrical/electronic and mechanical groups the effects of technological
diversification (a positive change in 1/CV) or technological concentration (a
negative change in 1/CV) are generally larger at the broader field level. In
contrast, the transport group shows that changes at the class level dominate.
The chemical group is inconclusive.

The chemical group (Figure 7.4) shows an almost cyclical pattern with two
decades of technological breadth of diversity being followed by an increase of
technological depth in 1950–60, then a further increase in technological breadth
in 1960–70 and relatively more depth again for the remaining two periods, reinforcing the changes observed in this period in the earlier figures in this chapter.
The electrical/electronic group shows less of a cyclical pattern but nevertheless technological diversification over the broad fields dominates the 1930–60
period whereas in the final three decades, whilst neither changes in diversity at
the field nor class level were particularly strong, they appear marginally stronger
at the class level. Similarly, the transport firms demonstrated strong positive
changes in broad technological diversity for the first 30 years and, in relative
terms, very little support for broad positive diversification in 1960–90. In
contrast, the mechanical group appears to consistently diversify more across
broad fields than across classes. Technological breadth in firm-specific combinations is seemingly more significant to this industry than technological
relatedness based on engineering and science. The chemical, electrical/electronic
and transport industrial groups therefore do lend some support to the proposition that firms have become less concerned with technological breadth over
time, although it is not absolutely clear that they substitute this for more technological depth. One factor that might account for such an observation could
be the change in the organization of competencies both within a firm and as
distributed across a network of firms. Generally, the perception is that any major
firm focuses on its key competencies, but maintains distributed portfolios over
a much wider range of technological areas in order to find, communicate and
understand potential network partners who may provide specialized technological capabilities.

7.3 COMBINING SCALE-INDUCED, DRIFT–OTHER
EFFECTS AND BREADTH–DEPTH ISSUES

The results so far in this chapter pay no account to the findings of Chapter 6.
That is, an increase in diversity sometimes occurs through drift effects

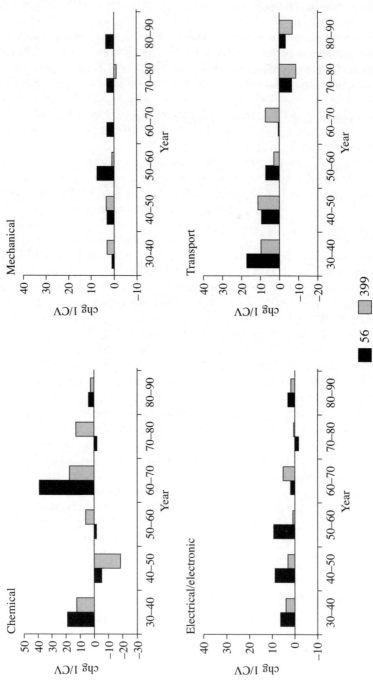

Figure 7.4   Change in technological diversity (1C/V)

associated with general increases in firm scale, whilst at other times (mainly more recently) diversification will occur even in the absence of any increase in firm size because of 'other' effects, which I there suggested were associated with the relatedness between the technologies themselves. The remainder of this chapter seeks to combine this matter with the breadth–depth issue of diversification dealt with in the sections above.

7.3.1   Types of Changes in Technological Diversity

Figure 7.5 identifies four possible combinations of change in diversity patterns. This is derived from the results of the shift-share analysis when applied to both the 56 technological fields and the 399 class levels respectively. Essentially, I am interested in the relative magnitude of the dominant effect (drift or other) at the 56 field level in comparison to the dominant effect at the 399 class level. If the drift effect at the field level dominates the 'other' effect at the class level, I regard this as change in diversity of type A in Figure 7.5. It should be clear from Figure 7.5 that type A relates to circumstances when the drift effect at the level of the broadly defined fields exceeds the effect (drift/other) driving the diversification/concentration at the class level. Type B is when the 'other' effect driving diversification/concentration at the class level is stronger than either drift or other effect on the field, and similarly for types C and D.

In Chapter 6 I found support for technological diversification to drift upwards in association with increases in firm size historically. Earlier in this chapter I found some support for broad diversification to have occurred across techno-

A	B
Drift (56) > Drift (399) Drift (56) > Other (399)	Other (399) > Drift (56) Other (399) > Other (56)
C	D
Other (56) > Drift (399) Other (56) > Other (399)	Drift (399) > Drift (56) Drift (399) > Other (56)

Figure 7.5   Types of change in technological diversity

logical fields more historically than recently. These two results in combination lead me to believe that diversification of type A would proliferate with greater frequency across the firms in each industrial group in earlier decades but will decline over time, whilst type B will be fairly scarce in earlier decades but become increasingly prevalent across firms.

7.3.2　Diversification Types Identified for each Industrial Group

Table 7.2 indicates the number of firms in each industrial group displaying one of the four possible patterns A–D.[4] My proposition about the more historical proliferation of type A loosely holds for the chemical, electrical/electronic and transport industrial groups, although my expectation of the emergence of type B in later decades applies only to electrical/electronics, and then only weakly. The types of change in diversity being experienced by each firm are thus more complex than a simple switch from broad, scale-induced, drift-like changes to more focused, technological depth-induced relatedness diversity.[5] The mode that does seem to become more widely adopted by firms across all four industrial groupings is C, where relatedness across broadly defined technological fields dominates either scale-induced drift or 'other' effects at the more detailed class level.

Table 7.2　Diversification types for each industrial sector

	1930–40	1940–50	1950–60	1960–70	1970–80	1980–90
Chemical	5A 0B	3A 1B	3A 0B	1A 1B	2A 0B	2A 0B
	0C 1D	0C 0D	1C 0D	2C 0D	2C 0D	2C 0D
Electrical/	4A 0B	3A 0B	2A 1B	3A 1B	2A 1B	1A 0B
electronic	2C 3D	4C 2D	3C 3D	2C 1D	2C 2D	5C 1D
Mechanical	3A 2B	6A 3B	3A 3B	4A 0B	0A 2B	5A 1B
	4C 2D	2C 0D	4C 1D	7C 0D	9C 0D	3C 2D
Transport	2A 0B	1A 2B	0A 0B	0A 1B	0A 1B	1A 0B
	2C 2D	1C 2D	4C 2D	3C 2D	2C 3D	3C 2D

Clearly changes in technological diversity over time do not conform to a simple trend. Despite the clear results of the individual contributions of Chapter 6 and the earlier part of the current chapter, it seems that when the two aspects of drift–other and breadth–depth are combined together, there is no simple replacement of changes in diversity of type A by type B over time. The true nature of changes in technological diversity is more complex. How might this complexity be explained?

Large firms are able to diversify into new technological areas as they have the resources to do so; however, the rising costs of R&D may also encourage them to diversify within their prior accumulated technological competencies. Given the assumption that the classes within a field are generally technologically closer to each other than to classes in different technological fields, one would expect more intra-field diversification across classes than inter-field diversification, because: (i) this enables the exploitation of economies of scope in the learning processes used to generate competence in one technological field, and (ii) the marginal costs of entry into a new class within an existing field of technological competence are likely to be lower than those of entering an entirely new field. However, balanced against this is the idea that not all classes within a field need necessarily be of equal value to the firm. The firm should not be discouraged from entering a distinct new class in a new field just because it is harder and more costly to do so in terms of the time, resources and learning effort to be committed to building up competence in this new area. When the firm does decide to enter a new class in a new field it seems reasonable to assume that it has done so for dynamic strategic purposes. The firm must have decided that this new area potentially offers rich technological opportunities for its technological development because the firm probably had to bridge a larger technological gap between the new technology and its existing competencies and therefore commit resources towards this activity. Therefore, when the size of a firm increases, it can use its resources either to diversify within fields as in Breschi et al. (1998, on the economies of scale and scope in technology utilization argument) or across fields into areas they perceive as crucial to their technological development and long run survival *à la* Piscitello (perhaps forgoing some of the potential economies afforded by intra-field diversification). The firm will have to consider the position of the fulcrum in this balance carefully.

When the firm shrinks, it is most likely to reduce its activity in those classes that are less vital to the firm's technological activities. This will probably be in fields where there are large numbers of classes in which the firm is active.[6] The firm will lose intra-field economies across classes and appear to concentrate within its technological classes, whilst remaining just as diversified across its technological fields. Hence, there is a skewness in the relationship between increase in firm size and the apparent effects it has on broad and deep diversification. Positive increases in size will probably affect technological diversity at both the field and the class level, but negative changes or decreases in size will appear to affect diversity at the level of the technological classes more greatly than at the level of the fields.

In summary, in the balance of the drift/other and the breadth/depth relationship, it seems that the shift from drift to other effects is a more important factor than whether changes in technological diversity occurred predominantly at the field or class level. This suggests that the primary motivating factor for changes in diversity has shifted from increases in firm size, to changes in the degree of technological relatedness between technologies, whether they arise through underlying principles or through firm- or industry-specific combinations. The issue of increasing technological complexity seems to place less pressure upon firms to face a trade-off between technological breadth and depth than we might have imagined. It seems that any trade-off between breadth and depth is partially a firm-specific decision, but also partially determined by industry needs. For the most part, relatedness through production linkages is becoming more prominent in each industrial sector and has been an important method of technological diversification in large firms in recent times. While relatedness through a common science or engineering base continues to be important, it is perhaps not as strong a motivator for the direction of technological diversification as might have been expected, even in the science-based industrial groups.

7.3.3 Trends within Firms

Whilst these technological diversification trends have been analysed at the industrial group level, it seems likely that a certain amount of detail regarding the individualistic, path-dependent behaviour of the firms in each of the industrial groups is being overlooked. Hence, trends of diversification types for each firm are given in Table 7.3.

In addition to emphasizing the heterogeneous nature of firms generally, and their individual path-dependent trajectories of technological evolution, a few other interesting features arise from Table 7.3. Within chemicals, it is evident that changes in the technological breadth of diversity (at the field level) are mostly associated with changes in firm size (A type diversification); for Union Carbide this has been the case throughout the time period analysed. In contrast, Du Pont never experienced changes in diversity of this sort. Apart from 1930–40, Du Pont has always experienced diversification through relatedness effects – across classes to enhance the depth of technological diversity in 1940–50, but for the remaining decades across fields to increase technological breadth. This would support Du Pont's more historical pursuit of related diversification, as recounted in the qualitative account of its history by Hounshell and Smith (1988).

Electrical/electronic firms are largely dominated by changes in diversity of types A and C, i.e. technological breadth irrespective of size or relatedness influences. However, General Electric and Westinghouse Electric stand out in this respect as they are dominated by type D – the pursuit of diversification across classes in a focused manner because of changes in firm size. This result may be explained by the sheer size of these two electrical firms, both being among the largest in this selection of very large firms.[7] Similar to the expla-

Table 7.3 Diversification patterns for individual firms

Chemical	Trend					
Firm	1930–40	1940–50	1950–60	1960–70	1970–80	1980–90
Union Carbide	A	A	A	A	A	A
Allied Chemical	A	A	A	C	A	C
Swiss IG	A	—	—	—	—	—
Standard Oil (NJ)	A	A	A	B	C	A
Du Pont	D	B	C	C	C	C
IG Farben	A	—	—	—	—	—

Electrical	Trend					
Firm	1930–40	1940–50	1950–60	1960–70	1970–80	1980–90
General Electric	D	D	D	B	D	D
Westinghouse Electric	D	D	D	D	A	A
Singer	C	C	B	A	A	C
Siemens	C	C	C	A	D	C
AEG-Telefunken	A	A	C	C	C	C
AT&T	A	C	C	A	B	C
RCA	A	A	A	C	C	C
Sperry	A	A	A	—	—	—
Burroughs	D	C	D	—	—	—

Mechanical	Trend					
Firm	1930–40	1940–50	1950–60	1960–70	1970–80	1980–90
US Steel	C	C	C	C	C	A
Bethlehem Steel	B	B	D	C	C	A
American Can	B	C	C	C	C	B
Krupp	C	A	C	A	C	C
International Harvester	A	B	B	A	C	C
Deere	C	A	A	A	C	A
Emhart	A	A	B	A	B	D
Allis Chalmers	D	B	B	C	C	D
Vickers	C	A	A	C	C	A
Eastman Kodak	A	A	A	C	B	C
Westinghouse Air Brake	D	A	C	C	C	A

Transport	*Trend*					
Firm	1930–40	1940–50	1950–60	1960–70	1970–80	1980–90
General Motors	D	B	C	B	D	D
Bendix	A	D	D	D	B	A
United Aircraft	A	D	D	D	D	D
Goodyear Tyre & Rubber	D	C	C	C	C	C
Firestone Tyre & Rubber	C	B	C	C	D	C
BF Goodrich	C	A	C	C	C	C

nation for GE's consistent concentration given in Chapter 5, the size of GE and Westinghouse enabled or encouraged them to be highly diversified technologically in 1930 through their product diversity, and it may be that because they were already highly diversified into most fields early on, there was little scope for them to diversify further, so they appear to diversify more within them over time and gain technological depth.

The mechanical firms, despite their heterogeneity, are dominated by types C and A – broad technological diversification. This is hardly surprising as mechanical products often involve systems based on complementary technologies; as such, broad knowledge rather than specialized knowledge in a few technologies would be more prudent. As diversity across fields (and in fact also across classes) through 'other' effects occurs with more frequency than that associated with the drift arising from increases in firm size, it seems that mechanical firms are well aware of the significance of technological relatedness in the evolution of diverse technological profiles, and thus serves to highlight the importance of technological relatedness as a firm-specific phenomenon. Finally, among the transport firms there is yet another and surprising split between the behaviour of the automotive and the tyre companies. Among automotive companies, type D is prevalent – drift effects arising from increases in firm size are leading to stronger technological diversification at the level of the detailed classes; among tyre companies, type C dominates – changes in technological breadth across fields due to changes in diversity through combinative relatedness is more popular. This anomaly is possibly explained by the nature of the firms in this sector. Automotive companies may originally have a wide range of technological experience in many fields as they are integrating various subsystems. Therefore any further increases in diversity manifest themselves as increased technological depth within these fields (just as in the GE case above). Tyre companies on the other hand are rather specialized equipment providers that supply automotive and other transport companies. Hence, originally their technological experience may be relatively narrow, but as they continue to expand and survive over time, they are required to develop an understanding of a wider range of technologies so that they have the underlying understanding of how their product fits in with other subsystems in, for example, an automobile or an aircraft, and what conditions their output will have to endure as part of that broader system.

7.4   SUMMARY AND CONCLUSIONS

Initiated by the findings in Chapter 5, this chapter has found that diversification can take place for at least two levels of classification – fields and classes.[8] The acceptance of the increasing cost of R&D and technological relatedness implying the use of a common source of scientific or engineering knowledge led to my expectation that technological inter-relatedness would encourage a firm to diversify more strongly across narrowly defined technological classes than across broader technological fields in the recent past. To determine this, I suggested that the relative strength of the *changes* in diversity might be greater at the class level in more recent times, whilst historically they might be greater at the level of the technological field. The analysis of this variable across decades did not reveal a clear-cut image of this sort, but was however suggestive of a *relative* decline in the extent of diversification at the field level and, implicitly, a relative increase at the class level, lending support to the original proposition.

The analysis up to this point had not, however, taken the influence of firm size into consideration, but Chapter 6 had established that across firms as a whole, technological drift effects arising through increase in scale had been a greater contributory factor to diversification in the earlier decades than in more recent times. The second half of this chapter sought to remedy this by combining the drift/other effects with the changes in diversity at the field and class levels to see if one effect consistently induced changes in diversity at one level or another. Four types of behaviour were identified.

The analysis of the four types of behaviour across and within firms in each industrial grouping highlighted that size-induced changes in diversity across broadly defined technological fields dominated the frequency of the changes in diversity in the earlier decades (type A) across all four industrial groupings, yet increasingly changes in diversity came to be induced by changes in technological relatedness effects rather than changes in size (type C). Moreover, the relatedness seemed to occur across both technological classes and fields, but predominantly the latter. This suggested that technological relatedness via its combinative use within specific firms or industries explained more of the technological diversity than would be predicted by an interpretation of technological relatedness as meaning commonality between technologies in their use of the underlying science base.[9]

It seems that the shift from size-induced diversification to diversification due to other effects has certainly taken place. I proposed that these other effects are partially accounted for by increases in technological relatedness. The reason for the rising importance of relatedness-induced diversification is that, during 1970–90, following a decade or more of strong increases in firm size, some firms' sizes were stagnating or even shrinking. Such firms may have had to reconsider their technological profiles of competence very carefully. I proposed that firms chose to eliminate some of those classes into which they had previously diversified (for the exploitation of scale and scope effects) when they were growing in size, in favour of remaining in those classes within the broader fields which were of central importance to them. A general reading of the competence-based literature suggests that this has in fact occurred. Corporate programmes have led to a renewed focus upon key[10] technological areas of central importance to their primary industrial interests, with activity in more peripheral technologies reduced to a level which either merely sustains their absorptive capacity or allows them sufficient competence to innovate design in product and processes but whose actual production, manufacture or execution might be conducted by a partner firm in their wider industrial network (Brusoni et al., 2001).

The finding with respect to the notion of a trade-off by firms between breadth and depth in an attempt to manage technological complexity is also significant, in that it suggests that the choice is not simple. Firms may be unable to substitute between technological depth and breadth directly, because industry-specific forces may constrain their decision-making, in terms of what technologies need to be combined in order to survive within the industry (especially in times of paradigmatic change). Sometimes the pressure from the industry may require technological diversification into areas that are related on a scientific or engineering basis, and at other times or in other industries the pressure may stem from the combination of technologies in use. However, firms also possess a considerable degree of autonomy with respect to the combinative use of technologies in use, and this would seem to dominate the desire to diversify into a new class just because it was close in scientific terms.

NOTES

1. The use of the word 'perception' is deliberate here. The reader may argue that the boundaries between technological sectors is somewhat arbitrary, being a construct of the original organization of the US patent class system (which was subsequently adopted and adapted in the database at Reading University). As a result some of the individual links between dissimilar sectors may not appear to be surprising. For example, in the chemical technological field 5

'chemical processes' is patent class 210 'liquid purification or separation (subclass 501–982)' yet in the mechanical technological field 16 'chemical and allied equipment' is patent class 210 'liquid purification or separation (subclass 1–500)'. However, the separation of the patent subclasses within the Reading database was conducted with good reason because, at times, the US patent class system itself was fairly arbitrary and inconsistent in its grouping together of dissimilar activities. For example, it placed certain chemical processes and mechanical devices together (as in the case of 'refrigeration' as explained in Chapter 2) which are of course related through production rather than scientific principles, yet the US patent class system would keep other production-based linkages quite separate, e.g. engines and electronic systems in automotives. The Reading database has therefore been adapted in its allocation of subclasses to classes and classes to fields, to best reflect inherent technological linkages rather than production-based linkages between which the US patent class system occasionally does not distinguish.

2. This criterion was selected after a closer inspection of the data.

3. Of course this may be linked to the use of patent data as mechanical products and processes are more easily invented around and reverse engineered, so secrecy may be used in preference to patents to protect intellectual property, thus affecting the patent-based measure of diversity for mechanical firms.

4. The number of firms in the chemical and electrical/electronic groups changes over time with the break up of the IG companies and the formation of Unisys via the Sperry–Burroughs merger, respectively. As such, for the purposes of the analysis they were omitted in the later decades.

5. In their analysis of significant innovations and *SIC sector* groupings, Pavitt et al. (1987, pp. 297–316) found that large chemical (and electrical/electronic) firms tended to enter into other three-digit product groups within the innovating firm's principal two-digit activity, while firms principally in machinery, mechanical engineering and instruments were more specialized in their innovative activities within their principal three-digit activity (p. 310). If one draws parallels between their two-digit and three-digit SIC groups with the technological fields and technological classes in this research, then the results here for the chemical and mechanical industrial groupings are analogous to theirs.

6. I have assumed that if the firm was active only in one class in the field (when there are numerous classes subsumed within the field), it would not have entered the field in the first place unless that single class was of significance, given the greater technological distance and the difficulties this entails.

7. Only AT&T exceeds these two electrical firms in 1930, but AT&T's production activities lie further downstream in telephone exchanges and more recently, telecommunications than GE or Westinghouse, who were both in the business of electricity generation. This difference might account for why AT&T does not also show a propensity to engage in changes in diversity of type D but prefers to diversify broadly across sectors instead.

8. As Penrose (1959, p. 107) has pointed out, there is an inherent ambiguity in the meaning of 'diversification'. Whilst she applies it to diversification across products, it applies equally across technologies. She condones attempts to establish its 'absolute' meaning, believing such acts are neither possible nor desirable. If the analysis were to be conducted with different levels of aggregation from the ones specified here, the patterns would be different in detail but the overall results would probably be similar when using one broad measure against one more narrowly defined measure.

9. In the situation where a very large firm splits up into smaller individual entities it might be expected that the entity that continues with the original firm's name will even show stronger concentration across sectors than across classes, as in the case of AT&T in the 1980s. The same would be true of Swiss IG and IG Farben when they split up in the 1950s.

10. I deliberately refrain from using the word 'core' in the Prahalad and Hamel (1990) sense because Granstrand et al. (1997) have since demonstrated that firms have distributed rather than core competencies.

8. Conclusions

8.1   INTRODUCTION

This final chapter summarizes the main findings of earlier chapters and brings together some thoughts on their implications for managers and academics.

This research was stimulated by my curiosity with respect to academic commentary on the growth of multi-technology corporations, growing relatedness between formerly distinct technologies and the process of technological fusion. To me, this meant that firms must be engaging in a process of technological diversification either as a deliberate strategy or because the wider environment enforced it upon them. But what did that process of diversification look like? How did firms search for and select from technologies? What stimulates technological diversification and how does this affect the firm's technological development? Would such diversification by firms begin to blur the technological boundaries between industries even if boundaries determined by product outputs remained distinct? What might be the implication of this? In the process of examining these questions an order of inquiry emerged to provide the structure of this current work. I have ascertained initial answers to most of my own curiosities and have summarized them below. However, I also recognize that in arriving at these answers many more questions are raised along the way that I have not attempted to answer here. Nevertheless, I hope that my findings might serve to initiate and encourage further investigations into the phenomenon of technological diversification and its implications for the evolution of corporate technological competence.

8.2   SUMMARY OF FINDINGS

Having introduced the main themes of interest in Chapter 1 and espoused the merits of patent data as a technological indicator in Chapter 2, I turned to consider technological patterns at the industrial group level. In particular, Chapter 3 considered the persistence of industry-specific competencies (Patel and Pavitt, 1994a, 1997) and found that even over a 60-year time frame, industries held persistent profiles of technological competencies. This supports the path-dependency view of technological development. However, this did not negate the other finding that each of the four industrial groups were extending the number of areas in which they were technologically active, even if they displayed no revealed technological advantage. Firms appear to hold both competencies in technologies crucial to the current era and capabilities in others, some of which could potentially become firm-specific competencies in the future. This complements Granstrand et al.'s (1997) finding that firms have distributed rather than core competencies. The outcomes of Chapter 3 were put forward as the long wave view and support the perception that even in the face of strong persistence, technological convergence between the industries has occurred.

Whilst industry-specific profiles were distinct and strongly persistent, this did not necessarily infer that this would be true at the firm level also. Factors that affected individual firms may not have been sufficiently strong to be registered at the more aggregate industrial group level, and so the aggregate industrial outcome might have appeared inherently more stable. Chapter 4 found that at the individual corporate group/firm level, persistent competencies also possessed longevity where the firm remained a consistent institutional entity. This confirmed the firm's role as a 'pool of resources' in the Penrosian sense and furthermore highlights its potential as a vehicle for institutional continuity. Even so, over a 60-year period, in a number of instances persistence did start to weaken largely through a process of diversifying incremental change although surprisingly, this was not a continuous process of erosion but a frequent occurrence motivated by technological or organizational factors.

The frequency with which diversifying incremental change was perceived across firms within Chapter 4 warranted a further examination of technological diversification as a separate phenomenon. Chapter 5, using an alternative and more direct indicator of technological diversification, confirmed the suggestive results of the previous chapter. It also indicated that technological diversification was both more widespread across firms and stronger within them, in historical decades than recent ones. This was surprising given the attention the issues of increasing technological complexity and inter-relatedness between distinct technologies had been getting in the literature in recent years. However, the work of Alfred Chandler (1990a) provided a basis for a possible explanation regarding the strength of the historical result. Consequently, an analysis involving the isolation of scale effects on technological scope and diversification from other effects (inter-relatedness, fusion, etc.) was attempted in the subsequent chapter.

Chapter 6 demonstrated that although there were some inter-industry differences, overall, firm size was positively associated with technological diversity. However, it suggested that beyond some threshold level, further increases in size might be associated with technological concentration (Cantwell and Santangelo, 2000). Studies from industrial economics (e.g. Gort, 1962 and Utton, 1979 from Pearce, 1983) provide some evidence that while firm size and industrial diversification were positively correlated for their full population of firms, amongst their largest firms the correlation disappeared. With more specific reference to innovation and technology, Kuemmerle (1998) posits that an optimal size for R&D laboratories exists. A similar relationship may also be true for technological diversification and the largest firms because innovation occurs not only within the corporate R&D facilities but also in the entire firm through a process of learning in production. Organizational issues will therefore come to the fore and organizational coherence may place bounds on the extent to which a firm may technologically diversify. However, the growth of the multi-tech firm has occurred and both Gambardella and Torrisi (1998) and Andersen and Walsh (2000) have empirical evidence that firms in the electrical and chemical industries have decreased their product diversity but continue to increase technological diversity.

The breakdown of the positive relationship between increases in scale and scope may have arisen because the effects of scale and scope were compounded. Further investigation found that in recent times, technological diversification has been associated less with increases in firm size. Indeed it can occur even when the firm shrinks in size. It seems that technological diversification was increasingly occurring independently of firm size (Chandler, 1990a, b, 1992, 1994) and in all likelihood, given other literature (Penrose, 1959; Rumelt, 1974; Chandler, 1966, 1990a; Markides and Williamson, 1994; Markides and Williamson, 1996) independently of concentration or diversification at the product level also. I have attributed technological diversification in recent years more to the influence of other factors such as the growing relatedness between technological fields.

Finally Chapter 7 considered the issue of technological relatedness explicitly and how this affects diversification. It examined technological diversification at both the field and class level because if relatedness between technologies lay in the use of common underlying knowledge of scientific and engineering principles then 'knowledge proximity' (Breschi et al., 1998) between classes *within* a technological field would be greater than *between* the fields themselves. This lay open the possibility that the analysis at the 56 field level may have been too aggregate and each field too broadly defined to detect this sensitivity. Indeed, I found a relative decline in diversification across the technological fields in favour of a relative increase in diversification across classes in later decades, suggesting that firms had changed to a more subtle or sensitive form of technological diversification over time.

I then examined this finding in the light of that from Chapter 6 to test my conjecture that relatedness would not be observed as strongly historically as it would in more recent times. If, historically, firms were not primarily concerned with technological diversification in its own right they would not have felt the importance of inter-relatedness between technological competencies as they diversified with their growth in size. This was found not to be the case. Size effects affected diversification as much at the class level as at the field level within firms. Both relatedness on the basis of underlying principles and on the basis of use in production and products exists, although there appeared to be greater technological relatedness between technological fields than I had expected, which was surprising given their considerable distinctiveness.

8.3 IMPLICATIONS

8.3.1 Persistent Industry Competencies

The persistence of industry-specific profiles of competence will act as a partial constraint on the direction of technological diversification for firms operating within that industry because these firms will be subject to the same forces emerging from technological trajectories that exert control over the industry's evolutionary pathway. Thus, an element of the direction into which firms may diversify will not be at the managers' discretion, just as Patel and Pavitt have found. This has implications for the nature of competition between firms and therefore firm policy.

Very large firms are generally perceived to exist in an oligopolistic environment, yet there are always threats to incumbents from new entrants (Eliasson, 1991). When disruptive technologies are involved (Christensen, 1997) smaller, creative, more flexible companies pose a threat. However for the most part, the nature of competition between such firms in an industry is largely stable. The greatest threat is perceived to come from those large firms that diversify beyond their existing markets, crossing traditional industry boundaries. Such firms have resources and other competitive advantages, which arise from being of equal size to incumbent firms, which otherwise form high barriers of entry to smaller potential challengers. However, the strength of technological persistence would suggest that the neoclassical perspective is lacking in explanatory power. It is not just the magnitude or quantity of generally available resources that matter, but the quality and suitability of the threatening firm's technological competencies for the destination industry's technological environment. A firm should probably only consider crossing industrial boundaries when the technological profile of competencies in the destination industry is similar to its present industry (Montgomery and Hariharan, 1991, p. 85), otherwise the firm has little chance of success.

For incumbent firms, it suggests that they should implement policies to maintain an interest in the wider technological environment, but that they should be especially vigilant in their monitoring and observation of technological developments occurring within industries that are technologically similar to their own, even if for the moment the industries do not appear to be in direct competition or may even be complementary. Such industries are likely to lie vertically within the production chain, up- or downstream. Technological similarity looks to be as much of a threat to incumbents as the magnitude of resources that come with size. For example, in the disk drive industry smaller newcomers have successfully challenged incumbents (Rosenbloom and Christensen, 1998).[1] Monitoring of this sort may have an additional benefit to merely pre-empting potential threats; it may also signal to firms potential technological opportunities which they might otherwise not have been aware of.

8.3.2   Convergence between Industries' Technological Activities

A closer inspection of the actual technological fields that caused increasing convergence between broad industrial groupings revealed that the areas of convergence were predominantly related to mechanical technologies, broader non-industrial technologies and more recently, electrical/electronic technologies. I suggested in Chapter 3 that firms will initially 'buy in' such technologies but over time, will find they need to specify equipment and processes to their particular needs and develop at least a degree of competence for this in-house (even if the actual manufacture is outsourced) (Brusoni et al., 2001). Technological convergence in a true sense does appear to be taking place and the existence of S-shapes at the general technological level confirmed is in the technological trajectories of individual firms also. It seems that the encompassing of new technologies to extend older competencies is a necessity so that firms do not become relegated to dinosaur status.

In the cases of certain technologies, this behaviour would complement Freeman and Perez's (1988) concept of meta-paradigms. Such socio-economic paradigms seem to take a long time to pervade society and the strengthening correlation coefficients between each pair of industries in each subsequent period are suggestive of a self-reinforcing, societal lock-in (Arthur et al., 1987; Arthur, 1989) to particular paradigms. So for example, the pervasiveness of computer technology is such that few industries have been left untouched by its influence, and so up to a point the technological activities of different industries have converged. Computing can be described as a general-purpose technology just as certain technologies in the mechanical paradigm have been in the past. Given the continuing strength of the mechanical paradigm even today, and if the pervasiveness of the mechanical paradigm is typical, it suggests that the pervasiveness of computerized technology we have witnessed so far is merely 'the tip of the iceberg' and that society should expect the electrical/electronic paradigm to continue to penetrate into our economies and societies even more deeply for some considerable time to come. As a result, academics still have much to learn about the pervasive effects of the ICT paradigm within electronics.

8.3.3   The Firm as a Repository of Persistent, Accumulated Technological Competence

Although persistence in technological profiles means that managers of firms are highly constrained in their choice of technological direction (Patel and Pavitt, 1997; Tidd et al., 1997) this persistence also acts as a solid foundation for the technological progression of the industry and economy as a whole if we view the firm as a repository of accumulated competence. This view holds an advantage over the Coasian transaction cost-based theory of firm approaches because the latter deals essentially only with the exchange of the potentially public element of technology – codified knowledge – and thus holds no obvious place for the notions of technological competence or productive capability. These elements can only be accumulated through internal learning processes within the firm, and thereby provide firms with the characteristics of technological persistence or stability, as such they have policy implications for the firm.

Whilst Schumpeter himself in his notion of 'creative destruction' and many writers subsequently have emphasized the tendency of technological change to transform and disrupt economies from time to time over longer periods, it is suggested here that this applies more to the spheres of activity that are largely exogenous to individual firms (the science base and the composition of products and markets), especially over longer periods, yet many large firms survive despite these changes. It seems the large firm provides a vehicle for potential institutional continuity, a means by which (through learning and experimentation) tacit capability or competence can be transformed to relate to and encompass new bodies of knowledge, to produce different products in order to serve and help to create new markets. Such a transformation may imply that the survival of the firm depends in the longer term upon the management of divisional and other organizational restructuring, but the firm's productive and technological system itself is potentially more stable.

The findings regarding technological persistence and the firm as a stable repository of competence also have implications for public policy. From the results portrayed here it appears that measures to deal with *institutional* failures are needed in order to support innovation, rather than measures addressing market failure. What is desired are institutional measures which encourage and support the development of more sophisticated systems of production, and the efforts devoted to collective learning within firms, which is in stark contrast to the conventional neoclassical view of technology policy as a remedy for market failure (Lall, 1994).

The theoretical and public policy implications outlined above have in common the conviction that what really matters is not so much how well markets do or do not work, but how tacit, social capability is generated through collective learning processes in production. Improving these learning processes normally means that the institutions must be adapted, with reference to their organization of social relationships.

The role of government should be to help lower the costs and facilitate the creation of tacit capability in firms, by addressing the problem of the development of more sophisticated systems of production, and increasing the propensity to seek profits through outward-looking innovation, rather than through wage-cutting or the search for positions of protected market power (Cantwell, 1995b). Additionally, if firms are not making the required investments in capability building and technological accumulation, it is insufficient for the government to merely support the provision of more education and skills as 'new growth theory' advocates if this knowledge and these skills do not match that sought by local firms. The most successful countries tend to be those in which government support for science and technology over a wide range has the vocal backing of innovative local firms, which wish to draw on and interact with knowledge and skills from many diverse areas, as opposed to purely market-based national innovation systems in which the public support of research is focused upon the areas of the most direct and immediate market potential for local companies (Nelson, 1993; Pavitt, 1995).

8.3.4 Implications of Scale and Scope in Technology

The findings of Chapters 5 and 6 together serve to focus attention on techno-logical diversification as a phenomenon in its own right. They indicate that technological diversification can occur independently of increases in firm size (Chandler, 1990a, b, 1992, 1994) and in accordance with other literature, inde-pendently of product diversification also (Penrose, 1959; Chandler, 1966, 1990a; Rumelt, 1974; Markides and Williamson, 1994, 1996). Technological diversi-fication can be engaged in passively as the firm grows, it may be necessitated by the emergence of new technological paradigms. However, technological diversification may also be engaged in with strategic intent, and scale and scope in technologies may not always be driven in the same direction. This has impli-cations for the management of diversity and this, in turn, is closely tied to organizational issues.

Although not expressly examined in this volume, organisational issues with respect to structure and behaviour have a long history (for example, Rumelt, 1974; Porter, 1985; Chandler, 1990a; Teece, 1993; Henderson and Cockburn, 1994; Hill, 1994; Marengo, 1995; Pavitt, 1998). I hinted at the importance of organizational considerations in Chapter 6. Combined with our increased under-standing of the difference between knowledge and know-how we are beginning to understand that a firm can possess a technological competence in order to understand its own needs and demands for a particular technology and yet not engage in the physical act of manufacturing that technology. It may rely on a network of partner institutions to do this (Richardson, 1972; Loasby, 1991, 1994, 1998; Hagedoorn and Narula, 1996; Teece, 1996; Granstrand et al., 1997; Quelin, 1997; Brusoni et al., 2001). Nevertheless, to be able to convey ideas and concepts between partners, the firm itself must possess sufficient competence in the technology internally. Partners can be useful for the outsourcing of non-essential elements of the product, but a deep understanding of the technologies involved may be necessary at times to provide the basis for selecting appropriate partners, the communication of ideas, and the development of further innovations. This might explain why the emergence of the networked firm and the firm as a network has occurred in the past decade or so, reducing firm size as they become more focused and lean and yet why we see firms continuing to technologically diversify. They are building up a portfolio of competencies to engage in communications with other firms and institutions.

Furthermore, managers must recognize the independence and interdependence between products, processes and technologies and triangulate their interplay with organizational considerations. They must do this so that they can develop elements within a network recognizing that different partners have different competencies, and different uses. Some partners may merely carry out instructions producing products and providing services, others may be more involved in the development of new technologies, provide specialist competencies or complementary products and processes in the value chain. The knowledge that is exchanged and the know-how that must be developed in each case will be different and recognition of this is important because these will, in turn, determine to a degree what the firm will be able to do in the future.

8.3.5 Diversification and Relatedness between Technologies

Given the importance of technological diversification in its own right, the findings of Chapter 7 are significant, as it goes some way to resolve what is implied by technological relatedness. Of the two definitions put forward, it seems that relatedness is essentially a firm-specific phenomenon, although general trends across firms within industries might be gleaned to indicate which technologies are more complementary than others in the industry-specific context. Relatedness appears to lie less in the sharing of common underlying knowledge than in the complementarity of technologies in their use in the production process. Firms will experiment and explore new combinations of capabilities and through a process of incremental and cumulative learning, will collect together those which are related in the context of the specific firm (Cantwell, 1998).

Even if there is general agreement between firms as to *which* technologies form industry-specific technological linkages, the '*how* they are related' (through production-linkages or underlying scientific and engineering principles) and *'to what extent* they are related' are likely to differ considerably between firms. This has implications for the firm when trying to use its external organization to enhance its internal organization's competencies. The choice of an appropriate technological partner will become even more important for those firms that chose to embark upon technological partnering and alliance strategies. If any one of the 'which', 'how' or 'to what extent' matters is perceived very differently by one potential technological partner the chances of the alliance being successful or even going ahead may be jeopardized. Even in the face of technological complexity and the growing use of network alliances, firms will require sufficient competence in an area to recognize the technological compatibility between themselves and elements in their external network and how developments in those areas might have implications for the current and future technological competencies they utilize in production or embody in products themselves. This is particularly true given the increasing use of different technologies in large systems. Those firms that fail to maintain a grip on technological complexity through diversification are likely to find themselves vulnerable, even if for the moment they are successful in their own field. Technological evolution is incremental, it is cumulative and it is continuous and changing. A failure to recognize this by firms will lead to their ultimate downfall in the future.

8.4   FINAL THOUGHTS

The suggestion that technological relatedness not only lies in shared underlying knowledge but also in the production process itself also requires further investigation. The nexus of technological combinations is highly complex. Technologies may be linked in production through vertical integration but there are also horizontal technological linkages across products and linkages between technologies within products. Even if products are linked by common technologies, these technologies may enter into each product at various different points in the vertical chain of production. I believe the work of Rumelt (1974) to be influential here. Parallels can be drawn between his notions of 'constrained' and 'linked' (product) diversification strategies with notions of technological relatedness based on (a) the exploitation of economies of scope and knowledge proximity and (b) relatedness in production, but the strength of these parallels needs to be investigated. Additionally, because technological complementarity and relatedness involve a high degree of firm specificity it seems that case study approaches would be very useful to enlighten us further about how firms perceive technologies to be related.

Much work is to be done regarding the independence and interdependencies between organizational issues, technologies and products. Considerable progress concerning the inter-linkages between technology, organization and competitiveness has been made (Dosi et al., 1998; Pavitt, 1998). But it would be interesting to examine how firms distinguish between those technologies they wish to maintain internally as their own competencies (perhaps core-distinctive and core-niche in Patel and Pavitt's, 1997 terminology) and those which they leave in the domain of their external networks but to which they have access (Loasby, 1991), and the impact this has had upon their organizational coherence and competitive performance.

I believe that the study of technological diversification has a great deal more to reveal about its nature and this is important because the phenomenon of technological diversification has the potential to affect so many areas of economic development and business strategy. With this research I hope to have made some small contribution towards this end.

NOTE

1. Christensen's work on disruptive innovations (1997) makes it clear that the smaller firms did not enter with new technologies or resources, but combined *existing* technologies with new values to produce disruptive innovations to challenge incumbents in the disk-drive industry.

Appendix to Chapter 2

Table A2.1   Full list of 399 technological patent classes and 56 technological fields, for the five broad technological areas

The chemical field

Technological fields (13)	Patent classes (57)
2 distillation processes	201 distillation: processes, thermolytic
	203 distillation: processes, separatory
3 inorganic chemicals	423 chemistry, inorganic
4 agricultural chemicals	71 chemistry, fertilizers
5 chemical processes	23 chemistry
	51 abrading (subclass 293–328)
	55 gas separation (subclass 1–99)
	62 refrigeration (subclass 1–122)
	134 cleaning and liquid contact with solids (subclass 1–42)
	156 adhesive bonding and miscellaneous chemical manufacture (subclass 1–479, 600–668)
	204 chemistry, electrical and wave energy (subclass 1–192, 900–914)
	210 liquid purification or separation (subclass 501–982)
	427 coating processes
	432 heating (subclass 1–53)
	518 chemistry (processes which include a Fischer–Tropsch reaction)
6 photographic chemistry	430 radiation imagery chemistry-processes, composition or product
7 cleaning agents and other compositions	106 compositions, coating or plastic
	252 compositions
	512 perfume compositions
8 disinfecting and preserving	422 process disinfecting, deodorizing, preserving or sterilizing, chemicals apparatus (subclass 1–43)
9 synthetic resins and fibres	260 chemistry carbon compounds (subclass 1–94, 666–683, 709–999)
	520 synthetic resins

521 part of the class 520 series – synthetic resins or natural rubbers
522 part of the class 520 series – synthetic resins or natural rubbers
523 part of the class 520 series – synthetic resins or natural rubbers
524 part of the class 520 series – synthetic resins or natural rubbers
525 part of the class 520 series – synthetic resins
526 part of the class 520 series – synthetic resins or natural rubbers
527 part of the class 520 series – synthetic resins or natural rubbers
528 part of the class 520 series – synthetic resins

10 bleaching and dyeing | 8 bleaching and dyeing of textiles and fibres

11 other organic compounds
260 chemistry carbon compounds (subclass 96–665)
530 chemistry, peptides or proteins; lignins or reaction products thereof
534 part of the class 532–570 series-organic compounds
536 part of the class 532–570 series-organic compounds
540 part of the class 532–570 series-organic compounds
544 part of the class 532–570 series-organic compounds
546 part of the class 532–570 series-organic compounds
548 part of the class 532–570 series-organic compounds
549 part of the class 532–570 series-organic compounds
552 part of the class 532–570 series-organic compounds
556 part of the class 532–570 series-organic compounds
558 part of the class 532–570 series-organic compounds
560 part of the class 532–570 series-organic compounds
562 part of the class 532–570 series-organic compounds
564 part of the class 532–570 series-organic compounds
568 part of the class 532–570 series-organic compounds
570 part of the class 532–570 series-organic compounds

12 pharmaceuticals and biotechnology
424 drug, bio-affecting and body treating compositions
435 chemistry: molecular biology and microbiology
436 chemistry: analytical and immunological testing
514 drug, bio-affecting and body treating compositions
800 multicellular living organism and unmodified parts thereof

51 coal and petroleum products
44 fuel and igniting devices
208 mineral oils; processes and products
585 chemistry, hydrocarbons

55 explosive compositions and charges
149 explosive and thermic compositions or charges

The electrical field

Technological fields (11)	Patent classes (69)
30 mechanical calculators and typewriters	235 register (subclass 61–89, 419–434) 400 typewriting machines
33 telecommunications	178 telegraphy 329 demodulators and detectors 332 modulators 367 communication, electrical: acoustic wave systems and devices 370 multiplex communications 375 pulse or digital communications 379 telephonic communication 455 telecommunications
34 other electrical communication systems	340 communications, electrical 341 coded data generation and conversion 382 image analysis
35 special radio system	342 communication, directive radio wave systems and devices 343 communication, radio wave antennas
36 image and sound equipment	84 music 181 acoustics 358 pictorial communication: television 381 electrical audio signal processing
37 illumination devices	313 electrical lamp and discharge devices 314 electrical lamp and discharge devices, consumable electrodes 315 electrical lamp and discharge devices, systems 362 illumination
38 electrical devices and systems	174 electricity, conductors and insulators 200 electricity, circuit maker and breakers 307 electrical transmission or interconnection systems (subclass 1–199, 586–999) 323 electricity, voltage magnitude and phase control system 328 miscellaneous electron space discharge device 330 amplifiers 331 oscillators 333 wave transmission lines and networks 334 tuners 335 electricity, magnetically operated switches, magnets and electromagnets 336 inductor devices 337 electricity, electrothermally or thermally actuated switches

338 electrical resistors

361 electricity, electrical systems and devices (subclass 1–432, 437–999)

363 electric power conversion systems

372 coherent light generators

439 electrical connectors

505 superconductor technology – apparatus, material, process

39 other general electrical equipment	62 refrigeration (subclass 123–999)
	136 batteries, thermoelectric and photoelectric
	204 chemistry, electrical and wave energy (subclass 193–499)
	219 electric heating
	236 automatic temperature and humidity regulation
	290 prime mover dynamo plants
	310 electrical generator or motor structure
	318 electricity, motive power systems
	320 electricity, battery and condenser charging and discharging
	322 electricity, single generator systems
	361 electricity, electrical systems and devices (subclass 433–436)
	373 industrial electric heating furnaces
	388 electricity, motor control systems
	392 electric resistant heating devices
	429 chemistry, electrical current producing apparatus, product and process
	437 semiconductor device manufacturing: process
40 semiconductors	307 electrical transmission or interconnection systems (subclass 200–585)
	357 active solid state devices, e.g. transistors, solid state diodes
41 office equipment and data processing systems	235 registers (subclass 375–386, 400–418, 435–457)
	360 dynamic magnetic information storage and retrieval
	364 electrical computers and data processing systems
	365 static information storage and retrieval
	369 dynamic information storage and retrieval
	371 error detection/correction and fault detection/recovery
	377 electrical pulse counters, pulse dividers or shift registers
	902 electronic funds transfer
52 photographic equipment	354 photography
	355 photocopying

The mechanical field

Technological fields (21)	*Patent classes (221)*
1 food and tobacco products	127 sugar, starch and carbohydrates (subclass 29–71) 131 tobacco (subclass 1–226, 291–999) 426 food or edible material: processes, compositions and products
13 metallurgical processes	29 metal working 75 metallurgy 148 metal treatment 164 metal founding (subclass 1–148) 228 metal fusion bonding (subclass 101–265) 419 powder metallurgy-processes 420 non-ferrous alloys or metallic compositions
14 miscellaneous metal products	4 baths, closets, sinks and spittoons 7 compound tools 10 bolt, nail, nut, rivet and screw making 16 miscellaneous hardware 24 buckles, buttons, clasps, etc. 27 undertaking 30 cutlery (subclass 1–165, 395–499, 501–999) 49 moveable or removable closures 63 jewellery 70 locks 108 horizontally supported planar surfaces 109 safes, bank protection and related devices 124 mechanical guns and projectors 132 toilet 135 tents, canopies, umbrellas and canes 138 pipes and tubular conduits 150 cloth, leather and rubber receptacles 160 closures, partitions and panels, flexible and portable 182 fire escapes, ladders, scaffolds 190 baggage 206 special receptacle or package 211 supports, racks 215 bottles and jars (subclass 100–367) 220 metallic receptacles 232 deposit and collection receptacles 248 supports 256 fences 267 spring devices 272 amusement and exercising devices 279 chucks or sockets 285 pipe joints or couplings 292 closure fasteners 312 supports, cabinet structures 383 flexible bags

403 joints and connections
411 expanded, threaded, headed, and driven fasteners –
    locked or coupled bolts
464 rotary shafts, gudgeons, housing and flexible
    couplings for rotary shafts
623 prosthesis (artificial body members), parts thereof
    or aids and accessories thereof

15 food, drink and tobacco 99 foods and beverages: apparatus
   equipment   127 sugar, starch and carbohydrates (subclass 1–28)
                           131 tobacco (subclass 227–290)

16 chemical and allied   34 drying and gas or vapour contact with solid
   equipment   51 abrading (subclass 1–292, 329–999)
                          55 gas separation (subclass 100–999)
                          68 textiles, fluid treating apparatus
                          118 coating apparatus
                          134 cleaning and liquid contact with solid (subclass
                              43–999)
                          156 adhesive bonding and miscellaneous chemical man-
                              ufacture (subclass 480–599, 669–999)
                          159 concentrating evaporators
                          196 mineral oil apparatus
                          202 distillation: apparatus
                          209 classifying, separating and assorting solids
                          210 liquid purification or separation (subclass 1–500)
                          261 gas and liquid contact apparatus
                          366 agitating
                          422 process disinfecting, deodorizing, preserving or
                              sterilizing, chemical apparatus (subclass 44–999)
                          494 imperforate bowl, centrifugal separators
                          502 catalyst, solid sorbent, or support thereof, product
                              or process
                          503 record receiver having plural leaves or a colorless
                              color former, method of use or developer thereof

17 metal working   59 chain, staple and horseshoe making
   equipment   72 metal deforming
                          76 metals tools and implements, making
                          81 tools
                          82 turning
                          83 cutting
                          163 needle and pin making
                          164 metal founding (subclass 149–999)
                          173 tool driving or impacting
                          225 severing by tearing or breaking
                          228 metal fusion bonding (subclass 1–100)
                          234 selective cutting (e.g. punching)
                          266 metallurgical apparatus
                          269 work holders
                          384 bearing or guides

407 cutters for shaping
408 cutting by use of rotating axially moving tool
409 gear cutting, milling or planing
413 sheet metal container making
474 endless belt power transmission and components

18 paper making apparatus 53 package making
162 paper making and fibre preparation
229 paper receptacles
493 manufacturing container or tube from paper

19 building material 65 glass manufacturing (subclass 138–999)
processing equipment 241 solid material comminution or disintegration
(subclass 132–999)
249 static moulds

20 assembly and material 186 store service
handling equipment 187 elevators (subclass 1–28, 30–999)
193 conveyors, chutes, skids, guides and ways
198 conveyors, power driven
212 traversing hoists
224 package and article carriers
226 advancing material of indeterminate length
242 winding and reeling
254 pushing and pulling implements (subclass 134–999)
258 railway mail delivery
271 sheet feeding or delivering
294 handling, hand and hoist-line implements
402 binder device releasably engaging aperture or notch
of sheet
406 conveyors, fluid current
410 freight accommodation on freight carrier
414 material or article handling

21 agricultural equipment 56 harvesters
111 planting
172 earth working
278 land vehicles, animal draft appliances
460 crop threshing or separating

22 other construction and 37 excavating
excavating equipment 171 unearthing plants or buried objects
404 road structure, process and apparatus (subclass
83–133)

23 mining equipment 166 wells
175 boring or penetrating the earth
299 mining or in situ disintegration of hard material

24 electrical lamp 445 electrical lamp or space discharge component or
manufacturing device manufacturing

25 textile and clothing 12 boot and shoe making
machinery 19 textiles, fibre preparation

	26	textiles, cloth finishing
	28	textiles, manufacturing
	38	textiles, ironing or smoothing
	57	textiles, spinning, twisting and twining
	66	textiles, knitting
	69	leather manufactures
	87	textiles, braiding, netting and lacemaking
	112	sewing
	139	textiles, weaving
	223	apparel apparatus
26 printing and publishing machinery	101	printing
	199	type casting
	270	sheet material associating or folding
	276	type setting
	281	books, strips and leaves
	282	manifolding
	283	printed matter
	412	bookbinding, process and apparatus
27 woodworking tools and machinery	142	wood turning
	144	wood working
28 other specialized machinery	15	brushing, scrubbing and general cleaning apparatus
	30	cutlery (subclass 166, 168–394, 500)
	79	button making
	98	ventilation
	100	presses
	116	signals and indicators
	140	wireworking
	141	fluent material handling, with receiver or receiver coating means
	147	coopering
	157	wheelwright machines
	169	fire-extinguishers
	194	check-controlled apparatus
	221	article dispensing
	222	dispensing
	227	elongated member driving apparatus
	254	pushing and pulling implements (subclass 1–133)
	277	joint packing
	291	track sanders
	300	brush, broom and mop making
	401	coating, implements with material supply
	425	plastic article or earthenware shaping or treating: apparatus
	453	coin handling
29 other general industrial equipment	48	gas, heating and illuminating
	91	motors, expansible chamber type
	92	expansible chamber device
	110	furnaces

	122	liquid heaters and vaporizers
	126	stores and furnaces
	137	fluid handling
	165	heat exchange
	184	lubrication
	185	motors, spring, weight and animal powered
	188	brakes
	192	clutches and power stop control
	237	heating systems
	239	fluid sprinkling, spraying and diffusing
	251	valve and valve actuation
	303	fluid pressure brake and analogous systems
	415	rotary kinetic fluid motors or pumps
	416	fluid reaction surfaces (i.e. impellers)
	417	pumps
	418	rotary expansible chamber devices
	431	combustion
	432	heating (subclass 54–999)
31 power plants	60	power plants
50 non-metallic mineral product	52	static structures (e.g. buildings)
	65	glass manufacturing (subclass 1–137)
	125	stone working
	215	bottles and jars (subclass 1–99)
	241	solid material comminution or disintegration (subclass 1–131)
	428	stock material or miscellaneous articles
	501	compositions: ceramics
53 other instruments and controls	33	geometrical instruments
	73	measuring and testing
	74	machine elements and mechanism
	128	surgery
	177	weighing scales
	187	elevators (subclass 29)
	235	registers (subclass 1–60, 90–374, 387–399, 458–999)
	250	radiant energy
	324	electricity, measuring and testing
	346	recorders
	350	optics, systems and elements
	351	optics, eye examining, vision testing and correcting
	352	optics, motion pictures
	353	optics, image projectors
	356	optics, measuring and testing
	368	horology – time measuring systems or devices
	374	thermal measuring and testing
	378	x-ray or gamma ray systems or devices
	433	dentistry

475 planetary gear transmission systems and
components
600 surgery
604 surgery
606 surgery

The transport field

Technological fields (7)	*Patent classes (21)*
42 internal combustion engines	123 internal combustion engines
43 motor vehicles	180 motor vehicles 296 land vehicles, bodies and tops
44 aircraft	244 aeronautics (subclass 1–13, 15–999)
45 ships and marine propulsion	114 ships (subclass 1–19, 26–999) 440 marine propulsion 441 buoys, rafts and aquatic devices
46 railways and railway equipment	104 railways 105 railway rolling stock 213 railway draft appliances 238 railways, surface track 246 railway switches and signals
47 other transport equipment	191 electricity, transmission to vehicles 280 land vehicles 293 vehicle fenders 295 railway wheels and axles 298 land vehicles, dumping 301 land vehicles, wheels and axles 305 wheel substitutes for land vehicles
49 rubber and plastic products	152 resilient tyres and wheels 264 plastic and non-metallic article shaping or treating process

The other (non-industrial) field

Technological fields (4)	*Patent classes (33)*
32 nuclear reactors	376 induced nuclear reaction, systems and elements
48 textiles, clothing and leather	2 apparel 36 boots, shoes and leggings 245 wire fabrics and structure 289 knots and knot tying 450 foundation garments

54 wood products

5   beds
217 wooden receptacles
297 chairs and seats

56 other manufacturing
   and non-industrial

14 bridges
40 card, picture and sign exhibiting
42 firearms
43 fishing, trapping and vermin destroying
47 plant husbandry
54 harness
86 ammunition and explosive-charge making
89 ordnance
102 ammunition and explosive devices
114 ships (subclass 20–25)
119 animal husbandry
168 farriery
231 whips and whip apparatus
244 aeronautics (subclass 14)
273 amusement devices, games
380 cryptography (cyphering and coding apparatus)
404 road structure, process and apparatus (subclass 1–82, 134–999)
405 hydraulic and earth engineering
434 education and demonstration
446 amusement devices, toys
449 bee culture
452 butchering

Appendix to Chapter 6

WORKED EXAMPLE

1. The RTA indices for each firm, in each of the 56 technological fields was calculated using:

$$RTA_{ijt} = (P_{ij}/\Sigma_j P_{ij})/(\Sigma_i P_{ij}/\Sigma_{ij} P_{ij})_t \qquad \text{(A6.1)}$$

where P_{ij} = number of patents accumulated by firm j in technological field i in a particular year, t. This was done on an intra-industry basis and repeated for each decade.

2. The inverse of the coefficient of variation of the RTA in a particular year (t) was calculated for each firm using:

$$1/CV_t = \mu_{RTA_t}/\sigma_{RTA_t} \qquad \text{(A6.2)}$$

This gave us a measure of a firm's technological diversity across the 56 technological fields in a particular year.

3. The size ($\Sigma_i P_{ij}$) and the diversity ($1/CV$) of the firms in year t were used in the following regression equation in a panel data estimation:

$$1/CV_t = \alpha + \beta \ln(size)_t + \varepsilon_t \qquad \text{(A6.3)}$$

Thus, the intercept and slope coefficient for each industrial grouping of firms (CEMT) was found for each decade between 1930 and 1990 (columns iii and iv in Table 6.1).

4. The average firm size (Av. LPAT) and average degree of technological diversity (Av. 1/CV) were calculated for each industrial grouping in each year (columns v and vi).

5. The observed change in the average firm size (Chg LPAT) and average degree of technological diversity (Chg 1/CV) between each decade were calculated (columns vii and viii).

6. The intercept and slope coefficients derived from the regression for the industry in year t, plus the observed average firm size in $t+1$ were used in the following equation:

Corporate technological competence

$$\text{Est. } 1/CV_{t+1} = \alpha_t + \beta_t \quad \ln(\text{size})_{t+1}$$

Columns: $\quad (ix)_{t+1} = (iii)_t + (iv)_t \; (v)_{t+1}$ (A6.4)

This gives an estimate of the technological diversity that would have been brought about purely by an increase in firm size in the absence of all other effects (Est. 1/CV, column ix). This equates to a movement along the regression line. For example, for Chemical between 1930 and 1940, the estimated level of technological diversity achieved through an increase in firm size would be:

$$\text{Est. } 1/CV_{1940} = -103.58 + 26.14 \,(7.29)$$
$$= 87.10$$

7. The hypothetical change in technological diversity between decades that would have been brought about purely by a change in firm size is given by:

$$(\text{Est. } 1/CV_{t+1}) - (\text{Av. } 1/CV_t) = (\text{drift})$$ (A6.5)

Columns: $\quad (ix) \qquad\qquad - (vi) \qquad = (x)$

For example, for Chemical between 1930 and 1940, the estimated change in technological diversity due to increases in firm size would be:

$$87.10 - 54.92 = 32.18$$ (A6.6)

8. The remainder of the observed change in technological diversity is therefore due to other effects such as technological necessity and is given by:

$$(\text{Av. } 1/CV)_{t+1} - (\text{drift})_{t+1} = (\text{other})_{t+1}$$ (A6.7)

Columns: $\quad (vi) \qquad\qquad - (x) \qquad = (xi)$

For example, for Chemical between 1930 and 1940, the estimated change in technological diversity due to other factors therefore must be:

$$69.18 - 87.10 = -17.92$$ (A6.8)

The signs associated with the two notional change effects (attained in steps 7 and 8) indicate whether 'drift' and 'other' independently contribute to or work against further technological diversification. Hence, when the figures in columns x and xi are both positive (or both negative), then the two work in the same direction with respect to technological diversification; when the two have opposing signs, they work in opposite directions. Graphically:

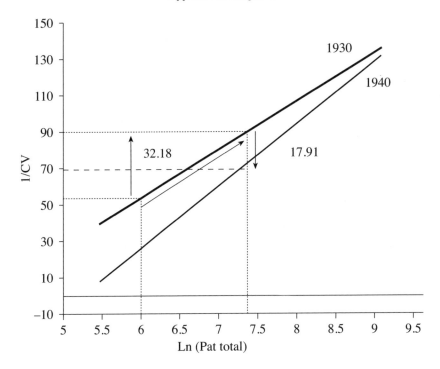

Figure A6.1   Chemical shift-share example, 1930/40

Bibliography

Andersen, H.B. (1999), 'The hunt for S-shaped growth paths in technological innovation: a patent study', *Journal of Evolutionary Economics*, **9**, 487–526.

Andersen, H.B. (2001), *Technological Change and the Evolution of Corporate Innovation*, Cheltenham, UK and Northampton, MA, USA: Edward Elgar.

Andersen, H.B. and V. Walsh (2000), 'Co-evolution within chemical technology systems: a competence bloc approach', *Industry and Innovation*, **7** (1), 77–115.

Archibugi, D. (1992), 'Patenting as an indicator of technological innovation: a review', *Science and Public Policy*, **19**, 357–68.

Archibugi, D. and M. Pianta (1992), *The Technological Specialisation of Advanced Countries: A Report to the EEC on International Science and Technology Activities*, Netherlands: Kluwer Academic Publishers.

Argyres, N. (1996), 'Capabilities, technological diversification and division-alization', *Strategic Management Journal*, **17**, 395–410.

Arora, A. (1995), 'Licensing tacit knowledge: intellectual property rights and the market for know-how', *Economics of Innovation and New Technology*, **4**, 41–9.

Arora, A. (1997), 'Patents, licensing and market structure in the chemical industry', *Research Policy*, **26**, 391–403.

Arthur, W.B. (1989), 'Competing technologies, increasing returns and lock-in by historical events', *Economic Journal*, **99**, 116–31.

Arthur, W.B., Yu U. Ermoliev and Yu M. Kaniovski (1987), 'Path dependent processes and the emergence of macro-structure', *European Journal of Operational Research*, **30**, 294–303.

Athreye, S. and G.N. von Tunzelmann (1997), 'Scale and scope in European industry', *Mimeo*, University of Sussex: UMIST and SPRU.

Basberg, B.L. (1987), 'Patents and the measurement of technological change: a survey of the literature', *Research Policy*, **16**, 131–41.

Baum, J.A.C. and J.V. Singh (1994), 'Organizational hierarchies and evolutionary processes; some reflections on a theory of organizational evolution', in J.A.C. Baum and J.V. Singh (eds), *Evolutionary Dynamics of Organizations*, New York: Oxford University Press.

Borkin, J. (1979), *The Crime and Punishment of I.G. Farben*, London: Andre Deutsch Limited.

Breschi, S., F. Lissoni and F. Malerba (1998), 'Knowledge proximity and firms' technological diversification', *Mimeo*, CESPRI – University Bocconi: Milan.

Bresnahan, T.F. and M. Trajtenberg (1995), 'General purpose technologies: 'engines of growth'?', *Journal of Econometrics*, **65**, 83–108.

Brusoni, S., A. Principe and K. Pavitt (2001), 'Knowledge specialisation and the boundaries of the firm: why do firms know more than they make?', *Administrative Science Quarterly*, **46** (4) 597–621.

Cantwell, J.A. (1998), 'Knowledge, capabilities, imagination and cooperation in business introduction', *Journal of Economic Behaviour and Organization* **35** (2), 132–6.

Cantwell, J.A. (1991a), 'Historical trends in international patterns of technological innovation', in J. Foreman-Peck (ed.), *New Perspectives on the Late Victorian Economy: Essays in Quantitative Economic History, 1860–1914*, Cambridge and New York: Cambridge University Press.

Cantwell, J.A. (1991b), The theory of technological competence and its application to international production', in D.G. McFetridge (ed.), *Foreign Investment, Technology and Growth*, Calgary: University of Calgary Press.

Cantwell, J.A. (1993), 'Corporate technological specialisation in international industries', in M. Casson and J. Greedy (eds), *Industrial Concentration and Economic Inequality*, Aldershot: Edward Elgar.

Cantwell, J.A. (1994), 'Introduction. Transnational corporations and innovatory activities', in J.A. Cantwell (ed.), *Transnational Corporations and Innovatory Activities*, London and New York: Routledge.

Cantwell, J.A. (1995a), 'The globalisation of technology: what remains of the product cycle model?', *Cambridge Journal of Economics*, **19**, 155–74.

Cantwell, J.A. (1995b), 'Innovation in the global economy', *University of Reading Discussion Papers in International Investment and Business Studies*.

Cantwell, J.A. and H.B. Andersen (1996), 'A statistical analysis of corporate technological leadership historically', *Economics of Innovation and New Technology*, **4**, 211–34.

Cantwell, J.A. and P. Barrera (1999), 'The localisation of corporate technological trajectories in the interwar cartels: co-operative learning versus an exchange of knowledge', *Economics of Innovation and New Technology*, **6**, 257–90.

Cantwell, J.A. and F. Fai (1999), 'Firms as the source of innovation and growth: the evolution of technological competence', *Journal of Evolutionary Economics*, **9** (3), 331–66.

Cantwell, J.A. and O. Janne (1999), 'Technological globalisation and innovative centres: the role of corporate technological leadership and locational hierarchy', *Research Policy*, **28**, 119–44.

Corporate technological competence

Cantwell, J.A. and O. Janne (2000), 'The role of multinational corporations and nation states in the globalisation of innovatory capacity: the European perspective', *Technology Analysis and Strategic Management*, **12**, 243–62.

Cantwell, J.A. and G.D. Santangelo (2000), 'Capitalism, profits and innovation in the new techno-economic paradigm', *Journal of Evolutionary Economics*, **10**, 131–57.

Chandler, A.D. (1966), *Strategy and Structure*, New York: Doubleday and Company.

Chandler, A.D. (1977), *The Visible Hand: The Managerial Revolution in American Business*, Cambridge, MA: Belknap Press.

Chandler, A.D. (1990a), *Scale and Scope: The Dynamics of Industrial Capitalism*, Cambridge, MA: Harvard University Press.

Chandler, A.D. (1990b), 'The enduring logic of industrial success', *Harvard Business Review*, **March–April**, 130–40.

Chandler, A.D. (1992), 'Organisational capabilities and the economic history of the industrial enterprise', *Journal of Economic Perspectives*, **16**, 79–100.

Chandler, A.D. (1994), 'The competitive performance of US industrial enterprises since the Second World War', *Business History Review*, **69**, 1–72.

Christensen, C.M. (1993), 'The rigid disk drive industry: a history of commercial and technological turbulence', *Business History Review*, **67**, 531–88.

Christensen, C.M. (1997), *The Innovator's Dilemma. When New Technologies Cause Great Firms to Fail*, Boston, MA: Harvard Business School Press.

Coase, R.H. (1937), 'The nature of the firm', *Economica*, **4**, 386–405.

Cohen, W.M. and D. Levinthal (1989), 'Innovation and learning: the two faces of R&D', *Economic Journal*, **99**, 569–96.

Dierickx, I. and K. Cool (1989), 'Asset stock accumulation and the sustainability of competitive advantage', *Management Science*, **35** (12), 1504–11.

Dodgson, M. (1991), *The Management of Technological Learning*, Berlin: de Gruyter.

Dodgson, M. (1993), 'Organisational learning: a review of some literatures', *Organization Studies*, **14**, 375–94.

Dosi, G. (1982), 'Technological paradigms and technological trajectories: a suggested reinterpretation of the determinants and directions of technical change', *Research Policy*, **2**, 147–62.

Dosi, G. (1988), 'The nature of the innovative process', in G. Dosi, C. Freeman, R.R. Nelson, G. Silverberg and L.L.G. Soete (eds), *Technical Change and Economic Theory*, London: Frances Pinter.

Dosi, G. and D.J. Teece (1993), 'Competencies and the boundaries of the firm', Centre for Research in Management, CCC Working Paper, University of California at Berkeley, Berkeley.

Dosi, G., D.J. Teece and S.G. Winter (1992), Towards a theory of corporate coherence: preliminary remarks', in G. Dosi, R. Giannetti and P.A. Toninelli (eds), *Technology and Enterprise in a Historical Perspective*, Oxford: Clarendon Press.

Dosi, G., D.J. Teece and J. Chytry (eds) (1998), *Technology, Organization and Competitiveness. Perspectives on Industrial and Corporate Change*, Oxford: Oxford University Press.

Duysters, G. and J. Hagedoorn (1996), 'The effect of core competence building on company performance', MERIT Working Paper 2/96–014.

Eliasson, G. (1991), 'Deregulation, innovative entry and structured diversity as a source of stable and rapid economic growth', *Journal of Evolutionary Economics*, **1**, 49–63.

Eliasson, G. (1994), 'Technology, economic competence and the theory of the firm – discussing the economic forces behind long-term growth', in O. Granstrand (ed.), *Economics of Technology*, Amsterdam: North-Holland.

Fai, F. and J.A. Cantwell (1999), The changing nature of corporate technological diversification and the importance of organisational capability', in P.E. Earl and S. Dow (eds), *Contingency, Complexity and the Theory of the Firm. Essays in Honour of Brian J. Loasby*, Cheltenham: Edward Elgar.

Fai, F. and G.N. von Tunzelmann (2001a), 'Industry-specific competencies and converging technological systems: evidence from patents', *Structural Change and Economic Dynamics*, **12** (2), 141–70.

Fai, F. and G.N. von Tunzelmann (2001b), 'Scale and scope in technology: large firms 1930/90', *Economics of Innovation and New Technology*, **10** (4), 255–88.

Feldenkirchen, W. (1998), 150 *Years of Siemens. The Company from 1847–1997*, Plitt, Oberhausen: Siemens A.G.

Feldman, M. and D. Audretsch (1995), 'Science-based diversity, specialization, localized competition and innovation', XIth World Congress of the International Economic Association.

Fisher, F.M. and P. Temin (1973), 'Returns to scale in research and development: what does the Schumpeterian hypothesis imply?', *Journal of Political Economy*, **81**, 56–70.

Fisher, F.M. and P. Temin (1979), 'The Schumpeterian hypothesis: reply', *Journal of Political Economy*, **87**, 386–89.

Foss, N. (1993), Theories of the firm: contractual and competence perspectives', *Journal of Evolutionary Economics*, **3**, 127–44.

Foss, N. (1996), 'Capabilities and the theory of the firm', *Revue d'Economie Industrielle*, **77**, 7–28.

Foss, N. (ed.) (1997), *Resources, Firms and Strategies: A Reader in the Resource-based Perspective*, Oxford: Oxford University Press.

Foss, N., C. Knudsen and C.A. Montgomery (1995), 'An exploration of common ground: integrating evolutionary and strategic theories of the firm', in C.A. Montgomery (ed.), *Resource-based and Evolutionary Theories of the Firm – Towards a Synthesis*, Netherlands: Kluwer Academic Publishers.

Freeman, C. and J. Hagedoorn (1995), 'Convergence and divergence in the internationalization of technology', in J. Hagedoorn (ed.), *Technical Change and the World Economy,* Aldershot, UK, and Brookfield, VT: Edward Elgar.

Freeman, C. and F. Louçã (2001), *As Time Goes By: The Information Revolution and the Industrial Revolutions in Historical Perspective,* Oxford: Oxford University Press.

Freeman, C. and C. Perez (1988), 'Structural crises of adjustment: business cycles and investment behaviour', in G. Dosi, C. Freeman, R.R. Nelson, G. Silverberg and L. Soete (eds), *Technical Change and Economic Theory,* London: Frances Pinter, 38–66.

Freeman, C. and L. Soete (1997), *The Economics of Industrial Innovation,* London: Cassell.

Freeman, C., J. Clark and L. Soete (1982), *Unemployment and Technical Innovation,* London: Pinter.

French, M.J. (1991), *The US Tire Industry. A History,* Boston, MA: Twayne Publishers.

Gambardella, A. and S. Torrisi (1998), 'Does technological convergence imply convergence in markets? Evidence from the electronics industry', *Research Policy,* **27**, 445–64.

GE (1996), *General Electric Source Book. Your Guide to GE Products, Services and Businesses,* GE Company Literature.

Granstrand, O. (1999), *The Economics and Management of Intellectual Property. Towards Intellectual Capitalism,* Cheltenham, UK and Northampton, MA: Edward Elgar.

Granstrand, O. and C. Oskarsson (1994), 'Technology diversification in "MUL-Tech" corporations', *IEEE Transactions on Engineering Management,* **14**, 355–64.

Granstrand, O. and S. Sjölander (1990), 'Managing innovation in multi-technology corporations', *Research Policy,* **19**, 35–60.

Granstrand, O. and S. Sjölander (1992), 'Internationalisation and diversification of multi-technology corporations', in O. Granstrand, L. Hakanson and S. Sjölander (eds), *Technology Management and International Business. Internationalisation of R&D and Technology,* London: Wiley.

Granstrand, O., C. Oskarsson, N. Sjoberg and S. Sjölander (1990), 'Business strategies for new technologies', in E. Deiaco, E. Hornell and G. Vickery (eds), *Technology and Investment. Crucial Issues for the 1990's,* London: Oxford University Press.

Granstrand, O., P. Patel and K. Pavitt (1997), 'Multi-technology corporations: why they have 'distributed' rather than 'distinctive core' competencies', *California Management Review,* **39**, 8–25.

Griliches, Z. (1990), 'Patent statistics as economic indicators: a survey', *Journal of Economic Literature*, **27**, 1667–707.

Hagedoorn, J. and R. Narula (1996), 'Choosing organizational modes of strategic technology partnering: international and sectoral differences', *Journal of International Business Studies*, **27**, 265–84.

Hall, B.H., A.B. Jaffe and M. Trajtenberg (2001), 'Market value and patent citations: a first look', UC Berkeley, Department of Economics Working Papers, Berkeley, CA.

Harhoff, D., F. Narin, P.M. Scherer and K. Vopel (1997), 'Citation frequency and the value of patented innovation', Discussion Paper: Wissenschaftszentrum Berlin.

Hart, P.E. (1983), 'The size mobility of earnings', *Oxford Bulletin of Economics and Statistics*, **45**, 181–93.

Helpman, E. (1998), *General Purpose Technologies and Economic Growth*, Cambridge, MA: MIT Press.

Henderson, R. and I. Cockburn (1994), 'Measuring competence? Exploring firm effects in pharmaceutical research', *Strategic Management Journal*, **15**, 63–84.

Hill, C.W.L. (1994), 'Diversification and economic performance: bring structure and corporate management back into the picture', in R. Rumelt, D. Schendel and D.J. Teece (eds), *Fundamental Issues in Strategy*, Boston, MA: Harvard Business School Press.

Hill, C.W.L. and G.S. Hansen (1991), 'A longitudinal study of the cause and consequences of changes in diversification in the U.S. pharmaceutical industry, 1977–1986', *Strategic Management Journal*, **12**, 187–99.

Hounshell, D.A. (1992), 'Continuity and change in the management of industrial research: the Du Pont Company, 1902–1980', in G. Dosi, R. Giannetti and P.A. Toninelli (eds), *Technology and the Enterprise in a Historical Perspective*, Oxford and New York: Oxford University Press.

Hounshell, D.A. and J.K. Smith (1988), *Science and Corporate Strategy: Du Pont R&D, 1902–1980*, Cambridge and New York: Cambridge University Press.

International Directory of Company Histories, 1988–1992, Chicago and London: St James Press.

Jacobsson, S. and C. Oskarsson (1995), 'Educational statistics as an indicator of technological activity', *Research Policy*, **24**, 127–36.

Jacobsson, S., C. Oskarsson and J. Philipson (1996), 'Indicators of technological activities – comparing educational, patent and R&D statistics in the case of Sweden', *Research Policy*, **25**, 573–85.

Jaffe, A.B. (2000), 'The U.S. patent system in transition: policy innovation and the innovation process', *Research Policy*, **29**, 531–57.

Kelm, M. (1995), 'Economic growth as an evolutionary process', University of Cambridge Working Paper, ESRC Centre for Business Research.

Klevorick, A.K., R.C. Levin, R.R. Nelson, and S.G. Winter (1987), 'Appropriating the returns from industrial research and development', *Brookings Papers on Economic Activity*, **3**, 783–820.

Klevorick, A.K., R.C. Levin, R.R. Nelson, and S.G. Winter (1995), 'On the sources and significance of interindustry differences in technological opportunities', *Research Policy*, **24**, 185–205.

Kodama, F. (1986), 'Japanese innovation in mechatronics technology', *Science and Public Policy*, **13**, 22–42.

Kodama, F. (1992) Technology fusion and the new R&D', *Harvard Business Review*, **July–August**, 70–78.

Kohn, M. and J.T. Scott (1982), 'Scale economies in research and development', *Journal of Industrial Economics*, **30**, 239–49.

Kohn, M. and J.T. Scott (1985), 'Scale economies in research and development. A reply', *Journal of Industrial Economics*, **33**, 363.

Kuemmerle, W. (1998), 'Optimal scale for research and development in foreign environments, an investigation into size and performance of research and development laboratories abroad', *Research Policy*, **27**, 111–26.

Lall, S. (1994), 'Industrial policy: the role of government in promoting industrial and technological development', *UNCTAD Review*, 65–89.

Langlois, R.N. (1995), 'Capabilities and coherence in firms and markets', in C.A. Montgomery (ed.), *Resource-based and Evolutionary Theories of the Firm – Towards a Synthesis,* Boston, MA: Kluwer Academic Publishers.

Langlois, R.N. and P.L. Robertson (1995), *Firms, Markets and Economic Change*, London and New York: Routledge.

Levinthal, D.A. and J.G. March (1981), 'A model of adaptive organizational search', *Journal of Economic Behavior and Organization*, **2**, 307–33.

Levinthal, D.A. and J.G. March (1993), 'The myopia of learning', *Strategic Management Journal*, **14**, 95–112.

Liebenau, J. (1988), 'Patents and the chemical industry; tools of business strategy', in J. Liebenau (ed.), *The Challenge of New Technology. Innovation in British Business since 1850*, Aldershot: Gower.

Loasby, B.J. (1991), *Equilibrium and Evolution: An Exploration of Connecting Principles in Economics,* Manchester: Manchester University Press.

Loasby, B.J. (1993), 'Knowledge, learning and enterprise', in U. Witt (ed.), *Evolutionary Economics,* Edward Elgar Reference Collection, Cambridge: Cambridge University Press.

Loasby, B.J. (1994), 'Organisational capabilities and inter-firm relations', *Metroeconomica*, **45**, 248–65.

Loasby, B.J. (1996), 'Organisational capability at Du Pont, 1890–1980', in P.E. Earl (ed.), *Management, Marketing and the Competitive Process*, Cheltenham: Edward Elgar.

Loasby, B.J. (1998), 'The organisation of capabilities', *Journal of Economic Behaviour and Organization*, **35** (2), 139–60.

Malerba, F. (1992), 'Learning by firms and incremental technical change', *Economic Journal*, **102**, 845–59.

Malerba, F., R.R. Nelson, L. Orsenigo and S.G. Winter (1999), '"History Friendly" models of industry evolution: the computer industry', *Industrial and Corporate Change*, **8**, 3–40.

Mansfield, E. (1986), 'Patents and innovation: an empirical study', *Management Science*, **32**, 173–81.

Mansfield, E., M. Schwartz and S. Wagner (1981), 'Imitation costs and patents: an empirical study', *Economic Journal*, **91**, 907–18.

Marengo, L. (1992), 'Coordination and organizational learning in the firm', *Journal of Evolutionary Economics*, **2**, 313–26.

Marengo, L. (1995), 'Competence, learning and organisational structure', *European Management and Organisation in Transition*, University of Reading, UK.

Markides, C.C. (1995), 'Diversification, restructuring and economic performance', *Strategic Management Journal*, **16**, 101–18.

Markides, C.C. and P.J. Williamson (1994), 'Related diversification, core competences and corporate performance', *Strategic Management Journal*, **15**, 149–65.

Markides, C.C. and P.J. Williamson (1996), 'Corporate diversification and organizational structure: a resource-based view', *Academy of Management Journal*, **39**, 340–69.

Marshall, A. (1919), *Industry and Trade: A Study of Industrial Technique and Business Organization*, London: Macmillan.

Meliciani, V. (1998), 'Technical Change, Patterns of Specialisation and Uneven Growth in OECD Countries', SPRU, University of Sussex: Brighton.

Mokyr, J. (1990), *The Lever of Riches. Technological Creativity and Economic Progress*, Oxford: Oxford University Press.

Montgomery, C.A. (ed.) (1995), *Resource-based and Evolutionary Theories of the Firm. Towards a Synthesis*, London: Kluwer Academic Publishers.

Montgomery, C.A. and S. Hariharan (1991), 'Diversified expansion by large established firms', *Journal of Economic Behavior and Organization*, **15**, 71–89.

Mowery, D.C. (1983), 'Industrial research and firm size. Survival and growth in American manufacturing, 1921–1946: an assessment', *Journal of Economic History*, **43**, 953–80.

Mowery, D.C. and N. Rosenberg (1979), 'The influence of market demand on innovation: a critical review of some recent empirical studies', *Research Policy*, **8**, 103–53.

Mowery, D.C., J.A. Oxley and B.S. Silverman (1995), 'Firm capabilities, technological complementarity and interfirm co-operation', *European Management and Organisation in Transition,* University of Reading, UK.

Narin, F., M.P. Carpenter and P. Woolf (1984), Technological performance assessments based on patents and patent citations', *IEEE Transactions on Engineering Management*, **EM-31** (4), 172–83.

Narin, F., M.B. Albert and V.M. Smith (1992), 'Technology indicators in strategic planning', *Science and Public Policy*, **19**, 369–81.

Nelson, R.R. (1988), 'Institutions supporting technical change in the United States', in G. Dosi, C. Freeman, R.R. Nelson, G. Silverberg and L. Soete (eds), *Technical Change and Economic Theory*, London: Pinter.

Nelson, R.R. (1992), 'The role of firms in technical advance: a perspective from evolutionary theory', in G. Dosi, R. Giannetti and P.A. Toninelli (eds), *Technology and Enterprise in a Historical Perspective*, Oxford: Clarendon Press.

Nelson, R.R. (1993), *National Innovation Systems: a Comparative Advantage*, Oxford: Oxford University Press.

Nelson, R.R. (1996), 'The evolution of competitive or comparative advantage: a preliminary report on a study', IIASA Working Papers.

Nelson, R.R. and S.G. Winter (1982), *An Evolutionary Theory of Economic Change*, Cambridge, MA: Harvard University Press.

Nonaka, I., R. Toyama and A. Nagata (2000), 'A firm as a knowledge-creating entity: a new perspective on the theory of the firm', *Industrial and Corporate Change*, **9** (1), 1–20.

Oskarsson, C. (1990), *Technology Diversification – the Phenomenon, Its Causes and Effects*, Department of Industrial Management and Economics, Chalmers University of Technology, Gothenburg, Sweden.

Oskarsson, C. (1993), 'Diversification growth in US, Japanese and European multi-technology corporations', *Mimeo*, Department of Industrial Management and Economics, Chalmers University, Gothenburg, Sweden.

Pakes, A. and Z. Griliches (1984), 'Patents and R&D at the firm level: a first look', in Z. Griliches (ed.), *R&D, Patents and Productivity*, Chicago: University of Chicago Press, 55–72.

Patel, P. and K. Pavitt (1991), 'Large firms in the production of the world's technology: an important case of "non-globalisation"', *Journal of International Business Studies*, **22**, 1–22.

Patel, P. and K. Pavitt (1994a), 'Technological competencies in the world's largest firms: characteristics, constraints and scope for managerial choice',

STEEP Discussion Paper (13), Science Policy Research Unit, University of Sussex, Brighton.

Patel, P. and K. Pavitt (1994b), 'The continuing, widespread (and neglected) importance of improvements in mechanical technologies', *Research Policy*, **23**, 533–45.

Patel, P. and K. Pavitt (1995), 'Divergence in technological development among countries and firms', in J. Hagedoorn (ed.), *Technical Change and the World Economy*, Aldershot, UK and Brookfield, VT: Edward Elgar.

Patel, P. and K. Pavitt (1997), The technological competencies of the world's largest firms: complex and path-dependent, but not much variety', *Research Policy*, **26**, 141–56.

Pavitt, K. (1984), 'Sectoral patterns of technical change: towards a taxonomy and a theory', *Research Policy*, **13**, 343–74.

Pavitt, K. (1986), '"Chips" and "trajectories": how does the semiconductor influence the sources and directions of technical change?', in R.M. MacLeod (ed.), *Technology and the Human Prospect. Essays in Honour of Christopher Freeman*, London and Wolfeboro N.H.: Frances Pinter.

Pavitt, K. (1987), 'International patterns of technological accumulation' in Hood, N. and Vahlne, J.E. (eds) *Strategies in Global Competition*, Croom Helm: London.

Pavitt, K. (1988), 'Uses and abuses of patent statistics', in A. van Raan (ed.), *Handbook of Quantitative Studies of Science and Technology*, Amsterdam: Elsevier, 509–36.

Pavitt, K. (1995), 'Some foundations for a theory of the large innovating firm', in G. Dosi, R. Giannetti and P.A. Toninelli (eds), *Technology and Enterprise in a Historical Perspective*, Oxford: Clarendon Press.

Pavitt, K. (1998), Technologies, products and organization in the innovating firm: what Adam Smith tells us and Joseph Schumpeter doesn't', *Industrial and Corporate Change*, **7** (3), 433–52.

Pavitt, K. (2001), 'Can the large Penrosian firm cope with the dynamics of technology?', SPRU Electronic Working Paper: Sussex.

Pavitt, K., M. Robson and J. Townsend (1987), The size distribution of innovating firms in the UK: 1945–83', *The Journal of Industrial Economics*, **35**, 297–316.

Pavitt, K., M. Robson and J. Townsend (1989), 'Accumulation, diversification and organisation of technological activities in UK companies, 1945–83', in M. Dodgson (ed.), *Technology Strategy and the Firm: Management and Public Policy*, Harlow: Longman.

Pearce, R.D. (1983), 'Industrial diversification among the world's leading multinational enterprises', in M. Casson and P.J. Buckley (eds), *The Growth of International Business*, London: Allen and Unwin.

Penrose, E.T. (1959), *The Theory of the Growth of the Firm*, Oxford: Oxford University Press.

Peteraf, M.A. (1993) 'The cornerstones of competitive advantage: a resource-based view', *Strategic Management Journal*, **14**, 179–94.

Peters, T.J. and R.H. Waterman (1982), *In Search of Excellence: Lessons from America's Best-run Companies*, New York: Harper.

Piscitello, L. (2000), 'Relatedness and coherence in technological and product diversification of the world's largest firms', *Structural Change and Economic Dynamics*, **11**, 295–315.

Porter, M.E. (1985), *Competitive Advantage: Creating and Sustaining Superior Performance*, New York and London: Free Press, Collier MacMillan.

Prahalad, C.K. and G. Hamel (1990), 'The core competence of the corporation', *Harvard Business Review*, **May–June**, 79–91.

Quelin, B. (1997), 'Appropriability and the creation of new capabilities through strategic alliances', in R. Sanchez and A. Heene (eds), *Strategic Learning and Knowledge Management*, Chichester: J. Wiley and Sons.

Richardson, G.B. (1972), 'The organisation of industry', *Economic Journal*, **82**, 883–93.

Rosenberg, N. (1976), *Perspectives on Technology*, Cambridge and New York: Cambridge University Press.

Rosenberg, N. (1982), *Inside the Black Box*, Cambridge: Cambridge University Press.

Rosenberg, N. (1994), *Exploring the Black Box: Technology and Economics*, Cambridge and New York: Cambridge University Press.

Rosenbloom, R.S. and C.M. Christensen (1998), 'Technological discontinuities, organizational capabilities and strategic commitments', in G. Dosi, D.J. Teece and J. Chytry (eds), *Technology, Organization and Competitiveness. Perspectives on Industrial and Corporate Change*, Oxford: Oxford University Press.

Rumelt, R.P. (1974), *Strategy, Structure and Economic Performance*, Cambridge, MA: Harvard University Press.

Rycroft, R.W. and D.E. Kash (1999), *The Complexity Challenge: Technological Innovation for the 21st Century*, Cassell Academic Publishers.

Saviotti, P.P. and S. Metcalfe (1984), 'A theoretical approach to the construction of technological output indicators', *Research Policy*, **13**, 141–51.

Scazzieri, R. (1993), *A Theory of Production: Tasks, Processes, and Technical Practices*, Oxford: Clarendon Press.

Scherer, F.M. (1965a), 'Corporate incentive output, profits and growth', *Journal of Political Economy*, **73**, 290–97.

Scherer, P.M. (1965b), 'Firms size, market structure, opportunity, and the output of patented inventions', *American Economic Review*, **55**, 1097–125.

Scherer, F.M. (1983), 'The propensity to patent', *International Journal of Industrial Organisation*, **1**, 107–28.

Scherer, F.M., S.E. Herzstein, A.W. Dreyfoos, W.G. Whitney, O.J. Bachmann, C.P. Pesek, C.J. Scott, T.G. Kelly and J.J. Galvin (1959), *Patents and the Corporation: A Report on Industrial Technology Under Changing Public Policy*, Boston, MA: Galvin, J.J. (privately published).

Schmookler, J. (1966), *Invention and Economic Growth*, Cambridge, MA: Harvard University Press.

Schumpeter, J.A. (1911), *Theory of Economic Development. An Inquiry into Profits, Capital, Credit, Interest, and the Business Cycle*, (transl. R. Opie), Harvard University Press, Cambridge, MA, 1934; repr. Oxford University Press, London, 1961.

Schumpeter, J.A. (1937), *The Theory of Economic Development*, Cambridge, Mass.: Harvard University Press.

Schumpeter, J.A. (1943), *Capitalism, Socialism and Democracy*, New York: McGraw-Hill.

Soete, L. (1987), 'The impact of technological innovation on international trade patterns: the evidence reconsidered', *Research Policy*, **16**, 101–30.

Soete, L. and S.M.E. Wyatt (1983), 'The use of foreign patenting as an internationally comparable science and technology output indicator', *Scientometrics*, **5** (1).

Stiglitz, J.E. (1987), 'Learning to learn, localised learning and technological progress', in P. Dasgupta and P. Stoneman (eds), *Economic Policy and Technological Performance*, Cambridge: Cambridge University Press.

Stopford, J.M. (1992), *The Directory of Multinationals*, Basingstoke and New York: Stockton Press.

Symeonidis, G. (1996), 'Innovation, firm size and market structure: Schumpeterian hypotheses and some new themes', Economics Department Working Papers no. 161, OECD: Paris.

Taylor, C.A. and Z.A. Silberston (1973), *The Economic Impact of the Patent System: A Study of the British Experience*, Cambridge: Cambridge University Press.

Teece, D.J. (1982), 'Towards an economic theory of the multiproduct firm', *Journal of Economic Behavior and Organization*, **3**, 39–63.

Teece, D.J. (1993), 'The dynamics of industrial capitalism: perspectives on Alfred Chandler's "Scale and Scope"', *Journal of Economic Literature*, **31**, 199–225.

Teece, D.J. (1996), 'Firm organization, industrial structure, and technological innovation', *Journal of Economic Behavior and Organization*, **31**, 193–224.

Teece, D.J. and G.P. Pisano (1994), 'The dynamic capabilities of firms: an introduction', International Institute for Applied Systems Analysis (IIASA) Working Paper WP-94-103.

188   *Corporate technological competence*

Teece, D.J., G.P. Pisano and A. Shuen (1990), 'Firm capabilities, resources and the concept of strategy', University of California at Berkeley.
Teece, D.J., R. Rumelt, G. Dosi and S.G. Winter (1994), 'Understanding corporate coherence: theory and evidence', *Journal of Economic Behaviour and Organization*, **23**, 1–30.
Teece, D.J., G.P. Pisano and A. Shuen (1997), 'Dynamic capabilities and strategic management', *Strategic Management Journal*, **18**, 509–33.
Tidd, J., Bessant, J. and K. Pavitt (1997), *Managing Innovation: Integrating Technological, Market and Organizational Change*, Chichester: Wiley.
Tushmann, M.L. and P. Anderson (1986), 'Technological discontinuities and organizational environments', *Administrative Science Quarterly*, **31**, 439–65.
von Tunzelmann, G.N. (1995a), *Technology and Industrial Progress. The Foundations of Economic Growth*, Aldershot, UK and Brookfield, VT: Edward Elgar.
von Tunzelmann, G.N. (1995b), Technology, Scale and Scope', UK Association of Business Historians, Warwick, UK.
von Tunzelmann, G.N. and Q. Wang (1997), 'The dimensions of complexity in production and management', Science Policy Research Unit SPRU: University of Sussex.
Wang, Q. and G.N. von Tunzelmann (2000), 'Complexity and the functions of the firm: breadth and depth', *Research Policy*, **29**, 805–18.
Wernerfelt, B. (1984), 'A resource-based view of the firm', *Strategic Management Journal*, **5**, 171–80.
Williamson, O.E. (1985), *The Economic Institutions of Capitalism*, New York: Free Press.
Winter, S.G. (1987), 'Knowledge and competence as strategic assets', in D.J. Teece (ed.), *The Competitive Challenge: Strategies for Industrial Innovation and Renewal*, Cambridge, MA: Ballinger.
Winter, S.G. (1991), 'On Coase, competence and the corporation', in D.J. Teece (ed.), *The Competitive Challenge: Strategies for Industrial Innovation and Renewal*, Cambridge, MA: Ballinger.
Zander, I. (1997), 'Technological diversification in the multinational corporation – historical evolution and future prospects', *Research Policy*, **26**, 209–27.

Index

oil crisis (1975) 105
oligopoly power 155
opportunity cost 2
organizational issues *see* business
    structure
Oskarsson, C. 32, 107
    Technological Diversification... 91
outsourcing 19, 20, 90, 114, 156
    see also business behaviour

Pakes, A. 30
partners *see* networking alliances
Patel, P. 6, 61, 65, 107, 155, 161
patents 29–45, 52, 91–2, 114, 115
    co-patenting 133
    as indicators of innovation 30–35
    lifetime of 36–7, 45
    Reading University database of 29,
        36–40, 45, 92, 133–4, 150
    Standard Industrial Classification of
        see Standard Industrial Classifi-
        cation
    statistical analysis 31–4
    US data on 29, 35–6, 38, 45, 91–2,
        114, 150
path-dependency
    in technological competencies 47–8,
        53–4, 67, 68–9, 87, 108, 152
Pavitt, K. 6, 17, 30–31, 61, 65, 91, 93,
    107, 107, 108, 151, 155, 161
Pearson's correlation coefficient 70
Penrose, E. T. 17, 24
    The Theory of the Growth of the Firm
    3, 6, 7, 15, 21, 22, 87, 90, 132,
    151
Perez, C. 156
persistence *see* technological persistence
Peteraf, M. A. 7
Pisano, G. P. 8
Piscitello, L. 26, 130, 133, 145
policy issues 157–8
policymakers *see* business policymakers
portfolio theory 15, 90, 159
price setting 18
problem-solving 10, 11, 14, 67
    see also learning
product complexity 89, 108
product diversification 3, 5, 9, 15, 16, 18,
    19, 26, 88, 140, 154, 158
    strategies for 160

technological diversification and 17,
    20–26, 108, 112–13
technological inter-relatedness and
    160
product interdependencies 19–20
product life 17, 108
product range 16, 88, 89, 108, 113
production costs 18, 90
production process 2, 6, 9, 10, 16, 90,
    157, 159
    mass production 113
    scale economies in 109, 110
    scope economies in 110
productive capabilities 11–12, 16, 57
    learning and 13–15, 154
profit making 158
protectionist measures 90
published papers
    as indicators of innovation 29–30,
        31–2

RCA 78, 98, 100
Reading University
    patent database 29, 36–40, 45, 92,
        133–4, 150
relatedness concept
    in technological diversification 15
research data 40–42, 52, 69–70
research and development (R&D) 12, 13,
    20, 35, 105, 113, 115
    diversification of 132
    intensity of 100, 111
    Schumpeter on 111, 129
    scale of 154
    scientific 29–30
research and development expenditure
    14, 16, 17, 30, 90, 111, 115
    increases in 131, 145
    public funding 17, 158
resource-based theory
    of business behaviour 3, 6–8, 15, 21,
        22, 90–91
revealed technological advantage (RTA)
    index 52, 54, 69–70, 92–3, 115, 135
    worked example using 173–5
Richardson, G. B. 6, 11
risk assessment 9, 90
Rosenberg, N. 10, 11
    Exploring the Black Box... 55